This book is due on the last date stamped below.
Failure to return books on the date due may result
in assessment of overdue fees.

FINES	.50 per day	

EGYPT
ON THE BRINK
FROM NASSER TO MUBARAK

TAREK OSMAN

YALE UNIVERSITY PRESS
NEW HAVEN AND LONDON

For information about this and other Yale University Press publications, please contact:
U.S. Office: sales.press@yale.edu   yalebooks.com
Europe Office: sales@yaleup.co.uk   www.yalebooks.co.uk

Set in Janson by IDSUK (DataConnection) Ltd.
Printed in the United States of America

Library of Congress Cataloging-in-Publication Data

Osman, Tarek.
Egypt on the brink: from Nasser to Mubarak / Tarek Osman.
   p. cm.
  ISBN 978-0-300-162752 (cl: alk. paper)
  1. Egypt—History—1952–1970. 2. Egypt—History—1970–1981.
  3. Egypt—History—1981–4. Egypt—Social conditions—1952–1970.
  5. Egypt—Social conditions—1970–1981. 6. Egypt—Social conditions—1981– I.
  Title.
  DT107.83.O76 2010
  962.05—dc22
                                                                    2010019706

A catalogue record for this book is available from the British Library.

10 9 8 7 6 5 4 3

2014 2013 2012 2011

CONTENTS

LIST OF ILLUSTRATIONS

LIST OF ILLUSTRATIONS

ACKNOWLEDGEMENTS

IT IS NOT easy writing a book about a complex country such as Egypt, especially with its varied political, economic and social history over the past six decades. So, my first debt of gratitude must go to the many authors, scholars and analysts whose writings, views, studies and assessments have guided me through the maze of Egypt's different worlds.

My commissioning editor at Yale University Press, Phoebe Clapham, provided invaluable support (from major insights to painstaking attention to detail) throughout the many months of writing *Egypt on the Brink*. To her, my warmest thanks are due.

Many friends and colleagues assisted me in writing this book. They provided information, shared insights and challenged ideas. I am especially grateful to David Hayes at Opendemocracy.net for giving me the precious gift of time (and for his sharp editing, which gave the book the fluency it would otherwise have lacked).

I also owe special thanks to the large group of independent-minded friends with whom I have enjoyed numerous animated discussions. I would like to name Marwa Gouda, Hany Salem, Nizar Sawaf, Nashwa Saleh, Mohamed El-Gohary, Diala Kabbara, Shereen Mukhtar, Farida Zahran, Yaser Marwan, Ahmed Karim El-Meligi, Leila El-Kashef, Liz Drachman, Nick Parker, Ahmed Abdeltawab, Mohamed El-Shentenawy, Karen Zein, Mark Landry, Nahla Gameel, Sherif Ahmed, Christina Karamanidou, Zeina Farouk, Janice Hughes, Sophie Crouch, Nouran Al-Hadi, Sherif Sami, Caroline Faraj, Charbel Abu Jaoude, Miri Frankel, Amina Kamel, Heather Klar, Ghada Souleiman, Tarek El-Sherbini, Mohamed Al-Ammawy, Mohamed Anis, Yousef Al-Essa, Dina El-Sherif, Berit Ronningen, Raschid Abdullah, Oguz Oktay, Cathy Dobson, Youlia Vladimirovna, Olfa Ben Yahya, Michael Graniani, Khaled Amin, and the young and insightful Gamal and Zainab Mahmoud Osman.

I am also appreciative of the help provided by the staffs of the library of The American University in Cairo, Bocconi University Library, the British Library, the library of St Antony's College at Oxford University and the British Government's National Archives in Kew for permitting me the use of their rich collections.

A NOTE ON TRANSLITERATION

COMBINATIONS OF ARABIC vowels and consonants take multiple pronunciations, depending on different linguistic variables. For those unfamiliar with the language, the multiple variants could sound complex and perplexing. Arabic also has a unique letter (*al-dhadh*), which does not exist in any other language. To achieve consistency and simplicity throughout the manuscript and in order not to confuse general readers unfamiliar with Arabic, Egypt or the Middle East, I have avoided Arabic terminology as much as possible except in cases where the point under discussion would be made clearer (or stronger) by invoking the Arabic, or at times Egyptianized, word.

Throughout the manuscript, I have included the name spellings, place names and terms that are in popular use in cited sources. When different versions were equally popular, I opted for the simpler option. For example, the *Koran* as opposed to *al'Qu'ran*, *Mohamed* as opposed to *Muhammad* and *Al-Jamaa Al-Islamiya* as opposed to *al'Jama'a al'islamiy'a*.

In a number of sections in Chapters 2, 4, 5 and 6, I have quoted Arabic poetry or interviewees' literal phrases, in which cases I have retained what I deem the most expressive sense of the verse or quotation, but in each case immediately preceded it with its English translation – for example, slavery (*al-sokhra*), foreigners (*al-khawagat*), the age of justice (*asr al adl*), the Christians of the Orient (*massihiyou al-sharq*), among a number of other examples.

For Egyptian cities, other than Cairo and Alexandria, I have used the spelling employed in cited academic sources, especially *The Cambridge History of Egypt*, Volume 2: *Modern Egypt from 1517 to the end of the twentieth century* (Cambridge University Press, 1998). I have omitted, however, the indication of vowel length.

For newly established places and organizations, I have opted for the spelling most commonly used in widely circulating English-language newspapers, for example, the *Shayfenkom* and *Kefaya* movements.

For
Amal Iskander-Samaan,
Mahmoud Ibrahim Osman
and Zamira Ismael

'If you have come to know what is not good for you, you may also think of it all as having been a sort of magical journey of finding out what is truly good for you.'

Naguib Mahfouz (in *Miramar*)

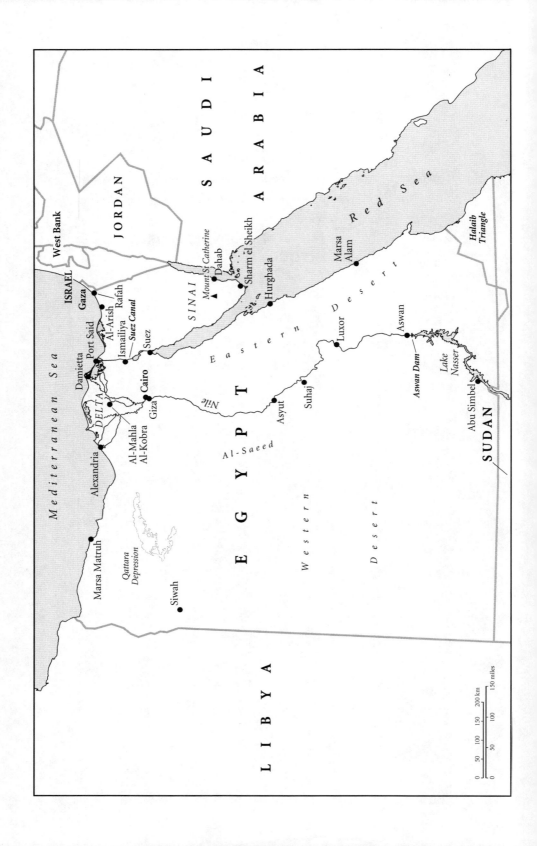

INTRODUCTION

SAMANTHA EGGAR UNINTENTIONALLY inspired millions of Egyptians. The American actress, in her role as the bubbly nurse in the 1960 film *Doctor Dolittle*, sang 'Fabulous Places': a song about a young American's desire to visit the glamorous cities of the world. She wanted to see London, Paris, Rome, Vienna and Cairo. If the song was remade today, fifty years later, Cairo would not feature in it. The worldly capital of the 1950s has lost its glamour, and turned into a crowded, classic third-world city. Cairo's descent mirrors a regression of the Egyptian society.

This book describes what has happened to Egypt and the Egyptians over the past half century: the changes that have taken place during that time period, the dynamics behind those changes, the state of Egyptian society today (at the beginning of the second decade of the twenty-first century) and the potential prospects of the society and the country in the foreseeable future.

* * *

Egypt's story should interest an international reader – not just because of its political twists (though there have been many of these, for example the move from being a staunch anti-colonial stalwart and political partner of the USSR to a solid American ally), its economic upheavals (such as the move from an austere socialist economy towards a merger and an extreme blur between decision-making and private economic interests) or moments and scenes of high-adrenaline (a coup, four widely covered wars, a presidential assassination live on TV and a landing in Jerusalem that was compared to the landing on the moon, among others), but because at the core of the story are dramatic changes in the values, customs, ways of looking at – and living – life, and even in the identities of the people. At the end of the first half of the twentieth century, Egypt was by and large an agricultural society; its people strongly attached to the land. Fifty years later, the country is the largest exporter of cheap labour in the Middle East and the Mediterranean basin, and a case study in brain drain – not to mention the thousands of Egyptian illegal immigrants crossing the Mediterranean in search of better lives on its northern shores.

The country that was a beacon for tranquillity, the society that was an example of peacefulness and tolerance – one that had never witnessed a civil war in over seven thousand years – has turned into the Middle East's most productive breeding ground of aggression. In three decades, Egypt witnessed an internal struggle between its government and armed groups working not only to overthrow the regime, but to overhaul the entire society; and an escalating tension between its two main religious groups. The country was also the birthplace of modern militant jihadism and the incubator of many of the groups that evolved to become international terrorist structures.

Reading Artemis Cooper's *Cairo in the War: 1939–1945*,[1] the reader sees a liberal, cosmopolitan society. Mohamed Hassanein

Heikal, Egypt's greatest journalist and the doyen of Arab political commentators, repeatedly described Egypt's influence in the Arab world and the Middle East from the 1930s to the 1960s not in terms of its political gravitas, or of its relatively advanced military might, but of its 'soft power': the Cairo and Alexandria that dazzled foreigners, seduced visitors, educated the region's elite, bred art and culture, hosted thousands of immigrants from Greece, Italy and Armenia as well as tens of thousands of Jews, and shaped a highly liberal, open society taking its inspiration from Paris and Rome. By the beginning of the twenty-first century, Egyptian society was devoid of cosmopolitanism, increasingly intolerant and highly conservative, even in comparison with other Arab societies in North Africa, the Levant and even the Gulf.

The world has changed drastically over the past five decades. South and East Asia have been transformed from under-developed economies and sleepy societies to vibrant, rich and creative ones. A country that was in the 1950s, according to the World Bank, in similar socio-economic circumstances to Egypt – South Korea – ended the century economically rich, technologically advanced and, crucially, socially developed in terms of the rule of law and the application of democracy. Some of the region's backwaters in the 1950s, such as Vietnam, emerged in the 2000s as economic stars with vibrantly modernizing societies. Most of the countries of Latin America have moved from crushing political and economic situations to become democratic nations actively engaging with the world. The economic turbulence that regularly afflicts Argentina and the troubling social gap in Brazil cannot eclipse the shining developments of the installation of democracy and the overall political and economic advancement that the societies of this continent have undergone. At the end of the first decade of the twenty-first century, the poverty of Bolivia is the exception compared with the developments in Brazil, Argentina, Chile and Peru.

Eastern Europe and Russia have founded for themselves new socio-economic realities, invariably better – even if far from ideal. The old civilizations of India and China have managed to turn their gigantic demographic masses into productive agents of development and richness. Close to 40 per cent of the combined population of the two nations are edging towards becoming middle class.[2] In Sub-Saharan Africa, despite decades of continuous civil unrest and in many cases outright wars and plundering, a large number of societies are emerging from their historically decrepit status, and are increasingly becoming investment destinations. Botswana, Liberia and of course South Africa lead the lot, but Zambia, Uganda and a few others are following behind. And of course the northern shores of the Mediterranean (Italy, Spain, Portugal and Greece) have pulled themselves out of relative poverty and dictatorship to secure their places in the heart of democratic, rich Europe.

In Egypt, society did not progress; on many fronts, it actually regressed. Politically, despite the introduction of a multi-party system in the 1970s and the undertaking, since then, of a number of parliamentary elections, democracy, the rule of law and the respect of the rights of the citizen have been diluted over the past six decades. The country's political system has descended to frightening levels of coercion, oppression and cruelty. Economically, despite significant improvements in the country's infrastructure (especially in utilities and telecommunications), and despite an average GDP growth rate of circa 6 per cent throughout the 2000s, Egypt comes in the lower 40 per cent of all *developing* countries in the UN's 2007 Human Poverty Index. This is a reflection of the difficulty of Egyptians' daily lives, from the crumbling education system and decrepit heath care, to humiliating transportation. There are more factories, bridges and highways, higher mobile telecoms penetration and increasing access to the Internet, but the economic development of the country, relative to the countries that used to be considered its international peers, has deteriorated significantly. In 2007, 32 per cent of the population were completely illiterate (42 per cent of women), 40 per cent of the population were at or below the international poverty line and GDP per capita (at purchasing power parity) was less than half that of Turkey and 45 per cent of South Africa's. And, crucially, there is not only a sense of confusion, resentment and rejection among the Egyptians – especially the younger ones, but increasingly an overarching feeling of an irreparable damage, a national defeat. The story of what happened to Egypt and the Egyptians, how and why, is interesting – albeit sad.

The story is also important. Egypt is the most populous country in the Arab world, Middle East and the Mediterranean basin. It is the birthplace and centre of a number of weighty ideas and trends, from the political, such as Arab nationalism, Arab–Israeli conflict and Arab–Israeli conciliation and peace, the artistic, such as pan-Arabic music, cinema and literature, to the noble, such as the peaceful co-existence of Christians and Muslims, and the perilous, such as modern Islamic militancy and tension between modernization and Salafism. Egypt is also next door to Europe and to the strategic energy reserves in the Gulf. It controls the Suez Canal, the world's most important trade route, and it continues to play a pivotal role in Middle Eastern geopolitics. The story of Egypt and the tumultuous changes shaping its society – and future – cannot safely be ignored.

Moreover, Egypt today presents perils and risks not only to the country itself and its society, but also to the region and the world. Many observers see it as 'a population bomb, a pollution epicentre, a laboratory for explosive terrorism, the flashpoint for communal Christian-Muslim riots, or ground zero for insurgent solidarities, such as anti-American protests and anti-IMF riots'.[3] The Cairo School of Urban Studies, led by Diane Singerman and Paul Amar, refuted the 'bomb' analogy as a 'myth'. The fact remains, however, that the Egyptian story entails a number of risks – to itself as well as to the wider world. To mitigate against them, these perils need to be understood.

Not only is the story interesting (because of its fascinating changes – on many fronts) and important (because of the significance of the country and the risks and perils inherent in today's Egypt), it is also quite perplexing. Despite the overall descent of the country and the multi-faceted failures of the state, and at many levels the society, there are spectacular cases of success and achievement. To a large extent, the Egyptian communities in the diaspora are very successful. Egyptians are one of the most educated communities in the United States (based on university degrees per capita); there is a thriving, and surprisingly large, community of Egyptian medical professionals in North America (Egyptians are the second largest community represented at Cleveland's Mayo Clinic[4]); Egyptians are vastly over-represented in American academia; they have a solid presence in high finance, especially in New York and London; Egyptians are among the most successful entrepreneurs in Italy (in central Milan there's a very high chance that you would eat an Egyptian-made pizza in an Egyptian-owned pizzeria); in addition to numerous cases of personal achievement (from the richest doctor in the UK,[5] to the world's most prominent fixed-income portfolio manager).[6]

There are also many successful examples inside the country. The Orascom group of companies are among the most successful and entrepreneurial businesses in emerging markets worldwide. El-Swedy Group is a leading infrastructure and alternative energy investor across Africa. The Middle East's most successful private equity firm, Citadel Capital, is a seven-year-old Egyptian business.

The United Nations Development Programme (UNDP) 2004 Egypt Human Development Report praised Egyptians' creation of highly successful private social support systems; this is a testament to the creativity of these often finance-strapped but ingenious not-for-profit organizations. Add to that four Nobel Laureates and a number of internationally renowned writers and artists – almost all of whom have lived, worked and developed their entire careers within the country. And amid the turbulence of today's Egypt, there is a new wave of creativity, positive momentum, international exposure and enthusiasm among the young Egyptians who represent more than 70 per cent of the population.

All of these examples make clear that despite the gloomy picture, there are positive elements within the Egyptian situation – cases that confirm the abilities and potential of the people and rule out simplifications about the 'inferiority of the culture' (as implied or explicitly said by some European politicians and commentators when discussing Arab cultures) or the collective self-mutilating generalizations of some modern Egyptian pessimists, such as Amal Donkol's short poem 'We are all losers' ('*Koluna Fashiloun*').

This book is not a political narrative of the country; politics is the background to the story of the book and it permeates the social shifts and swings that the story recounts. It is not a history of the country in the past half century; it will not recite political or social events, and though there is an underlying chronological order running throughout the story, the book is not a sequence of events and incidents presented in order. The book is also not a socio-economic study of the country; it will link economic and financial circumstances to social trends and events in the story of the Egyptians over the past six decades, but it will not adopt a singular disciplinary method in looking at that story. Nor is the book a political anthropological account of those millions living on the banks of the Nile. Not only is the author not qualified to do this, but also political anthropology is fundamentally a study of the people through looking at the structure of their society and their political institutions and systems. The book will not study the structures of society, nor will it dwell much on the political institutions of the country (most of which are dysfunctional to start with). It is a multi-disciplinary attempt to tell the story of the Egyptians, as a people, and how they – and their society – have changed.

THE STRUCTURE OF THE BOOK

The book is divided into eight chapters. Chapter 1 presents the liberal, glamorous, cosmopolitan – and seemingly of high potential – Egyptian society at the end of the first half of the twentieth century; it will focus on the different schools of thought that accompanied the birth of 'Egyptianism', and especially the Egyptian liberal experiment during that period.

Chapter 2 presents Nasser and Arab nationalism. It tries to explain how the external glamour of late 1940s and early 1950s Cairo and Alexandria, the atmosphere of prosperous content, the conspicuous European influences on Egyptian society and the aura of liberalism – especially in the country's cultural produce (most evident in Egyptian cinema and music), were all but decorative societal features, concealing fractures and cracks (from a monstrous level of poverty embedded in a severely unequal distribution of wealth to a muted rejection by millions of the wave of Europeanization and Mediterranean-ism that swept the country from the 1920s to the 1950s). This chapter will also address the transformation of Nasser from the leader of a *coup d'état* with an ambitious development programme to a 'hero', and how his project managed to alter the politics, economics and structure of Egyptian society. The chapter also reflects on the future of Arab nationalism as a political movement in Egypt and whether or not it has the potential to rise as a possible challenger to the current regime.

Chapter 3 tells the story of Islamism in Egypt: how the mortifying fall of Arab nationalism, combined with a Sadat-led coup on all the values and notions of Arab nationalism, brought about a divorce from the past; and how that divorce combined with the emerging power of petrodollars (from the mid-1970s onwards) pushed swaths of the Egyptian middle class (and those on the verge of becoming middle class) into the arms of a new Egyptianized Salafism. This chapter will address the changing role of the Muslim Brotherhood – from an ally of President Sadat (during the mid-1970s) to the most effective and challenging rival of the regime, and how the group evolved from a nervous political structure in the 1970s (drawing most of its power and resources from outside Egypt, and trying anxiously to find its place in the Egyptian society – especially after its prosecution during Nasser's times) to a mature, deeply rooted organization with a sophisticated strategy-in-action. The chapter will also recount the story of militant Islamism in the country, the change in the role of Al-Azhar (the oldest Islamic university in the world and the Sunni world's seat of learning) in the past half century, the relationship between the regime and the Islamic movement and the new facets of the movement that are increasingly addressing and targeting young Egyptians. The chapter will also study the nature of the Islamic movement's interaction with the West (mainly after its excellent showing in the 2005 parliamentary election), and whether or not that new positioning might enable it to evolve into a genuine challenger of the regime. The chapter will close with an assessment of the main predicaments facing the Islamic movement today.

Chapter 4 discusses how the new moneyed classes that flourished as a result of the transformative socio-economic changes that Egypt witnessed in the 1970s and 1980s have meshed with the regime, resulting in a blur between political decision-making and special economic and financial interests; and how, in turn, liberal capitalism emerged as the regime's increasingly polished dogma and doctrine. Here, we present the regime's socio-economic policies from the 1970s to the 2000s, and their exacting and transformative results on Egypt's middle class. This chapter will also emphasize how the regime (especially after the meteoric rise of Gamal Mubarak, the president's son) and its capitalist allies were keen on asserting the liberalism of their form of capitalism, as opposed to the Islamic capitalism espoused by the capitalist forces within the Islamic movement. Chapter 4 also focuses on the assets and liabilities of the liberal capitalist movement in Egypt – most notably Gamal Mubarak himself.

Chapter 5 assesses the changes that have occurred in the relationship between Egyptian Christians and their society over the past six decades. The chapter discusses the emergence of 'Christianism' in Egypt, as a reaction to the increasingly dominant Islamization; and how the rising sectarianism of society is affecting not only the relationship between the two religious groups, but also – it can be argued more importantly – the Egyptian identity, social cohesion, the society's exposure to the world and the make-up of the Egyptian character. This chapter also looks at the factors that are currently changing Egyptian Christians' interaction with (and dynamics within) their society.

Chapter 6 covers President Mubarak's period in office. After the different wars, conflicts and impassioned political and economic upheavals of the 1960s and 1970s, Egypt needed a tranquillizer, a calming drug to soothe the cuts and relieve the pains. Mubarak, with his relaxed demeanour and cosy deportment – backed by the gravitas of his military experience – seemed to be that tranquilizer. And yet, over the many years of Mubarak's rule, the lack of a national project, the absence of grand strategic goals or even clear directions, combined with the man's lack of interest in 'connecting' with his people, led to a growing feeling of disenchantment, which under the deteriorating socio-economic conditions, and the rise of multiple opponents, evolved into active opposition and a significant dilution in the regime's legitimacy. This chapter also examines the strategic descent of Egypt as a political power during Mubarak's era. In this section, it will be argued that unlike the assessments of many political observers in Egypt, Mubarak's foreign policy was not a continuation of that of Sadat (without Sadat's glamour and appeal); rather, it was a strategic decision to alter the Egyptian project, redirect Egypt's foreign policy and pursue new strategic objectives. This section will compare (and present the inherent clashes between) the Egyptian Arabic project, the Saudi Islamic project and the Israeli Middle Eastern project. The chapter will close by depicting how most Egyptians, after almost thirty years of Mubarak's rule, feel unimpressed or embittered, and how the Mubarak regime is increasingly in a political quandary with perilous ramifications.

Chapter 7 examines the country's most important demographic segment: the 70 per cent under thirty-five years of age. This chapter discusses the gloomy situation of many of these young people: mediocre education, poverty, disenchantment, increasing violence, and 'opting out' – and yet looks as well at the encouraging potential of the rising role of the private sector; the revival in the country's civic society; the new waves of modern, refreshing Egyptian 'young' culture; and, interestingly, young Egyptians' attempts at forging their own Egyptianism. The chapter assesses how the demographic composition of Egypt is a blessing as well as a curse: how the diverse initiatives and contributions of today's young Egyptians could trigger a new developmental phase for Egypt – or fail to materialize, leaving the country to anger, anguish and anxiety.

Chapter 8, the conclusion, examines three dynamics that would have a strong influence on the future of the country. The first is the dynamic at the top of the Egyptian scene: the interaction between the traditionally influential military and intelligence circles and the new moneyed clique – with a special focus on how that interaction would play out in the period post-President Mubarak, when there is a new administration that lacks the experience – and crucially the military credentials – of Mr Mubarak Senior. The second dynamic concerns Egypt's foreign policy in the period post-Mubarak. This section will argue that there are a number of factors that could well pose significant challenges to the foreign policy of Egypt's next administration and that could potentially compel it to undertake a strategic change in that policy. It will also discuss the idea that there is a strategic void in today's Middle East that presents Egypt's next administration with a historic opportunity to reshape the country's positioning in the region. The third dynamic is the interaction between Islamism and liberal capitalism, with especial regard to the cultural orientation of the majority of young Egyptians.

WHY THIS BOOK

Most, though not all, of the topics and themes presented in the book have been covered in rich literature. The overall theme of the book, however – the story of Egypt and the Egyptians in the past half century and the outlook of their future – is new. A small number of books were published in the early twenty-first century that attempted to explain Egypt. Collectively, they focused on the socio-economic changes that had altered Egyptian society over the past few decades; analysed the dynamics of the struggle between the regime and the Islamic movement; and reported from/about Egypt: a number of thematic snapshots, taken from a number of scenes in today's Egypt. This book, however, is intended as a serious and detailed analysis of the key factors that have affected the country's recent past and present, and the ones shaping its future.

This book is addressed to an international reader, interested in an important country, the turns and changes of which have ripple effects on its wider region and the world, or merely intrigued by a story of immense social change. The book's scope is ambitious. The Egyptian story over the past six decades has been complicated; the country's future is a function of a number of interconnected variables and dynamics; reporting the important details and analysing the crucial dynamics require elaborate effort. However, the book is not trying to be an authoritative reference on any of the topics or dynamics it is covering. It will draw on (and point to) the rich literature available on each of the topics it covers to achieve its objective of telling the story.

It is hoped that general readers who know little about Egypt, but are interested in its story, will find the book informative as well as entertaining. Perhaps it will also be a starting point for students embarking on studying modern-day Egypt. And for readers with in-depth knowledge of the country, the book presents new narratives and arguments that challenge existing dogmas and perceptions.

CHAPTER 1

EGYPT'S WORLD

THE CLASSICAL GREEK historian Herodotus described Egypt as 'the gift of the Nile'. Indeed, for millennia the great river has nourished and sustained this land as one of the most fertile agricultural areas of the world. From its source in Ethiopia's catchment plateaus, it courses across Sudan's swamps to enrich the narrow valley along its banks with a dense blanket of natural fertilizer. The Nile gave life to the valley and the Delta, its cycles of inundation and recession governing the eternal seasonal cycles of plantation and harvest. The guarantee of abundance was the foundation of an economic stability that allowed the inhabitants of the region to trade their maize and wheat for luxury goods from the Levant, Greece, Mesopotamia and central and east Africa.

The spread of international trade (from Greece eastwards, from Africa upwards and from Persia westwards) made Egypt wealthy. Its location at the intersection of many routes of exchange, including the Silk Road that linked Europe to western Asia to India and southern China, made it also one of the world's most important geo-strategic spots.

Almost every major civilization in the Mediterranean basin and the Middle East (and later Europe) envied Egypt's pivotal placing and coveted its riches. Greeks, Persians, Mesopotamians, Romans; Arab Muslims from the peninsula; the later Islamic empires of the Fatimids, Ayyubids, Mamelukes[1] and Ottomans; Napoleon's France and colonial Britain; even Hitler's Germany – all invaded and tried to subjugate the Delta and valley. Thus, as much as geography and nature have been generous to the Egyptians, history has treated them harshly. For Egypt fell to almost all of its invaders, and throughout the country's long history its inhabitants have been reduced to the status of second-class citizens in their own country – and, at times, outright slaves to foreign rulers.

Egypt's status under foreign rule alternated from being an important province (as in the Greek, Roman, Arab Islamic, Ottoman and British empires) to being the base of an expanding state (as it was under the Fatimids, Ayyubids and Mamelukes). In almost all cases, the country's resources (from the riches of the land to the toil of the people) were employed to serve the interests and campaigns of these foreign rulers, with little regard for the development and betterment of the Egyptians themselves.

Most historians regard Mohamed Ali, who ruled Egypt from 1805 to 1849, as the 'founder of modern Egypt' and the architect of its first developmental project. Mohamed Ali, who was of Albanian origin, came to Egypt as a soldier in an Ottoman garrison only to witness Napoleon's invasion and conquest in 1798. Napoleon's campaign was a failure. The French were unable to maintain order; Egyptians revolted more than five times in less than three years. Nelson destroyed the French navy at Abukir in the Battle of the Nile just a few weeks after the invasion. Napoleon's siege of Acre in 1799 broke down, and his commanding general in Egypt, Kleber, was assassinated. In 1801, the French withdrew. By manipulating the religious

15

establishment and eliminating the remnants of the Mamelukes, Mohamed Ali managed to fill the political void, and gain control of the country. His experience of France's weapons, ships, scientific knowledge and sophisticated administrative systems convinced him that the nascent state should dispense with Ottoman heritage and embrace a Europeanized destiny. In 1808, Mohamed Ali broke with the Ottoman legacy of four centuries (since Selim I's conquest of Egypt in 1517) by confiscating all of the country's land, thus rendering worthless all its title deeds and establishing himself as its sole owner.

The redistribution that followed benefited his family. In the 1850s, they controlled more than half of all of Egypt's farmland. By the late 1880s, and after a major wave of land divestment following the exile of Khedive Ismael, Mohamed Ali's grandson, the family continued to own more than a fifth of the country's land.[2] The redistribution also profited a select group of Albanian and Turkish officers and soldiers of fortune who had stood by Mohamed Ali in his military and political adventure; and some of those who had lobbied the court of the Ottoman Sultan in Istanbul in favour of acknowledging him as the ruler of an independent state within the empire.

The Ottoman Sultan had nothing to offer but official recognition. For more than a century, the Ottomans' grip over Egypt had been loosening as a result of the control of the warrior Kazdagli family over the country. The 1760s witnessed an attempt by Bulutkapan Ali Bek (also known as Ali Bek the Great – the most prominent member of the family) to expand Egyptian control over the Levant at the expense of the Ottomans. The territorial losses that Ali Bek had inflicted on the Ottomans gave an indication of the impotence of the Sublime Porte to defend its Arab realm. Ali Bek's expansions were only curtailed because he was betrayed by his son-in-law Mohamed Bek Abu Al-Dahab, who succeeded Ali Bek in ruling Egypt, for two years. In their attempt to regain control over Egypt, the Ottomans commissioned their Syrian viceroy, Ahmed Pasha Al-Gazzar ('the Butcher') to 'study the situation in Egypt and recommend a strategy for an expedition to regain control over the country'. Though he stressed the strategic importance of Egypt, Ahmed Pasha's assessment of Egyptians was damning: 'since ancient times, the people of Egypt have been expert in deceit and treachery', he said, before recommending a ruthless campaign in the country.[3]

Mohamed Ali instigated major economic changes: the overhaul of Egypt's irrigation system, the first innovation in this vital activity for more than 400 years; the introduction of new crops (mainly cotton), which promised attractive cash returns; and the organization of manufacturing and industry in an early form of vertically integrated value chains (the cotton was processed in weaving factories situated near the centre of the Delta to optimize transport costs). The story of cotton in Egypt has been a corollary of the story of wealth and power in the country. The Egyptian cotton industry benefited from a fortuitous historical coincidence. At the time that the Egyptian cotton farms and factories were increasing their capacity and production, America's cotton farms (most of which were concentrated in the southern states) were greatly suffering as a result of the country's civil war. The area devoted to cotton cultivation in Egypt increased more than threefold in less than fifteen years, and the exponential rise in cotton prices during the period resulted in significant returns for major owners of Egyptian farmland. In his memoirs *I Lived My Life amongst Those People*,[4] Mohamed Farghali Pasha (the king of cotton in Egypt) gives insights into the industry and its links to Egypt's political and finance circles.

Mohamed Ali also reorganized Egypt's political system by cutting the executive links to Istanbul (albeit remaining, in theory, a vassal of the Ottoman Sultan); established strict control over trade and tax collection; concentrated decision-making in a central structure administered by French and Turkish bureaucrats; opened French-style training schools to educate students to become engineers, doctors, teachers and technicians; and sent more than 350 of Egypt's brightest minds to train in Paris and Rome.[5]

But Mohamed Ali's key initiative was the creation of an independent, modern army based in Egypt. The Pasha disbanded the mercenary troops on whom the weak Mamelukes that had ruled Egypt in the seventeenth and eighteenth centuries had relied; he brought in a number of Turkish, Albanian, French and Italian officers to form the nucleus of a professional army command; created a fully fledged fleet; and established a military conscription system. The army, over the next few decades (especially under the leadership of his son Ibrahim Pasha from the 1810s to 1830s), expanded the new Egyptian state to incorporate Palestine, the valley adjacent to Mount Lebanon, almost the whole of today's Syria, Sudan and Al-Hijaz, the holy Islamic shrines in Mecca and Medina, and the eastern domains of Najd (Ibrahim Pasha captured and flattened the Saudis' capital of Diraiyah – now a suburb of Riyadh, arrested the Saudi emir Abdullah Ibn Saud and sent him to Istanbul, where he was beheaded). Ibrahim Pasha proved to be a gifted strategist and military commander, and after his successive victories the Ottoman Sultan asked him to lead a campaign to suppress the Greek uprising of 1824. The achievements of the army and its rapid growth triggered more economic developments: a new munitions factory (the first ever in the Middle East) in Etay Al-Baroud, a specialist textile and clothing plant in Al-Mahla and major developments at the ports of Alexandria and Damietta.

Mohamed Ali realized that Napoleon's ships, which had anchored in Alexandria in July 1798, had awakened the country to modernity,[6] and that his project would need to continue the wave of rejuvenation. And, indeed, he enabled thousands of Egyptians to benefit from unprecedented opportunities in terms of education, trade with Europe and the rebuilding of national infrastructure. In the subsequent period,[7] especially during the reign of his grandson Khedive Ismael, his achievements were built on by broadening education far beyond the military sciences and recruiting European technicians to modernize agriculture, the Nile and the maritime transport system.

Ismael was determined to make Egypt 'a part of Europe'. It was during his reign that Egypt's railway, including Cairo's splendid Al-Mahatta (central station), was built. Ismael adorned Cairo with Paris-, Rome- and Vienna-inspired buildings, palaces, parks and quarters. In effect, he commissioned the building of modern Cairo. 'Paris on the Nile' or the 'finery of Cairo', Al-Ismailiya – a district to which Ismael gave his name – comprised large, wide avenues, piazzas, *belle époque* buildings and urban public gardens.[8] He was a major patron of the arts and created the Cairo Opera House, another architectural jewel. He founded Dar-Al-Kuttub (the National Library), an ambitious project that started with more than 250,000 volumes, most of which were gathered from Egyptian, Levantine, Turkish and European collections, and which grew to become the region's largest library and one of the cultural treasures of the world. Ismael established the Egyptian Geographical Society, the House of Literature, the National Observatory, the National Antiques Museum and the Giza Zoo. He modernized Cairo and Alexandria by developing municipal services – from the supply of gas and water, to official policing, to a modern sewage system and street lighting. In the international arena, Ismael was keen to have Egypt represented in international conferences on issues ranging from health and hygiene to post and telegraphy.[9] The epitome of Ismael's attempts to market his Egypt internationally, and especially in Europe, was the opening of the Suez Canal in 1869. This was marked with almost a full month of celebrations, an all-expenses-paid festival to which many European notables were invited (led by Empress Eugenie of France) – 'the century's grandest party'.[10]

Mohamed Ali's and Ismael's efforts were the basis of a developmental project, but at heart it was not an 'Egyptian' one. Mohamed Ali's largesse over landownership did not extend to Egyptians themselves. None of his key managers or administrators was Egyptian, and Egyptians, though subjected to the new conscription system, were not allowed to graduate as officers, let alone commanders or leaders. Neither Mohamed Ali nor any of his descendants (up to King Fuad, who ascended to the throne in 1917) even spoke classical Arabic, let alone mastered the Egyptian variant (Turkish was the language of administration up to the second half of the nineteenth century, when a breed of Europe-educated Egyptian bureaucrats began to take leading roles in government agencies and ministries, and started to Arabize the the administrative system). Mohamed Ali's and Ismael's developmental project was dynastic – the vision of intelligent and ambitious men trying to build an empire based on a rich country that they had managed to subjugate.

Before the 1952 coup that ended the Egyptian monarchy, Mohamed Ali (the founder of the ruling dynasty) was presented in Egyptian educational history books as a Muslim leader who earned Egyptians' trust and admiration after he liberated them from the Mamelukes and defended them against the injustices of the Ottomans. Post-1952, however, and after the fall of his dynasty, the Pasha became a 'foreign adventurer' who subordinated the country and its people.

It is difficult to find out what ordinary Egyptians of the time thought of Mohamed Ali's and Ismael's project. However, the work of Abdelrahman Al-Kawakibi, arguably the most rigorous sociologist in Egypt at the time, casts some light on this. In his book *The Characteristics of Oppression and the Demises of Slavery* (published in 1900; the Arabic title of the book is a linguistic treat), Al-Kawakibi noted that the country had witnessed revival at the hands of 'men of will', but devastation 'at the union between political subjugation and religious absolutism'. He could not have been more prescient. Mohamed Ali, his son Ibrahim and Ismael were indeed 'men of will' who had reawakened and transformed Egypt. But in consolidating all powers in their hands (and those of their family), dismissing any notion of checks and balances and allying themselves with Al-Azhar (the religious power in the country), the governing system they established was, from ordinary Egyptians' viewpoint, domineering.

Despite the exclusion and the condescension with which Egyptians were treated, Mohamed Ali's and Ismael's project produced major upheavals in Egyptian society. Modern administration and education, exposure to the West, industrialization, the opening of trade and with it huge immigration to Egypt from abroad – all this in combination triggered the emergence of an Egyptian middle class composed of engineers, doctors, teachers, lawyers, civil servants, merchants and traders, and even some landowners.

The story of landownership in Egypt is the story of wealth and power in the country. In the first few decades after Mohamed Ali's confiscation of the land, the largesse was not extended to Egyptians. Mohamed Ali, possibly out of a racist disposition, or more likely because of a calculated political strategy, kept Egyptians outside the realm of wealth and power. Egyptians' access to these prizes came as a result of three factors. The first was the creation of the Egyptian army. A number of notable Egyptian families, from different regions in the Delta and

Al-Saeed (Southern Egypt), were tasked to find the young men who, through the conscription system, were to become the backbone of the budding Egyptian army. The best performers were rewarded with swaths of fertile land. The second factor was intermarriages. In the second half of the nineteenth century, an increasing number of up and coming Egyptians, especially in the fields of law, medicine and education, married into leading Turkish and Anatolian families that had settled in Egypt. In many cases, such marriages were alliances between heirs to Ottoman aristocratic families and aspiring Egyptians who had specific value to add to such unions of convenience – typically influence in a particular region in the Delta or Al-Saeed. The third reason was circumstantial. In the 1880s and 1890s, following the exiling of Khedive Ismael and the resulting strife within the royal family, thousands of acres of the family's land holdings were liquidated, sold by junior members of the royal family or by Ismael himself to settle major personal debts. Egyptian notables were among the most voracious buyers.

The social structure was changing. Whereas in 1800 at least 90 per cent of Egyptians were poor peasants, by 1900 more than 25 per cent of the population of 10 million lived in Cairo, Alexandria and the Delta's main cities, and could be counted as lower middle class or working class.[11] The economy was by and large in the hands of the royal family, its Turkish-Albanian-European entourage and the thousands of foreigners who had settled in Egypt from the mid- and late-nineteenth century; yet Egyptians, and especially the increasingly influential landowners, were rapidly climbing the political and socio-economic ladder.[12]

Egyptianism was coming of age. The royal family insisted on Egypt's independence from the Ottoman Empire. It was notable that, after the defeat of his army in south-eastern Turkey, Mohamed Ali's sole request to the Ottoman-British victors, at the London Peace Conference in 1840, was that they guarantee his family's rule over Egypt, not the sustenance of any of his political or territorial achievements. Exactly the same thing happened again in the 1860s. Ismael secured for himself the title of Khedive (Turkish for 'viceroy', a title first invoked by Mohamed Ali and later acknowledged by the Ottoman Sublime Porte in 1867), and more importantly, a Sultanic edict sanctioning succession by primogeniture in his line, in lieu of the seniority principle that the Ottomans had previously sanctioned for Mohamed Ali. Egyptianism manifested itself in other developments as well: complete detachment from Turkey following the weakening and subsequent fall of the Ottoman Empire in the aftermath of the First World War, the creation of an Egyptian army and the major expansion of the middle class. An Egyptian view of the country, the world and the future began to emerge. This historical moment was ignited by the British occupation of Egypt in 1882, itself the culmination of increasing British influence in the country (symbolized both by Ismael's mounting indebtedness to British banks and merchant houses, and the Ottomans' increasing reliance on Britain as a strategic ally against Russia and the Habsburgs).

The British entry into the Middle East in general, and Egypt specifically, is typically presented as an economic decision, the result of the country's desire to control the Suez Canal and thereby secure the road to India. True, but, in essence, it was a strategic move. In the first half of the nineteenth century, the Ottomans were increasingly weakened against the Russian Empire, which was keen on extending its borders (or influence) to the 'warm seas' of the Mediterranean and the Red and Dead Seas, as well as expanding its protection to the Orthodox Christians of the Ottoman Empire. At the same time, Mohamed Ali and his son Ibrahim Pasha were trying to push their ruling and territorial holdings into the northern frontiers of the Levant and parts of Turkey itself. Britain, having just expelled the French from the Middle East, and seeing that the Ottomans were clearly falling into an unredeemable decline, was not keen on the emergence of a new power in the Middle East – whether Russia or Mohamed Ali's Egypt. Hence, Britain acted almost as a protector of the Ottomans, first against the Russians and later against Mohamed Ali. Britain came to the Ottomans' aid in their efforts to push back Ibrahim Pasha's army, and forced Egypt to sign the Treaty for the Pacification of the Levant in 1840, which ensured that the Ottoman Empire would remain intact despite the ambitions of both the Russians and Mohamed Ali.[13]

In the 1860s and 1870s, Britain's influence in Egypt soared. British banks and merchant houses were among the leading financiers of Egyptian–European trade. Britain was heavily involved in the financing of the Suez Canal, and the governance of the company that managed the project. Britain also asserted its role as the protector of foreign (and especially European) minorities in the country. In 1880 and 1881, a growing number of Egyptian army officers, led by Ahmed Urabi, started to revolt against Khedive Tawfiq (Ismael's son), whom they regarded as a pawn of the British. In September 1881, a military garrison commanded by Urabi besieged Tawfiq's palace, and forced him to dismiss his government, install a new one in which the rebellious officers featured heavily, and move to Alexandria. Soon after, Britain sent warships to Alexandria to reinforce the khedive's position. The chain of events culminated in the Tel El-Kebir battle in September 1882 in which the British forces annihilated Urabi's garrisons. It marked the beginning of Britain's occupation of Egypt.

The occupation of Egypt by a European power further boosted Egyptianism. Mohamed Ali's modernization efforts,

Ibrahim Pasha's military expansionism and Ismael's developmental project seemed to have catapulted Egypt from a lagging Ottoman province into a modern, independent state. The occupation shattered those achievements. The poems of Abdullah Al-Nadeem[14] (Ahmed Urabi's chief propagandist) urged Egyptians to resist the occupiers and 'the fall back into decay', a reference to Egypt's 'dark days' under the Ottomans and the Mamelukes. The occupation was also a defining moment in the history of Mohamed Ali's family. Khedive Tawfiq was generally perceived to have collaborated with the British against the Egyptian army. Mohamed Ali's descendants were no longer seen as 'men of will' but, to quote Al-Nadeem, turncoats and 'agents of the nation's enemies'.

There were various popular insurgencies against the new occupiers, and political resistance was also reflected in the creation of the National Party (an attempt to formulate an Egyptian political interest and rhetoric independent of that of the royal family of Mohamed Ali's descendants). These efforts culminated in the 1919 revolution, the largest uprising against the British to date. Egyptians continued to struggle for an independent state, and for the full representation and equality of its citizens. To a large extent, the efforts bore fruit, for in 1922 the British government recognized Egypt's independence (though London continued to govern the country by proxy until 1945). The Egyptian monarchy (Mohamed Ali's dynasty) realized that it had to accommodate the emerging Egyptianism. King Fuad, Khedive Ismael's youngest son, agreed to sign up to a constitutional monarchical system whereby almost all executive powers were held by the government, which was answerable to a nationally elected parliament. The Egyptian political elite, with wide support from the Cairene and Alexandrian middle classes, drafted the 1923 constitution. This was the first civic constitution in the Middle East; it enshrined parliamentary representation, separation of authorities, universal suffrage and the respect for civil rights, and divided the parliament between a house of representatives and a senate.[15]

The creation of Al-Wafd ('the delegation') – which came together to argue Egypt's case for independence at the Paris peace conference in 1919 – was a milestone for the rising Egyptianism. Al-Wafd grew to become the country's most popular and influential political party; it spearheaded the development of the 1923 constitution; and with the determination of its founding fathers (especially Saad Zaghloul Pasha, the iconic leader of Egypt's struggle for independence) ushered in the country's parliamentary life. Al-Wafd's creation was a representation of Egypt's search for identity; it was driven by assertive intellectuals (mostly lawyers, teachers and writers) who predominately represented the upper segments of the expanding middle class and sought to found political independence on the 'demands of the Egyptian nation'.

That was a historical first, at least since the fall of the pharaonic state. The crumbling of the Ottoman Empire and the emergence of a 'Turkish' identity in its place had allowed other identities to surface, in cultural and political contexts alike. (The period witnessed the Hashemites' quest to create a number of Arab states, detached from the Ottoman Empire and centred round the Arabic identity; the same dynamics were also taking place among the Kurds, Greek Cypriots and other erstwhile Ottoman subjects.) But in the case of Egyptianism, the modernization and exposure to Europe that Mohamed Ali's and Ismael's project had heralded (and which continued throughout the last decades of the nineteenth and first of the twentieth century) led to sophisticated political thinking which aimed to install democracy and true representation in Egypt. In the same vein, Al-Wafd's leaders were trying to redesign Egyptian politics according to a Western, liberal-democratic model.

Egyptians had traditionally been compelled to accept whatever political and cultural orientation was forced upon them; now they were taking the lead in choosing their society's identity, direction and frame of reference. The emerging Egyptianism was an amalgamation of the views of spirited movements, political leaders, activist groups and clandestine cells, all trying to shape a fluid situation.

One school of thought, among the many contenders, was the Salafist movement. The word *salaf* in classic Arabic is a noun meaning 'predecessor'. In Islamic historical studies, the *salaf* typically refers to the Prophet Mohamed's companions and their immediate followers, with a focus on the period of the four 'Rightly Guided Caliphs'. The Salafists, who venerate Islam's early pious communities, believed that the weakening of the Ottoman Empire (the guardian of Sunni Islam) – especially with regard to the colonialist British and French, and the subsequent fall of the Islamic caliphate – would lead to a dilution of Islamic culture and open the way to Western (infidel) subjugation of Muslims. Their fears were exacerbated by Egypt's own modernization – especially the increasing take-up of civic education at the expense of the religious equivalent based at Cairo's eminent Al-Azhar. At that time, a number of leading educators were taking the initiative in developing secular education in Egypt, for example, Yaqoub Artin, the under-secretary of education from 1884 to 1906; Amin Sami, who directed the Mubtadayan School – one of the earliest and largest secular schools in the country and the alma mater of a number of Egyptian politicians in the first half of the twentieth century; and Mohamed Rifaat, who led the founding of the Higher Teachers' College, the first Egyptian establishment to train non-religious teachers. The Salafists were also concerned with the increasing intellectual divisions within the religious establishment itself, where some of the country's leading scholars were championing the need to revisit ideological contexts and the society's modus vivendi. To prevent what they perceived as a decline into western-ization and to preserve the status quo, the Salafists focused their efforts on the party that they thought would stand by traditions and 'anchor values': the Palace.

Al-Azhar lent strong moral support to Sultan Abbas Hilmy and later to King Fuad, and many in the religious establishment went along with King Fuad's ambitions to establish a new caliphate based in Egypt. When it became clear that this was not possible, the Salafists resorted to proselytizing among the people (especially young Egyptians) with the aim of encouraging them to embrace Islam anew and return to what were understood as the early traditions of austere Muslim piety. The Muslim Brotherhood, which Sheikh Hassan Al-Banna established in the 1920s in Ismailiya, was (and continues to be) the most important product of these mobilizations.

The Salafists gained ground in some quarters and became serious socio-political players. But their orientation towards the past was against the forward-looking spirit of the age, and in addition was at odds with the really inspiring development in Islamic thinking at the time – one that offered not a return to the past but a creative adaptation of Islamic thinking to the present.

The progressive project of Mohamed Ali and Ismael had prompted many Islamic scholars, especially within Al-Azhar, to explore intelligently revisionist paths of thought that aimed to redefine Islam's role in a rapidly changing society. Sheikh Refaa Rafae Al-Tahtawi (1801–73), the *imam* of one of Mohamed Ali's educational missions to France, described his lengthy encounter with Europe in *Al-ibriz fi talkhis Baris* (translated and published in France as *L'or de Paris* (*Paris's Gold*)). Al-Tahtawi's treatise presented favourable, if not uncritical, impressions of France and of modern European culture. The author acknowledged that 'there is a lot to learn from them', that Egypt needed to embrace 'Western society's values' and 'review how we function'.[16]

In *Osman's Dream*, Caroline Fenkel describes the role of Rashid Pasha and his protégé Ahmed Cevdet Pasha in modernizing the Ottoman government during the nineteenth century. Like Al-Tahtawi, Rashid and Cevdet argued that Islamic thinking is wide and flexible enough ('an ocean without shores') to absorb the tenets of modernity. Despite championing progress and systemic changes within the empire, they considered Islam the fundamental 'framework within which reform was to take place'. But Al-Tahtawi's view preceded the Ottomans'. Al-Tahtawi's assessment was the first time that a venerable Islamic scholar, from the core of the Islamic theological establishment, unabashedly advocated a complete overhauling of Egyptian values and acceptance of Western 'ways' and norms.[17]

Sheikh Mohamed Abdou (1849–1905), Egypt's grand *mufti* at the time, also responded to the waves of change the country was experiencing. He argued for the compatibility between Western contributions and the tenets of Koranic Islam (that is, freed from the backward-looking social, tribal and cultural contexts that he believed had been imposed on the 'rational religion').[18] Abdou campaigned for the introduction of modern sciences into Al-Azhar University's curriculum; he repeatedly pressed for an educational system based on 'reasoning' rather than 'rejection', and reminded his colleagues inside the religious establishment that a score of Islam's brilliant scholars (such as Imam Al-Ghazali) considered the study of logic obligatory for students of theology and jurisprudence. Abbas Mahmoud Al-Akkad continued the trend, focusing on 'the adaptive genius of Islam and Koranic philosophy'. The self-taught Al-Akkad, arguably

Egypt's most compelling Islamic thinker in the twentieth century and dubbed 'the giant of Arabic literature', was a prolific writer. He is most remembered for his *al-abkareyat* series: an examination of the *'geniuses'* of God, Jesus Christ, Prophet Mohamed, the Koran and a number of key Islamic figures, as well as for his novel *Sarah*, the account of his own sad love story. But Al-Akkad's production extended to essays and books ranging from comparative literature to harsh political tirades against the country's key political parties at the time, to voluminous studies of Islamic history and detailed critiques of a number of Western schools of philosophy, especially the Existentialist school.

These Islamic reformists sought to free Egyptian society from its backward-facing perspective and reliance on abstruse theologizing which failed to gain social purchase. The Salafist project lacked the intellectual rigour to confront Abdou and Al-Akkad (and others), as well as the thrust to push through; it would have to wait until the mid-1970s to seize the society's socio-political momentum.

The 'easternists' among Egyptian politicians offered another option for the country. Seeing the political void in the Middle East following the fall of the Ottoman Empire, they aspired to a major Egyptian role in the region. Egypt was the region's centre of gravity and political heavyweight, they argued; it had a regional vocation imbuing it with respect and reverence, and a seductive 'soft power' that attracted the region's elite, whether for education or entertainment.[19] Believing that Egypt's future lay with the Levant, Iraq, Iran and the Arabian peninsula, the easternists sought to establish strong relationships with the rising Saudi family, accommodated the Hashemites (in Jordan and Iraq), established through marriage a political alliance with Iran,[20] and sponsored attempts to formulate an Arabic political forum (which evolved, in 1945, into the League of Arab States).

The Palace and some of Egypt's leading politicians at the time[21] had championed the easternists' efforts, but their thinking did not have a wide appeal on the Egyptian street. Egypt for at least twelve centuries had been governed under a strictly Islamic framework, and most Egyptians considered themselves not 'easterners' or even Arabs as much as Muslims. The orientation towards the East did not resonate with Egyptians' accumulated historical experience. In addition, the project was inconsistent: its initial foray was mainly towards Iran, the region's other major demographic and political power, but after the deterioration of the Iranian–Egyptian relationship in the 1940s, it refocused on Arabism (a variation that excluded Persian Iran, diluted Islamism and highlighted the Arabic cultural heritage).

The easternists were also more concerned with grand strategic visions than Egyptians' daily lives, at a time when Egyptian society was suffering great social inequality. In addition, they were close to the Egyptian monarchy when that institution was losing its credibility, and so the Eastern project lacked a charismatic and credible leadership that was able to mobilize enough popular support behind it. But the most important reason for the project's limited appeal was that Al-Wafd (by far the most popular political party in the country, and the reservoir of the era's charismatic leaders) opposed it. Al-Wafd represented the liberal Egyptian movement, which, in subtle and restrained ways, wanted to continue Khedive Ismael's dream of 'putting Egypt in Europe' – not in the East.

The liberals' project was more comprehensive, popular and better structured than the easternists'. At its heart was the move from dynastic rule to constitutional monarchy, centred on a nationally elected parliament. Al-Wafd's leadership established its legitimacy and the foundations of the Egyptian liberal experiment by pioneering the 1923 constitution and fighting the

Palace to defend it. Throughout the 1920s and 1930s, Al-Wafd led a spirited campaign trying to contain the Palace's influence and cement the notion of the 'supremacy of the constitution'. Parliamentary records reveal numerous quarrels between Al-Wafd's representatives and Palace loyalists.[22] Al-Wafd fought various real electoral competitions with a number of political parties. The new political system was not perfect, but it did introduce genuine constitutionalism, political pluralism, cross-class participation in the political process and enshrined democracy and civil freedoms.[23]

The experiment also incorporated a commitment to capitalism – from respect for private ownership to free trade and open markets. And though the country's economic system at the time was concentrated in the hands of a limited class at the society's upper echelons, the capitalist dynamism of the era added vigour and vitality to the overall experiment. The Alexandria Bourse (the fourth largest worldwide) and the Cairo stock exchange were sizable, international markets. In fact, the story of the Alexandria Bourse – or the Alexandria Futures Exchange – is an interesting representation of Egyptian society's capitalism – and cosmopolitanism – in the first half of the twentieth century; the Bourse's board of directors included Muslim, Christian and Jewish Egyptians in addition to Egyptianized foreigners who had settled in the country. Egyptian commodities companies (especially in cotton and sugar) were active players in international markets, with significant international holdings and investments. Large retail brands competed in product diversity and glamour with (and were not far behind in terms of revenue from) leading London and Parisian retail empires. The accumulated wealth and the emergence of an Egyptian middle class had its counterpart in the development of Egyptian civil society – welfare associations, community development and professional advocacy agencies, feminist groups and trade unions. For the first time in the country's history, there were active social groups detached from any religious or political backing.

Free trade, open markets and vast opportunities for wealth creation turned Egypt into a regional commercial and trading destination. One consequence was a flow of immigrants; the number of foreigners in the country rose from 10,000 in the 1840s (the first relatively reliable census) to around 90,000 in the 1880s, and more than 1.5 million by the 1930s. The major immigrant populations included Greeks, Jews and Armenians.[24] The ensuing cosmopolitanism infused Egyptian society with tolerance, open-mindedness and glamour – adding to the country's 'seductive soft power', and gave the liberal experiment a certain international appeal.

In a vibrant political, economic and social scene, culture and the arts flourished. The 1920s, 1930s and 1940s witnessed a literary effervescence. Vast numbers of novels and plays challenged conventional norms and presented a society at ease with embracing westernizing modernity. In theatre, pioneering artists such as Fatima Rouschdie and Naguib Al-Rihani introduced popular comedies as well as melodramas (Al-Rihani 1889–1948, 'the father of Egyptian comedy', worked with his lifelong friend Badeih Khairy on Egyptianizing a number of French theatre hits and presenting them in Egyptian theatre, and later cinema). Egyptian cinema, introduced in the early 1920s by Italians and Armenians living in Egypt, was boosted by the creation of Studio Misr (under the patronage of Talaat Harb Pasha, the era's most prominent capitalist). Egyptian directors of the 1930s and 1940s rendered the dynamism of the society in comedy, tragedy and melodrama. Egypt's musical innovators – most prominently Mohamed Abdel Wahab,[25] Farid Al-Attrash[26] and Umm Kulthoum[27] – took leading roles. Mahmoud Saeed (1897–1964)

produced his best paintings during the 1930s and 1940s –
including some of his famous nudes that challenged society's
norms and tested the boundaries of its tolerance.[28] The period
also witnessed Mahmoud Mukhtar's finest sculptures, from
Nahdat Misr ('Egypt's Renaissance'), which continues to stand
across the gates of Cairo University, to *Isis – the Egyptian Mother
Goddess*, to *The Mermaid* – his rendering of 'the ever-beautiful
Egypt'. There are a number of books on Mukhtar's work, in addition to the museum devoted to his career. Waleed Aouni's
Mahmoud Mukhtar and the Khamassen Winds, a captivating chore-
ographic rendering of Mukhtar's representation of *Al-Khamassen*,
the quintessential Egyptian springtime wind, is a creative visual
tribute to the artist.

But the liberal movement's leading sage was Taha Hussein, a
determined secularist who revolutionized the study of Arabic
literature and Islamic history. Hussein, an Al-Azhar scholar who
completed his doctorate at the University of Montpellier with a
period at the Sorbonne, was, for a brief time, Egypt's education
minister. He is most remembered for his autobiography *The
Days (Al-Ayam)* and the novel *The Prayer of the Curlew* (a story of
love crushed by the society's strict conservative traditions). But
Hussein's most important work, and his major contribution to
the cultural stimulation of the era, was a serious examination of
how Egypt's liberal spirit (in the 1930s and 1940s) could be
reconciled with Islam. His book *The Future of Culture in Egypt*[29]
argued for what came to be called 'the Ideology of Pharaonism',
which asserted the uniqueness of Egypt's culture and identity, as
opposed to eastern-ism or Islamism. Hussein also conducted a
rare and frank study of Islam's 'Great Sedition' (the division that
followed the assassination of the third caliph Osman Ibn Aafan,
and led to the emergence of the Sunni versus Shi'ite schools of
thought in the Muslim world). He also made a daring study of

the development of Islamic thought in which he challenged the religious establishment in Egypt to acknowledge the contributions of the Hellenic and ancient Egyptian civilizations on a number of leading Islamic schools of thought.[30] Other major figures in the liberal movement were Ahmed Lutfi Al-Sayed (the driving force behind the creation and first president of Fuad I University, later Cairo University, the first secular graduate educational institution in the country), Salama Mousa and Tawfik Al-Hakeem, one of the leading playwrights in Egyptian theatre. Al-Hakeem's most important contribution to Egyptian literature was a series of plays and short stories that revolve around the theme of divine justice and judgement; the first of these was *The People of the Cave (Ahl Al-Kahf)*. In his later years, Al-Hakeem wrote two books, *The Prince of Darkness* and *My Dialogue with God*, which severely antagonized the Egyptian religious establishment. In general, the period was the heyday of Egyptian culture and art.

The liberal experiment, and especially its focus on Europeanizing society, could have been perceived as an attempt to sever Egyptian society from its historic and cultural heritages. But the progressive schools of thought that had evolved inside Al-Azhar (or the Islamic movement in general) – from Al-Tahtawi to Mohamed Abdou to Al-Akkad – were ammunition against such an argument. At the same time, the Muslim Brotherhood (the key opposition to Al-Wafd's liberal programme) seemed mired in a dictatorial, backward-looking structure and mindset. At the Brotherhood's 1935 Organizing Congress, a number of resolutions were adopted demanding complete obedience from all members; declaring that the Brotherhood's programme 'embodied Islam'; and dictating that every diversion from that programme would be considered an offence to the religion. This allowed leading liberals to claim that their project was not merely compatible with Islam but (unlike the Muslim Brotherhood) represented the religion's true nature.[31] The liberal Islamists' endorsement also cemented the liberal experiment's concept of 'citizenship' in a secular state where Muslims, Christians, Jews (and others) enjoy equal rights and bear equal responsibilities – as opposed to the Ottoman Empire's (and other Islamic states') distinction between Muslims living in *Dar-al-Islam* (Islam's abode) and non-Muslims (mainly Christians and Jews) who were considered *ahl-dhimma* (individuals living under the protection of the Islamic State, yet obliged to pay *Al-Jizya*, poll tax). 'Nationalism is our religion' became a famous Wafdist slogan. Citizenship was a cornerstone of the Egyptian state and of the definition of Egyptianism – the embodiment of a whole nation in an inclusive identity, based not on religion but on the modern notion of civic society.[32]

But the liberal experiment's dynamism (from a promising political system to economic progress, to cultural vivaciousness to glamour and allure) was not a social panacea. The struggle between the Salafists and the liberals (with unwise intervention from the young King Farouk) descended from intellectual debates and heated articles to waves of assassination that took the lives of two prime ministers, a number of prominent politicians, as well as that of Sheikh Hassan Al-Banna. At the same time, Al-Wafd, the liberal movement's leading champion, underwent a strategic transformation: its legendary president, Al-Nahas Pasha ('the leader of the nation') was growing old, and increasingly reliant on a clique of young politicians drawn from some of the country's leading landowning families. To many observers, Al-Wafd seemed to be shifting its orientation and political allegiance from the middle and lower classes that had been its base for more than three decades to the rich landowning families and a corrupt and sleazy Palace.[33] New players also sprang up on Egypt's political scene, challenged Al-Wafd and increasingly made inroads into its political base. The Democratic Party and especially its fiery spokesperson, Fathi Radwan, gained immense popularity by attacking the King and the 'Palace's interventions in the country's political life'. Misr Al-Fatah (Young Egypt), a movement – later a party – founded by Ahmed Hussein and Ibrahim Shoukry, led a courageous campaign in the parliament and the media to 'expose and change' the deteriorating socio-economic conditions. By adopting provocative political campaigning techniques such as printing pictures depicting devastating poverty under headlines such as 'these are your subjects, your Majesty', Misr Al-Fatah attracted swaths of the country's angry young men.

The political tensions and cracks in Al-Wafd's credibility coincided with the economic difficulties associated with the Second World War, in which Egypt was a key front. These difficulties included extreme income differentials and a lack of social mobility. They also brought to light the fact that, despite the economic development that Egypt had undergone in the first half of the twentieth century (in industry, infrastructure, as well as exposure to international markets and technology), the country's middle class was growing at a very slow pace. By the late 1940s, around 5 per cent of the population controlled more than 65 per cent of the country's asset base (private companies and traded stocks); more than 20 per cent of all Egyptian peasants were landless while around 3 per cent of the population held around 80 per cent of all cultivated land; and foreigners continued to exert dramatic influence on the economy. In general, the liberal experiment seemed to have failed to put forward a development programme for the country's poor, who continued to constitute more than 80 per cent of the entire population.[34]

The liberal experiment also failed to address a fundamental change that was taking place in Egyptian society. The increasing number of schools in the Nile Delta and Al-Saeed, the growth in print media, and the rising penetration of radio inspired thousands of young peasants to discard rural life and land cultivation and pursue secondary education (and for relatively affluent young men, higher education), as a route to more prestigious careers in law, business, teaching and the budding public service. This social change within the fellahin class altered the relationship between the country's peasants and the landowning elite who dominated the country's political life. Increasingly, the peasants became more aware of their rights and demanded better working conditions and lower rents on leased lands. In certain cases, tensions broke out, as in 1951 when hundreds of villagers in Behout (in the Nile Delta) attacked the properties of Al-Badrawi family, one of the richest in Egypt at the time and a key ally of Al-Wafd.[35]

At the same time, the head of the Egyptian state, King Farouk, was embroiled in a series of scandals. In 1951, he accepted a bribe from Ahmed Aboud Pasha in return for dissolving Naguib al-Hilali's government, which had been investigating a number of Aboud's business practices; the King's name was also mentioned in investigations into the illegal procurement of weapons for the Egyptian army during the 1948 war against Israel; and his colourful personal life was a feast for the international and local tabloids.[36] In the wider world, colonialism was fading, and the winds of independence and nationalism blowing from India, China and other Asian corners were reaching the Arab world and Egypt itself. Change was in the air; the question was whether leading forces inside Egypt (within the country's political elite, and mainly Al-Wafd) would be able (and willing) to lead such change (and in what form), or whether the country would be taken unawares.

In January 1952, as a result of a chain reaction of provocations and confrontations between the British army, the Egyptian police, the Palace and Al-Wafd, a number of riots in some Cairene neighbourhoods descended into anarchy and mayhem. Thousands of protestors marched on downtown Cairo, breaking into retail shops, cafes, cinemas, hotels, restaurants, theatres, nightclubs and even the country's Opera House, splashing them with petrol and setting some of them alight. Within hours, the riot spread from Al-Ismailiya district (the heart of *belle époque* Cairo) to other neighbourhoods, and took the lives of tens of Egyptians.[37] By the end of the day, swaths of Cairo's historical centre were consumed in flames and lost forever. The 'Cairo fire' – in which young Egyptians burnt the centre of their capital while the country's rulers and elite watched in fear and impotence – signalled the end of an era: it was a clear indication that the regime had no future.

A political war of wills between the Palace and Egyptian army officers over the composition of the board of directors of the Officers' Club in this context became a symbol of a wider contest over Egypt's political future. Al-Wafd, despite its historic role of representing the middle class, avoided intervening in the confrontation. Al-Nahas Pasha sought to placate the Palace, and failed to show leadership at a crucial time. All other political parties lurked in Al-Wafd's shadows, leaving a glaring void in the country's political life. (Al-Wafd's popularity from the 1920s to the 1950s, drawing on the immense charisma of its founder Saad Zaghloul Pasha, relegated many of Egypt's brightest politicians to the political periphery. The story of Egypt's Liberal Constitutional Party is a case in point. The party, despite comprising some of Egypt's exceptional political and economic minds of the time, could not extend its appeal beyond parts of the Cairene and Alexandrian intelligentsia. Some historians argue that beside Zaghloul's charisma, Al-Wafd employed vulgar populism that many prominent – and highly refined – politicians could not – and would not – take up.)

In July 1952, while Al-Wafd's leaders were relaxing in St Moritz and Cannes, a number of armed brigades mounted a coup against King Farouk. The people poured joyfully into the streets, and cheered on the young officers who led the coup as agents of change. This swift action, conducted by less than a hundred officers – almost all drawn from junior ranks – ended the country's political experiment of the previous half century. In less than twelve months, the young officers abolished monarchism, established republicanism, put an end to the country's parliamentary system, abolished political parties and jailed (or sidelined) almost all the key politicians of the 'bygone era'. The July 1952 coup quickly turned into a revolution that – with the people's blessing – initiated a new phase in Egypt's history. The almost immediate popular endorsement enabled the young officers to jettison the institutions, norms, modus operandi and even accumulated experience of the liberal experiment. The officers, chief among them the rising star Gamal Abdel Nasser, discarded the past as well as the present and launched a transformative political and social project. Egypt changed forever.

CHAPTER 2
NASSER AND ARAB NATIONALISM

MANY AFICIONADOS OF Arab cinema recall a famous scene in *Nasser 56*, the film made to commemorate the Suez War of October/November 1956. An old Egyptian woman from Al-Saeed, the region from which Gamal Abdel Nasser hailed, gets a chance to talk to Nasser in private. She hands him a wretched, flimsy pair of trousers that used to belong to her grandfather. She tells Nasser that the man was, like millions of Egyptian youths, taken from his village into slavery (*al-sokhra*) to join the brigades digging the Suez Canal. And like many of those millions, he never returned; he died young, far away from his family and his home, in a country that remained under colonial rule.

'Why did he die? For what? And who brought such death upon him?' she exclaims. Since then, generations had passed, yet the Suez Canal – for which her grandfather had died – remained in the hands of the foreigners (*khawagat*). He, Nasser, having nationalized the Suez Canal Company, is now the rightful owner of the pair of trousers. He, to her and millions like her, has avenged the crimes inflicted on the exploited, broken masses.

This scene – filled with much more drama than the above description conveys – drew tears from millions of viewers, in Egypt and across the Arab world. At that moment in history Gamal Abdel Nasser was in their eyes doing much more than nationalizing the vital economic asset the Suez Canal represented, more than evening the score with yesterday's powers. He was asserting national pride; standing up against the imperialist powers that had dominated the region for decades; emotionally freeing millions of oppressed Arabs and Egyptians; through his actions – and thus in his person – effecting the rebirth of Egyptian (and Arab) dignity.

In that moment, and at the high point of his rule, Gamal Abdel Nasser was, to the vast majority of Egyptians, a classic example of Thomas Carlyle's 'hero': 'the man with savage sincerity', who 'comes into historical being to lead his people', who 'represents the aspirations of generations before and beyond him', 'the man whose valour is value' and 'whose work is achievements and calamities' (for only mediocre people yield mediocre results). No wonder that even at the depths of Nasser's greatest defeat – after the Six-Day War against Israel of June 1967 – Umm Kulthoum, the Arab world's grandest diva, sang to him, on behalf of millions: 'Stay, you're the hope' ('*ebka fa'anta al-amal*'). No wonder that on his death in September 1970, more than 6 million people from all over Egypt marched behind and around his coffin in tumultuous scenes.

Even today, four decades after his death, Nasser symbolizes for millions all over Egypt an unfulfilled dream of a saviour who died while preaching, even (as Nizar Kabbani, the Arab world's most renowned modern poet, described him) 'the last prophet'.

The scale of the popular veneration of Gamal Abdel Nasser in Egypt, or indeed in the wider Arab world, is arguably greater than that of any other political leader since the Prophet Mohamed.

Much has been made of Nasser's own efforts to cultivate and then manipulate his own heroic image, in which the media played a central role – portraying his acts of solidarity with the poor, broadcasting dozens of songs and poems lauding his achievements and projecting him as the architect of a redemptive grand Egyptian and Arab strategy against the imperialist powers.

The interplay in the Nasser 'phenomenon' between genuine expression of popular romantic feeling and state-sponsored propaganda may sometimes be hard to disentangle. But behind it lies a vital historical fact: that Gamal Abdel Nasser signifies the only truly Egyptian developmental project in the country's history since the fall of the pharaonic state. There had been other projects: a Greek one in Alexandria, an Arab–Islamic one under the Ummayads (the first dynasty to rule the Islamic world after the end of the era of the 'Rightly Guided Caliphs'), military–Islamic ones under Saladin and the grand Mamelukes, a French one under Napoleon's commanders and a dynastic (Ottoman-inspired) one under Mohamed Ali Pasha and Khedive Ismael. But this was different – in origin, meaning and impact. For Nasser was a man of the Egyptian soil who had overthrown the Middle East's most established and sophisticated monarchy in a swift and bloodless move – to the acclaim of the millions of poor, oppressed Egyptians – and ushered in a programme of 'social justice', 'progress and development' and 'dignity': a nation-centred developmental vision.

This was a momentous event: the first time, in thousands of years, that a native Egyptian had ruled Egypt and articulated a coherent vision of its future. Since the fall of Egypt to Alexander the Great in 332 BC, arguably every single ruler of Egypt had been a foreigner – from the Ptolemic Greeks to the Romans, to the Persians, to the Romans again, to the Arab Muslims (under various different dynasties), to the North African Fatimids, to the

Kurd Ayyubids, to the Mamelukes, who hailed from various parts
of Turkey and the Caucasus, to the Albanian and Anatolian
Mohamed Ali Pasha dynasty. True, Egypt had always managed –
as many of the country's historians have argued – gradually to
assimilate successive foreign rulers and invaders, and the cultures
they brought with them, into parts of its rich native melting
pot. Alexander the Great pronounced himself the son of Ra
(the Egyptian sun god). His successors became pharaohs and
Nile queens – from Ptolemy the First to Cleopatra (the Seventh,
to be specific). The Arabs shunned their desert ways and turned
native. Saladin made the country his home. Most of the Turks
who came with the Ottomans and later the Mohamed Ali dynasty
never left. But their culture and that of Egypt's other rulers, in
origin and formation, were foreign. Nasser's was not. The tall,
dark and poised man from Al-Saeed was to most Egyptians one
of them, even a reborn pharaoh reincarnated from the depths of
the country's history, a giant risen from the muddy Nile itself.

Most, but not all. Tawfik Al-Hakeem, one of Egypt's most
renowned twentieth-century writers, described Nasser as a
'confused Sultan' pursuing grand – but ultimately empty –
dreams; a man armed with rhetoric, but no real plan of action.
Such criticism grew in the later 1970s, as the immediate post-
Nasser years gave way to the period of economic opening up
(*al-infitah*) under Anwar Sadat, and the entire Nasserite project
was assailed as a failure rooted in a lack of dynamism.

If anything the exact opposite was true. Nasser's development
programme was frenetically action-oriented as well as rich in
rhetoric. In the space of a few years following the July 1952 coup
that abolished Egyptian monarchism, Nasser overhauled Egypt's
entire political system; sidelined the political class that had
ruled Egypt for half a century, replacing the Turco-dominated
aristocracy with ordinary Egyptians, who at least in theory

represented the will and aspirations of the masses; emasculated all political parties; tried (and in many cases imprisoned) most of the key politicians of the 'bygone era'; created a new constitutional order; and established a new system based on an ultra-powerful presidency supported by an executive government, the legitimacy of which was derived from the consent (albeit without formal electoral channels) of the people.

The country's liberal political experiment from the 1920s to 1940s (which had been led by Europe-inspired and oriented landowners and capitalists, as well as writers, teachers and lawyers) was terminated, to be replaced by a strongly socialist and populist doctrine (led by a military bureaucratic elite). It all amounted to the most comprehensive political upheaval in Egypt's history since Napoleon's campaign at the end of the eighteenth century.

The economic underpinning of the Nasserite transformation was twofold. The first pillar was a dramatic reform of Egypt's grossly unequal pattern of landownership. Land reform was not Gamal Abdel Nasser's brainchild. Makram Ebeid Pasha, in September 1945, presented to the government a fully drafted bill aimed at enhancing the percentage of fertile land owned by small landowners (*seghar mulak al-aradi*), whom he defined as those owning less than fifty acres. Ibrahim Shoukry, a scion of a large landowning family (and later the head of Egypt's Labour Party), was a loud parliamentary voice (in the 1940s) advocating a series of propositions aimed at reforming the dramatically skewed landownership structure in Egypt. Also Abdel Rahman Al-Rafei Pasha, in 1948, came up with a similar proposal, though more oriented towards the laws governing the sale and purchase of land. Yet the disparity remained. In 1950, more than one-third of all fertile land was owned by less than 0.5 per cent of Egyptians, while another third was shared among 95 per cent of mostly poor farmers.[1] Such vast concentration, in a mainly agrarian economy where land was almost the only real reservoir of wealth, entailed a major skewing of wealth generation and accumulation – not only in agriculture and agribusiness, but across all economic fronts. The distorted landownership structure lay at the heart of the injustices Nasser wished to purge.

His policy in this area had immense social effects as well as proving to be a masterstroke of populist politics. Land reform was enacted through enforcing a 100-acre ceiling on the size of any single family's holding; ending absentee ownership; capping rent on leased lands; strengthening the legal rights of peasants (*al-fellahin*); and, crucially, confiscating hundreds of thousands of fertile acres from major landowners and distributing them to millions of landless peasants. Today, almost five decades later, the footage of Nasser distributing landownership titles to poor peasants in drab *jalabeyas* is still a powerful – and moving – symbol of the rise of the poor classes (*Al-Tabaquat Al-Fakeera*) and the transformation of a feudal system into one based on 'equity and progress'. Salah Jahin, Egypt's foremost songwriter of the last half century, pithily celebrated the arrival of 'the age of justice, the age of Nasser' (*'Asr Al-Adl, Asr Abdel Nasser'*).[2]

The second pillar of Nasser's economic revolution was the public sector. This new class of state-owned factories, companies and enterprises was, as with the land-reform drive, in effect created in the late 1950s and early 1960s from the proceeds of the nationalization of almost all of Egypt's sizable businesses. The underlying philosophy was also similar: to remodel the structure of wealth by transferring ownership from a narrow capitalist class at the very top of the country's socio-economic pyramid to millions of ordinary employees, poor labourers and struggling workers.

This newly created public sector was also the vehicle through which Nasser launched a major industrialization drive. This involved a host of large-scale projects and installations: the Middle East and Africa's largest steelworks in Helwan; Naghammadi's Aluminium Complex; the major expansion of the cotton-weaving factories of Al-Mahla Al-Kobra; the founding of steel factories in Alexandria; the creation of the car-assembly lines in Al-Nasr; the push to manufacture consumer goods in Al-Masane Al-Harbeya; and, most importantly, the completion of the High Dam in Aswan, which enabled the electrification of the whole country, not least the remote villages of the Delta and Al-Saeed regions.[3]

Nasser was indeed a revolutionary, fired by an absolute determination to change society. The combination of the land-reform programme and the creation of the public sector resulted in around 75 per cent of Egypt's gross domestic product (GDP) being transferred from the hands of the country's rich either to the state or to millions of small owners. The closest parallel to such a large-scale social programme had been in the early days of Mohamed Ali Pasha's rule in the early nineteenth century.

Nasser's detractors accuse him of vulgar populism, anti-hierarchal spitefulness and deep hatred of liberal capitalism. This is a very simplistic view. The political, social and economic changes he oversaw, which turned the July 1952 coup into a revolution, drew on the bedrock legitimating principle of the people's consent. To a large extent, Nasser's greatest social achievement (and arguably his most courageous decision) was to build his power base on a philosophical imperative: the need to win a sweeping mandate from the people. This bottom-up approach aimed to translate the desires and wants of the people into state policies and national socio-economic strategies. It was, again, the first time in Egyptian history that a 'pharaoh' had sought to serve the people and adopted their agenda, rather than imposed his on them.

For some years, the chemistry between the 'hero' and his people indeed seemed to fuel Nasser's comprehensive project. 'The forces of progress and development' were transforming the 'working society'; the highly ambitious industrialization programme, the major advances in agriculture and cultivation, the momentum of the public sector, the High Dam and increasingly a relatively large military build-up seemed to be turning Egypt from a poor and lethargic economy into an exemplary developmental case study. The country's economy grew at an average rate of 9 per cent per annum for almost a decade. The extent of cultivated land increased by almost a third (an achievement that had eluded Egyptians for more than a millennium); the contribution of manufacturing to GDP rose from around 14 per cent in the late 1940s to 35 per cent by the early 1970s. Manufacturing was also rapidly becoming the country's largest employer. And by 1970 (the end of Nasser's rule), 'out of 21 less developed countries surveyed by the OECD, Egypt had by far the largest share of labour force employed in manufacturing, despite the inclusion of more developed countries such as Argentina and Chile'.[4] Unemployment and inflation were at record lows throughout the 1950s and the first half of the 1960s. Egypt also made great advances in technological development in the Nasser years (especially through cooperation with India and Czechoslovakia). The country seemed to be striding forward, to the extent that the World Bank was even comparing the 'Egyptian developmental experiment' with that of leading emerging markets such as South Korea.[5]

But the deeper appeal of the Nasserite project was not in growth rates or development programmes. The 'hero' was manifesting himself through the 'will of his people' – and nothing demonstrated that will more than the nationalization of the Suez Canal Company. From its opening in 1869, the Canal was operated by the Universal Company of the Suez Maritime Canal, which was initially owned by Khedive Ismael and a score of French institutional and private investors. Following his debt crisis in 1875–6, the Khedive and his sons were forced to sell their shares to their leading creditors, a number of British banks and merchant houses, in a series of transactions engineered by the British government under Benjamin Disraeli. In 1888, the Ottoman government signed the Convention of Constantinople which declared the Canal an international (not Egyptian) neutral zone under British protection. The Canal's strategic importance soared in the First and Second World Wars, and later as a result of the discovery of oil in the Arabian Peninsula; it was arguably the most important strategic asset in the Middle East.

There were tumultuous consequences following the Suez Crisis of 1956 – the tripartite attack on Egypt by Britain, France and Israel following the nationalization of the Canal ended in a humiliating failure that effectively ended the careers of two prime ministers, Anthony Eden in Britain and Guy Mollet in France. For Gamal Abdel Nasser it resulted in him being catapulted to a transcendent political status. He was now both an Egyptian hero and an Arab one, capable of 'defeating the nation's enemies' and 'representing Arab dignity'.[6]

In the post-Suez decade, the Egyptian 'giant' aggregated the power of its increasingly impressive developmental programme and the glamour of its new assertive regional and Arab nationalist role to become the Arab world's centre of political gravity. Egypt became the main supporter of the Algerian revolution against French colonial rule; the sole backer of the Yemeni revolutionary forces that revolted against the country's monarchical regime; the emulated model of a number of regimes in Syria; the example for all rebel movements in the Gulf; and, in the late Nasser period, the inspiration of Muammar Gaddafi's 'revolution' in Libya. Even beyond the region, Nasser's moves were elevating Egypt into a leading third-world power. Along with Jawaharlal Nehru (India's pioneering prime minister) and Marshal Tito (Yugoslavia's president), Nasser emerged as one of the architects of the Non-Aligned Movement, which was founded in Belgrade in 1961 as a bloc of 'independent nations' detached from both NATO and the Warsaw Pact. Almost all African 'freedom fighters' came to him for guidance, moral support – and funds. All Soviet leaders from Nikita Khrushchev to Alexei Kosygin praised their 'brave friend'. Zhou Enlai, Mao Zedong's successor, described Nasser as 'the giant of the Middle East'. Che Guevara made a pilgrimage to Cairo, the world's new capital of 'revolutionary support'. From Bandung (the Indonesian town where in 1955 the first conference of newly independent Asian–African states was convened) to Beirut (the Arab world's capital of media, entertainment and culture in the 1950s and 1960s), Nasser was the region's unrivalled hero.[7]

*　*　*

The dominant views among analysts of ordinary Egyptians' fascination with Nasser and his grand project tend to be bifurcated: they see it either as a form of national hysteria (wherein a third-world country with a more than 50 per cent illiteracy rate becomes enamoured by the fiery, yet empty, rhetoric of a military dictator) or as a moment of historic awakening (where an old nation with a rich history coalesces behind a historic figure who carves an immortal mark by meeting his people's profound longing for regeneration). The excessive emotional charge aside, in reality Nasser's project did resonate with Egyptians' sense of where history had led them and the direction in which they wanted to go, even if they could not necessarily have articulated it themselves.

The country's history, they believed, had been dominated by centuries of oppression and quasi-slavery inflicted on millions of Egyptians by foreign rulers from different parts of the world. That injustice needed to be corrected. The Egyptian psyche was in a condition of perpetual waiting for 'one of us' to free the country from its oppressors. Externally too, Egypt was yearning to resume its traditional role of regional leader. Within its own borders, Egypt is a poor country with few resources, scores of problems and limited potential. In its role as the political heart of the Arab world, the region's cultural trendsetter and the centre of debate and action, Egypt can transcend its limitations and expand its capacities. All of Egypt's great rulers have been aware of these components of the country's collective psychology – as have great swaths of the people. The Egyptians took to Nasser's project because it was an imperative based on the country's historical experience (a point elaborated in Chapter 6, where Egyptians' acceptance of Nasser's project is contrasted with their hostility towards the country's foreign policy from the 1970s onwards).

Nasser's project was also the sole non-Islamic political and developmental programme in the country's modern history. This is a crucial issue in Egypt, where Christianity has always been part of the national psyche; especially so given that in the first half of the twentieth century Egyptian Christians played a very prominent role in the country's public life. Nasser's project was given an inclusive, 'national' appeal by its emphasis on civic notions such as social equality, identification with the poor and Egypt's role as the leader of the Arab world (free of any Islamic dimension).

Nasser's fierce confrontations with political Islam (discussed in Chapter 3) led many commentators to consider him an enemy of Islam. That was hardly true, for Nasser saw the religion as the civilizational framework for his Arab nationalist project.

Mohamed Hassanein Heikal, Nasser's closest advisor, describes Nasser's 'appreciation of the cultural and civilizational role of Islam in Egypt and the Arab world'; that appreciation, however, did not extend to political identity. His project was uncompromisingly civic. Heikal, as well as other Nasserites, stresses Nasser's awareness of the historic role of eastern Christians (*massihiyou al-sharq*), and especially Egyptian Copts, in the region's long history. That awareness certainly played a role in his emphasis on 'Arabizing', rather than 'Islamizing', his political venture.

Perhaps Nasser's relationship with Al-Azhar University, the Sunni world's pre-eminent seat of learning, is the most telling example of how he saw the role of Islam in his grand project. Nasser ended the historical tradition of having Al-Azhar's Grand Sheikh elected by the institution's Council of Great Scholars. He put strict limitations on the institution's social role. He forced Al-Azhar to expand its curricula beyond languages, philosophy and jurisprudence to include natural and social sciences – basically diluting Egyptian Islamism's grand seat of learning and turning it into an ordinary university.[8] And subtly but steadily, he transformed Al-Azhar from the country's most vocal – and arguably most influential – independent body into a mere arm of the regime. Yet, at the same time, Nasser had an amicable working relationship with Sheikh Shaltout, Al-Azhar's legendary Grand Sheikh of the 1950s and 1960s. Also, in a number of cases Nasser used Al-Azhar to counterbalance the influence of the Muslim Brotherhood, the Islamic movement's leading political player.[9] And it was from inside Al-Azhar's grand hall that he delivered one of his most memorable speeches, on the eve of the tripartite attack on Egypt in 1956. Nasser's embrace of Islam (as civilization) and repudiation of Islam (as government, political movement or governing framework) was arguably one of his most brilliant balancing acts; the one that endeared him to Egyptian Christians without antagonizing the vast majority of Egyptian Muslims, and defined his project in purely national hues.

Interestingly, that civic nature of the Nasserite project resonated well beyond Egypt's borders. Forty years after his death, many distinguished Arab Levantine Christian families continue to invoke 'his model' as the one they would accept in their interaction with 'the state and their Muslim neighbours'. The writings of the veteran Lebanese journalist Ghassan Tueini, the long-time editor of *An-Nahar* newspaper and an icon in the Lebanese Christian community, show that many Arab Christians viewed Nasser's project as 'inclusive and linked to the Levant's Arabic heritage'.

Nasser's positioning of Arab nationalism as 'Egypt's historical calling' was not an accurate representation of the country's former engagements in its wider region. Pharaonic Egypt's expansion in the Levant was aimed at the subjugation of 'barbaric tribes' and bringing them within 'the realm of Raa's (the Egyptian sun god) shadow on earth (the Pharaoh)'. The military campaigns that introduced Islam to North Africa were undertaken under the banner of the Islamic Ummayad Empire. Egypt's struggle against the Tatars and the Crusaders was strictly 'Islamic jihad' under-taken by Kurdish, Turkish and Caucasian Sultans. Mohamed Ali's battles were carried out under an Ottoman flag and fuelled by the ambitions of an Albanian–Turkish family. Nasser's 'Arabism' was thus almost unprecedented in Egypt's long history.

Nasser did not even invent Arab nationalism as a political identity. The easternists led the way towards the 'Arabic East'. Michel Afleq, the Sorbonne-educated Arab Christian political philosopher who founded the Al-Baath (Rebirth) party in 1941, pioneered the call for an Arab political front.

But Nasser's vision (and genius) was in moulding Arab nation-alism as the cultural identity of the nation that spoke Arabic, suffered the occupation of the same European powers and shared the same history under the Mamelukes and Ottomans. Nasser's project benefited from the intellectual infrastructure that the easternists had laid out in the 1930s and 1940s and from Al-Baath's propaganda in the Levant. His brilliance, however, was in popularizing Arabism; Nasser was not like the immaculately dressed, rich easternist Pashas; he was not the Francophone Michel Aflaq; he was 'a man of the people'.

His emphasis on the secular Arab nation also resonated well with the idea of the modern state introduced and given momentum to by the Arabs' interaction with Europe in the late nineteenth and early twentieth century. His project was not a relapse to the past; it came across as modernization, development and progress.

Nasser's personal experience also played a role in his insistence on Arabizing, rather than Islamizing, his project. Nasser spent his formative years in Alexandria when the city was buzzing with cosmopolitanism and liberalism, and when Egypt as a whole was at the apex of the liberal experiment. Nasser's defining experience was his participation in the 1948 war against Israel. He fought alongside Palestinian farmers – Muslims as well as Christians, who saw themselves as Arabs. The strategic struggles he studied as a young officer (the Arab revolt against the Turks and the British–French carving of the Middle East into respective spheres of influence) defined 'his people' as 'Arabs' not 'Muslims'.

Nasser's venture was further helped by the weakness – at that time – of its key competitors. The Muslim Brotherhood then (as now) was the undisputed leader of Egyptian political Islamism. But the Brotherhood of the 1950s was hardly a mighty opponent. After the wave of violence of the previous decade in which the Brotherhood's 'secret apparatus' was implicated, the death of the group's founder Sheikh Hassan Al-Banna and the Brotherhood's failure to challenge the emerging nationalism of the July 1952 revolution, Nasser found a painless political opportunity to abolish the Brotherhood, banish its leaders, imprison scores of its members and send the group into the political wilderness.

Egyptian liberalism was also in a dire state. As discussed in Chapter 1, the liberal experiment of the 1920s to 1940s had produced weighty thinkers such as Taha Hussein and Tawfik Al-Hakeem; triggered the emergence of a liberal Islamism; generated a cultural wave, the fruits of which included one of the world's earliest film industries, a thriving literary and theatre scene, the world's fifth oldest opera house and scores of architectural gems in downtown Cairo and on Alexandria's corniche's boulevards. Egyptian liberalism's facade was alluring. But, to most Egyptians, it lacked a substance that they could relate to. It failed to reform the country's corrupt and debilitated monarchy; it failed to put forward a development programme for the country's poor who constituted the vast majority of the population; it failed to 'Egyptianize' the cultural themes and currents it had imported from London and Paris; and it failed to secure its cultural advances in institutional terms (so that they translated into a better educational system, job opportunities, improved living standards or more dignity for ordinary Egyptians in their own country).

The liberal constitutional experiment that the Egyptian political scene had witnessed in the 1930s and 1940s remained the province of Cairo's and Alexandria's elite and upper middle class. The liberal cultural fashions of the same period were detached from the crushing living standards of the peasants in the Delta and Al-Saeed, as well as the poor in the country's urban areas. It was no surprise then that the vast majority of people on the Egyptian street cheered Nasser's repudiation of the 'bygone era'

(which conveniently lumped together the monarchy, the aristo-
crats, the landed gentry and the different political parties – from
the liberal and secular to the conservative and religious). Nasser's
political and socio-economic plans emerged as the country's sole
and compelling project with a substantial, expansive mandate.

Nasser's external competitors, as well as his internal ones,
were weak. The Arab world was wide open to the Nasserite
project. Syria and Iraq were consumed by a series of destabilizing
coups. Lebanon, as usual, was embroiled in its sectarian divisions. Its president, Camille Shamoun (1900–87), tried to put
together a political front that defined itself in opposition to
Nasser and his project. But Shamoun's alliance with the United
States, his ultra-capitalist ethos and – crucially – the conspicuous
Christianism of his front left him with no chance to stand
opposed to the mighty Nasserite Arab nationalist movement.
King Hussein in Jordan was fighting for his survival. Morocco
was witnessing an open war between King Hassan and the
leaders of his army, who had repeatedly tried to assassinate him.
Even Saudi Arabia, the only real viable competition to Nasser,
was torn between its classic 'passivist' tendencies (the wing led by
King Saud) and a more assertive stance based on an evolving
Islamic ideology (a wing led by Prince – later King – Faisal).

The non-Arab world at the time seemed buffeted too by winds
of change that offered political opportunity: the retreat of imperialism from the Middle East and Africa and the conspicuous
weakening of yesterday's masters (the British and the French),
the upbeat mood following the Bandung conference and later
the Suez Crisis, the echoes of the revolution in Cuba, the
struggle against apartheid in South Africa, the moral terms in
which President Dwight Eisenhower characterized US foreign
policy and (later) the euphoria that followed the election of John
F. Kennedy. And amid the positive atmosphere, the Arab world

was looking for its own change of direction. Nasser saw the chance and grabbed it. Cairo quickly became the sanctuary of 'revolutionists' from all over the Arab world, who praised Nasser as 'the guardian of freedom and Arab dignity'.

The Voice of the Arabs (*Sout Al-Arab*), Nasser's far-reaching radio station, became a propagandist vehicle par excellence, conveying the leader's fiery speeches to the Arab world from 'the Ocean to the Gulf'; even Egyptian cinema and music were mobilized to market the notion of the 'rising Arab nation' led by its 'historical leader'. A new adaptation of the Saladin story was made into a smash-hit film, in which the Kurdish leader who fought the Christian Crusaders in the name of Islam was transformed into 'the servant and the leader of the Arabs fighting the invading Westerners'. Scores of Egyptian (and Arab) songwriters and singers thrilled the Arab masses by singing of 'Arabic dignity', 'the grand nation', 'our destiny: Arabic unity' and 'Nasser: our own hero'. The Egyptian socio-economic developmental project was transformed rapidly into a pan-Arabic 'historical and transformational' political dream. Nasser, the Egyptian (Saeedi) hero, was remodelled into a modern-day Saladin.

And like Saladin, the hero was up for a fight. A growing number of voices in the Arab world and elsewhere argue that Nasser was seeking a strategic and just peace with Israel. It is certainly true that at various moments, Nasser avoided a direct confrontation with Israel; moreover, he repeatedly entertained discussions about potential solutions to the Arab–Israeli struggle, and acted as an intermediary in intra-Arab conflicts. But there is no escaping the fact that Nasserite Arab nationalism was on a clashing path with three strong forces in the Middle East: Saudi Arabia (and with it most Arab monarchies), the United States and Israel.

Nasser saw the revolutionary fervour that he unleashed in the Arab world as an unstoppable political tsunami. He denounced the 'regressive regimes' in the region, especially Saudi Arabia's. The Saudis – with their absolute monarchy, Wahhabi-Salafi Islamism, starkly capitalistic ethic, highly conservative social codes and alliance with the West in general and the United States in particular – represented everything that Arab nationalism of the Nasserite variant was not. Nasser proclaimed that 'the Arabs' oil should be for the Arabs'. He attacked Saudi Arabia's – as well as Jordan's and monarchical Iraq's – reliance on the West, lack of courage and 'disregard for the aspirations of their people'. In his eyes – and in his loud, far-reaching, highly influential speeches – those 'regressive regimes' were 'agents of the West, working against the will of the nation'.

In normal circumstances, such rhetoric could have been dismissed or ignored. But after the Suez Crisis, Nasser's appeal soared; the 'historical hero' seemed to have 'cut the tail' of the British and French empires in the Middle East; after challenging France by arming and bankrolling the Algerian revolutionaries, he had the courage to send thousands of his troops to Yemen, on the Saudi borders, to support the revolutionaries in their coup against the country's antiquated royal regime. Nasser's project appeared to be a true revolutionary avalanche. Syria begged to unite with Egypt under his leadership. Several Iraqi leaders invited him to Baghdad to announce Iraq's inclusion in the 'United Arab Republic'. Lebanon's Muslims and Druze hailed him as their leader. A special friendship emerged between Nasser and the philosopher-cum-politician Kamal Jumblatt, the Druze's feudalistic leader. Though the two men's backgrounds could not be more different, they shared a view of the Arabs' 'road towards salvation'. Jumblatt's quasi-sanctity in the Levant helped propel Nasser's appeal in the region. In Damascus, the people literally carried his car above their heads while singing for his life. The Nasserite project was increasingly becoming *real*; something akin to a 'United Arab World' could, at the time, be envisaged; it was impossible to dismiss or ignore his project.

What lay underneath that United Arab World – more import-ant than questions of economic integration, defence treaties or open borders – was the potential of a macro-developmental project that could use Arab oil as 'a weapon in the confrontation with the West', claim complete control of all strategic paths across the Arab world (including Aden, the last British protectorate in the Middle East, and the Strait of Hormuz, through which more than 40 per cent of all of the world's energy requirements pass, as well as the Suez Canal) and mobilize tens of millions of people in a vital strategic area. That threatening possibility put Nasser and his project squarely against US strategic interests in the region.[10]

Paradoxically, there were strong arguments for some sort of an accord between the United States and Nasser. Nasser's political venture was fundamentally secular; unlike most Arab states, Nasserite Egypt was envisioned to be a modern, non-religious state – a concept congruent with US principles and political beliefs. The Nasserite project was also the sole, viable alternative to political Islam in the Arab world, which had a fundamental dispute with the West in general and the United States in particular. Nasser also positioned his project (and mobilized his internal security forces) against Egyptian Communists.

However, the clash between the United States and Nasser was inevitable. Nasser played a leading role in terminating the British presence in the Middle East. And with the populist appeal and unrivalled command over the people's emotions that he enjoyed post-Suez, the 'hero' was unwilling to baulk at confronting the 'new colonialists' seeking to inherit British assets in the Middle East.

The confrontation with the United States transcended mere geopolitical calculations to become a clear and present danger.

With the British relinquishing their bases in the Gulf, the duty of protecting the strategic oil reserves fell to the US military. At the same time, Nasser's forces, after playing a crucial role in dethroning the Yemeni monarchy, were gaining ground just a few hundred kilometres away from Saudi's Eastern Province, the world's largest reservoir of oil. That 'danger' came a short time after America had doused another threat in the Gulf. In 1953, the CIA, under its legendary commander in the Middle East, Kermit Roosevelt, orchestrated the overthrow of Iran's Prime Minister Mossadeq, whose closeness to the Soviets and plans to nationalize all of Iran's oil assets were deemed intolerable perils to US interests in the region. America was not looking forward to confronting yet another 'hostile' nationalist project. To many American strategists, Nasser was becoming Cairo's Savonarola.

A number of analysts (especially from the Nasserite camp) accuse the United States of belittling Nasser and reducing him to 'yet another Arab terrorist'. This is not true. The United States and Britain launched propaganda wars against Nasser; they personalized their battle with him. But unlike in the cases of Saddam Hussein, Yasser Arafat or even Osama bin Laden, American commentators and decision-makers did not disparage Nasser; President Lyndon Johnson called him 'an obstacle' and 'an adversary to our interests in the region'. America gave Nasser his due – as a serious enemy.

The United States' perception of the Nasserite threat was exacerbated by the Egyptian leader's closeness to the USSR. In his memoir, Yevgeny Primakov (who had held a number of senior positions at the KGB and later at Russia's Foreign Intelligence Service, and was Russia's prime minister from 1998 to 1999) described Nasser not only as 'a friend' but, interestingly, as 'a rare phenomenon of genius in the Arab World'.[11] In 1955, Egypt became the first country from outside the Soviet bloc to buy weapons from the Soviets, in what came to be known as the Egyptian–Czechoslovakian arms deal. Nasser was increasingly very close to the then Soviet leader Khrushchev; the Soviets' highly generous financing of the High Dam, and Khrushchev's well-publicized visit to Aswan to commemorate the finishing of the dam's first phase, seemed to many in the West to represent Soviet infiltration of the Middle East – a stone's throw from the strategic oil reserves of the Gulf.

Nasser's personal behaviour towards the West, and especially the United States, did not help. He coldly rejected the Eisenhower doctrine which sanctioned the deployment of American forces in any Middle Eastern country to defend 'the territorial integrity and political independence of the region's nations against armed aggression from any nation controlled by international commun- ism', almost single-handedly destroyed the Baghdad Pact (a mili- tary organization created in 1955 under British auspices and an American nod of approval comprising Iran, Iraq, Turkey and Pakistan, with the objective of containing the USSR by building a line of allied countries on its southern borders) and publicly condemned 'the West's unending attempts to subjugate our lands'. Nasserites emphasize that Nasser's opposition to the Baghdad Pact stemmed from a strategic view that recognized the pact as a 'Western vehicle' to assert its control over the region, pull it away from potential closeness to the Soviets and crush the Arab nation- alist project. In reality, personal rivalry played a role as well. At the heart of the story of the Baghdad Pact is the personal antipathy between Nasser and Iraq's strong man, Nuri Al-Said Pasha. Nuri Al-Said, an aristocratic capitalist Anglophile with a special fond- ness for Savile Row suits and high-end Scottish malt, was the natural opposite of everything Nasser represented.[12]

Nasser's steadfastness in the face of Western, and especially American, interests in the Middle East made up a significant part of his domestic and regional appeal. He delivered 'his people's dreams' in a real political avalanche, and using his charisma, and his brilliant and far-reaching propaganda, he positioned himself as the 'people's hero' standing up to the 'imperialists, colonialists', and even to 'mighty America'.

But if the United States viewed Nasser's project as infuriating and potentially destabilizing of a region of strategic importance, Israel considered it fatal. Nasser's Arab nationalism adopted highly confrontational rhetoric against Israel; more, it defined itself in opposition to the Israeli project of becoming an integral part of the Middle East. Nasser's position was that all 'Arabic lands' (as the Arabs define them) belonged to the Arabs; that Israel (an ally of the United States and the West) was an 'arrow directed at the heart of the Arab world'; that there was a civilizational and generational war between the Arabs and Israel; that armed struggle against Israel was valid and necessary (though not necessarily in any particular short- or medium-term time-frame); and that the struggle with Israel was not a Palestinian–Israeli struggle, but an Arab–Israeli one.

Nasser, as Mohamed Hassanein Heikal repeatedly stressed, recognized that Egypt's national security extended far beyond its borders, well into the East (in the Levant and up to Iraq and Turkey), and that Israel's true function in the Middle East was to divide the Arab world – a 'Western military base' at its heart. That line of thinking positioned Israel, unequivocally, as not only an occupier of Arab Palestine, but as 'the nation's strategic enemy'. Nasser considered Israel's mere existence a threat to the Arabs' strategic interests, and especially to the objective of coalescing the disparate states into a grand Arab nation.

The Nasserite view here drew upon Egypt's long experience with wars. With the sole exception of Napoleon's campaign in Egypt, every single invasion the country witnessed in its history had come from the East. Sinai, throughout thousands of years, has been the invaders' route into the country. Egyptian rulers and strategists, from Tuthmosis III (the great New Kingdom's warrior Pharaoh) and Saladin to Mohamed Ali and Nasser saw Palestine and the Levant as Egypt's link to its domain of influence in the East. Egypt's political presence in the Levant was deemed a tenet of Egyptian grand geostrategy. Occupiers of Palestine and the Levant, from the Hittites to the Crusaders, to – now – Israel, were not only a potential threat to Egypt, but strategic adversaries of 'its project in the East'.

Israel was accustomed to ignoring such inflammatory, yet empty, rhetoric when it came from lesser men with little legitimacy in their own countries; when it came from Nasser (with his legitimacy, dramatic appeal and sweeping project), Israel had to take note. The Nasserite project was the most significant strategic challenge it had faced since its creation.[13]

The full story of the Six-Day War between Israel on the one hand and Egypt, Syria and Jordan on the other in June 1967 is beyond the scope of this book. Arab nationalists contend that the war was a deliberate trap for Nasser, a calculated attempt to strike the Arab nationalist project and discredit its hero. Israel's official record represents the war as the culmination of a chain of events started by border tensions between Israel and Syria, followed by Nasser's rushing to support Syria, and reached its climax with Nasser's May 1967 decision to expel the United Nations Emergency Force from Sinai (where it had been stationed since the end of the Suez Crisis in 1957) and close the Strait of Tiran (in the Red Sea) to all ships flying Israeli flags. Intentions and narratives aside, what is undisputable is that Israel occupied Sinai, the West Bank (previously under Jordanian guardianship), the Syrian Golan Heights and Jerusalem (with all the emotional and historic connotations attached to the city), obliterated three-quarters of the Egyptian air force and crushed the backbone of the Egyptian and Syrian armies.[14] This effectively marked the end of the Nasserite project. President Sadat, years later, commented that Nasser did not die on 28 September 1970 but on 5 June 1967 (the day the war broke out).

He was right. The defeat had a devastating impact on Nasser's health – and his ego. Much more importantly, it redefined how the people, ordinary Egyptians (the hero's true constituency), saw him. The hero, the historical giant, the dream, was revealed to be a mere inept leader presiding over a failing system. He trusted military commanders who proved to be incompetent and hopeless (King Hussein of Jordan once described Marshal Amer, the general commander of the Egyptian army in 1967, as 'retarded'); the great leader rushed into a battle only to be trounced in less than a week. The Arab nationalist project lost its momentum and its appeal. No longer were Nasser's actions 'historic', no longer was 'the nation moving on a generational stride towards victory'. Nasser became mortal: merely the president of a poor, third-world country that had been humiliatingly defeated in a war. For the first time ever, Egyptians rioted against Nasser; in March 1968, thousands of university students took to the streets to condemn what they saw as lenient verdicts on the military leaders 'responsible for the 1967 setback', and later in the same year, workers in different factories held strikes against the regime.

The society experienced a psychological dilemma. Right after the defeat, most Egyptians rejected Nasser's emotional resignation, delivered live on TV; that night, millions filled Cairo's streets hailing his name, demanding that he 'return to lead'; society felt 'orphaned' by Nasser's potential disappearance from the helm. Yet the same millions who poured into the streets singing his praises felt cheated, let down – and made their bitterness clear. The scar was not of the military defeat, but of the crumbling of the belief in the hero. In the eyes of the millions who once believed in him, the messiah no longer walked on water; he almost drowned.

There are hundreds of Arabic sources that reveal the dramatic fall in Nasser's status in the Egyptian and Arab psyche following the 1967 war. But perhaps modern Arabic poetry – especially the later work of Salah Jahin, and Nizar Kabbani's 1967–8 collection – is the most touching. Right after the defeat, Kabbani wrote:

> Friends, the ancient word is dead; the ancient books are dead; our speech with holes like worn-out shoes is dead; our poems have gone sour; women's hair and nights have gone sour; my grieved nation, in a flash, you turned me from a poet writing for love and tenderness to a poet writing with a knife; our shouting is louder than our actions; our swords are taller than us; friends, smash the doors; wash your brains; grow words, pomegranates and grapes; sail to countries of fog and snow; nobody knows you exit in your caves; friends, we run wildly through streets; dragging people with ropes; smashing windows and locks; we praise like frogs; turn midgets into heroes; in mosques, we crouch idly; write poems and proverbs; and pray God for victory.[15]

The defeat in 1967 had vast strategic implications. Nasser, unlike almost any other Arab leader, truly represented his people's will. A military defeat of such dramatic magnitude was a direct blow to the people's – and the nation's – determination. True, Egyptians poured into the streets, 'rejecting the war's results' and showing their resolve to fight, but at a deeper level, the immense damage done to the 'dream', to the people's drive, had a lasting impact on their relationship with the ruling regime and their trust in the solidarity between the ruler and the masses.

The war also confirmed a hypothesis held by many of Nasser's detractors in the Arab world: that Israel's strategic vision and decision-making processes at the time were vastly superior to Egypt's. Israel, despite the acrimonious divisions between the sidelined Ben-Gurion's camp and the ruling Levi Eshkol's government, was able to master a complex decision-making process (a war on multiple fronts) and overwhelm the regime led by Egypt's 'historical hero', despite the fact that the war was the culmination of a chain of events instigated by the Egyptian regime itself. Also the level of support Israel received from the United States before and during the war (an almost unlimited supply of weapons and information and, more importantly, a clear guarantee that the United States would not allow an Israeli defeat) dwarfed anything the Soviets had offered Egypt. The differences between the American and the Soviet modus operandi aside, this was a clear indication of the importance of the 'Israeli project' to the United States as opposed to that of the 'Arab nationalist project' to the USSR.[16]

The June 1967 rout was reminiscent of Mohamed Ali Pasha's defeat in 1840. 'The strategic opponents of the Egyptian project' dealt it a devastating blow. In 1840 Britain forced Mohamed Ali to abandon his dreams of building an empire and extending Egypt's domain to the Levant and the southern and eastern frontiers of the Ottoman Empire. In 1967, Israel and the United States forced Nasser to curtail his Arab nationalist dream; Egypt was to recoil from its leading pan-Arabic role to focus on its new, urgent adversity.

In the last three years of his rule, from the 1967 defeat to his death in 1970, Nasser seemed to be in a race with time – as if he knew he was shortly going to die, and was trying to correct his mistakes. He almost completed the rebuilding of the armed forces, made wide changes in government, initiated and managed the war of attrition against Israel (with frequent and irregular raids against

Israeli targets and units in Sinai intended to inflict casualties), mended relationships with the Saudis and with King Hussein in Jordan, all the while – admirably – continuing the ambitious industrialization programme. Yet his speeches of the time showed (in tone as much as in substance) that Nasser recognized that his project had lost its charm, that his relationship with ordinary Egyptians had changed forever and that his 'hero status' was gone. In the frenetic efforts of the last years of his life, the wounded messiah seemed determined to atone for his own sins.

The problem, however, was that by this stage there were many sins. Some of the key pillars of Nasser's project proved greatly lacking. The public sector evolved into a Soviet-style system of sterile thinking, a deathbed for talent, a site of mediocre resource allocation, inefficiency, suffocating bureaucracy, waste and decrepit management; in no way could it support lasting economic development in the country. Many of Nasser's detractors argue that land reform precipitated a dramatic retreat of Egyptian agribusiness: that the replacement of sophisticated, well-capitalized large landowners by low-skilled and poor peasants resulted in lower quality products, no concern for the long-term subsistence of the land, poor marketing of strategic Egyptian crops such as cotton and a continued erosion of links to international markets (especially in Europe).

The accusations against the Nasserite project go beyond the economic to the social and political. Nasser supplanted Egypt's liberal experiment with a suffocating military bureaucratic system. That halted the potential progress towards a genuine liberal democracy in the country, and ended Egypt's then close interaction with the West in general and Europe in particular. This had a lasting impact on society's development. In addition, Nasser's obsession with controlling the media remained very much alive in the continuing immense influence of the Egyptian government's media apparatus. More broadly, Egypt remains at heart a police state with a sad human-rights record: one of Nasser's imprints on the Egyptian political scene. Though torture and political coercion had certainly existed in monarchical Egypt, Nasser institutionalized them. There are disturbing accounts of the systematic torturing of Muslim Brotherhood members in the 1950s and 1960s and the collective punishment of Egyptian Communists: all distressing examples of the immense power of the country's interior ministry and intelligence services, which repeatedly trounced any rule of law.

Arab cinema is again the best conveyor of that legacy. In *Al-Karnak*, an Egyptian film produced in the mid-1970s, the leading Egyptian actress Souad Hosni brilliantly exposed what a broken soul would look like, after her character – an aspiring postgraduate student – was humiliated, tortured and raped in 'Nasser's prisons'. Filmgoers remember her slow walk on Cairo's Nile Corniche, a silent tear on her cheek – a grief-filled representation of the crushing of Egyptians under a cruel police state: Nasser's own.

But despite the severity of that record, Nasser's cardinal sin was his failure to leverage on his status. Nasser, undoubtedly, was Egypt's twentieth-century hero. Unlike his successors, Anwar Sadat and Hosni Mubarak, and certainly unlike all of his predecessors, Nasser represented the will and aspirations of the vast majority of the Egyptian people. They gave him an unlimited mandate, a political carte blanche. But he failed to use that mandate to transform his (and his people's) dreams into lasting institutions; he failed to convert his revolution into a state. Nasser's defeat in 1967, as well as the various flaws of his project, could have been seen as impediments in a historical march. The Nasserite project in Egypt could have been analogical to the Napoleonic one in France: it defined the nation, despite a dramatic military defeat and disastrous economic consequences. But it did not. Unlike Napoleon, Nasser did not leave behind a state – merely an ill-defined aspiration.

The main reason Nasser could not establish a state was that all of the new vehicles that he had created in the country, the pillars of his project – the new economic system after land reform, the societal changes that the industrialization and the nationalization policies had ushered in and the new Arab nationalist identity and foreign policy – were all personified in him; intentionally or not, the Nasserite socio-political venture revolved around the man himself. He failed to link his project with the major advances of the liberal experiment that had preceded him. He portrayed his project as starting, in effect, from scratch. That cutting-off from the past suited the revolutionary positioning of the project, and the glorification of the 'hero'. But it meant that Nasser severed his project from its context: the past and the historical flow that had led to it. That disconnection made his project, almost, an aberration in Egypt's modern life. And crucially, it diluted the project's chances of survival. The consent of the people, the basis of legitimacy upon which the entire Nasserite project had been based, was positioned as a mandate for the man himself – not for the project. When the man ceased to exist, the mandate was withdrawn. The project's vehicles (which were supposed to have evolved into the state's lasting institutions) appeared to have been just administrative means, drawing their power from the leader's own legitimacy, the people's consent to *him* – rather than from a system imbuing those new vehicles with institutional legitimacy.

The personification of Nasser's developmental project also put time pressure on the whole venture. Glorifying the hero neces-sitated very rapid moves and quick wins. Each year, every major speech had to herald new achievements. The land reform, the spreading of the public sector, the call for Arab nationalism could have evolved more slowly, allowing these transformational enterprises to mature and the people to develop alongside in order to make the best of them. That did not happen. The speed of these social changes outpaced the development of Egyptian society and the people. Land reform and asset nationalization resulted in a far more equitable land and asset distribution across the economy, but the new owners and managers were hardly on a par with the grand objectives of the developmental endeavour they were leading; the historical context and bold objectives of Arab nationalism transcended the realities of a poor, less developed society.

The lack of institutionalization and the personification of the project made it relatively easy for his successors (who came with very different convictions, strategies and programmes) to steer the country away – completely – from the Nasserite project. Sadat, for example, abolished Nasser's socialism; altered Egypt's strategic orientation from Arab nationalism and a close friendship with the USSR to an alliance with the United States; shunned progressive revolutionism and joined Saudi-led Arab conservatism; diluted the public sector in favour of a resurgent capitalism; and reversed the regime's relationship with its people: from a bottom-up legitimacy based on the masses' consent to top-down imposition of power. (This is discussed in Chapter 4.)

Arab nationalism, from the 1970s to the 2000s, has been in political retreat. Only one Nasserite candidate won in Egypt's parliamentary election of 2005. Not a single student union in any Egyptian university is controlled by Nasserite Arab nationalists. A respectable politician, Aziz Siddqui – arguably the father of Egyptian industrialization in the 1950s and 1960s, and one of the most esteemed Arab nationalists – failed to secure a single seat for his electoral group in any significant Egyptian election during the 2000s. The Islamic movement in Egypt, from the late 1970s, managed to occupy the political space in the country that had been the domain of Nasserite Arab nationalism, and to monopolize the representation of the country's middle class.

Despite all this, Arab nationalism is not necessarily destined for oblivion. Many of the observers who believe that Nasserite Arab nationalism is condemned to the political periphery fail to comprehend the major changes that the Nasserite project effected in Egypt. Nasser seized the political landscape with a thunderous coup, abolished monarchism, installed republicanism, reformed the agricultural sector, eliminated entire social strata and created others, built whole new industries, introduced groundbreaking political systems, entered into wars (close and far away), triggered a regional political wave (inspiring revolutions and social overhauls across the whole Arab world) and altered the country's social character.

The Nasserite project's vehicles remain, despite their weaknesses and their failure to evolve into institutions, the main pillars of Egyptian government and authority. Almost sixty years after the 1952 coup, Egypt is still ruled by the military establishment that Nasser's revolt brought to power. The Nasser-made Egyptian bureaucracy (predominantly in the public sector) remains the government's nerve centre and key administrative arm, even after successive waves of privatization. Egypt, despite decades of close association with US interests in the Middle East, and three decades of peace with Israel, still designs its foreign policy in accordance with the dynamics of the Arab–Israeli struggle. The Egyptian parliament retains commitment to the Nasserite doctrine that 50 per cent of representatives come from the peasant and labouring classes.[17] The official legitimacy of the Egyptian regime is still based on the Nasserite revolution of 1952.

Arab nationalism's failures and defeats in the last thirty years could also be a political asset. It may have been consigned to the political wilderness since the mid-1970s, but Arab nationalists can convincingly distance themselves from the policies and strategies (internal and external) that have shaped today's Egypt. Arab nationalists could market themselves as a clear slate: recalling the emotional power of the Nasserite project, while projecting it as a new force detached from its disappointments.

Today's external forces could also help to propel Arab nationalism. The election of Barack Obama, his pronounced new approach of interacting with the Arab world on the basis of mutual respect and cooperation and his decision to make Egypt a centre of that effort (including the choice of Cairo for his chief message to the Islamic world) – all compel Egypt to consider fresh ideas in response. Gamal Mubarak and the liberal capitalist venture (discussed in detail in Chapter 4) are one reaction. But that project cannot be separated from the long reign of Gamal's father, President Hosni Mubarak – with all of its problems. The Islamists offer an alternative project that could engage with the Obama/new-American calls on Egypt. But unlike George W. Bush's aggressiveness and hubris, Obama's wise engagement and astute communication would not promote jihadism, antagonism and fervent rhetoric – the classic imprints of political Islam in dealing with foreign policy. Arab nationalism, drawing on the best of the Nasserite project while having the flexibility to imbue it with modern pragmatism, could evolve to become a fresh platform with new ideas and policies – one that corresponds to Obama's (and the West's) calls on Egypt to return to its regional role in cooperative, rather than confrontational, modes.

But to leverage these factors, Arab nationalism would need to reinvent itself. Such an intellectual exercise – what to include from its mixed legacy (its successes and failures) and what to create and accrue – is an opportunity as well as a challenge. Forty years after his death, Nasser now is an idea much more than a president with specific achievements and failures, especially to the more than three-quarters of Egyptians who were born after the man's death. Such potent notions as 'the leader of the Egyptian revolution', the 'historical hero' and 'the representation of the Egyptian will' can also be flexibly moulded, shaped and employed in whatever new foreign policy and developmental programme a new Arab nationalism chooses.

The challenge, however, is that such a reinvention of Arab nationalism calls for a leader with immense talents and courage – something Arab nationalism has failed to produce since Nasser's death. It is also becoming increasingly difficult because the major figures in Nasserite and Arab nationalist thinking – from Mohamed Hassanein Heikal to almost all of the president's other close aides – are yesterday's men (all are in their ninth decade), unable to connect with young Egyptians. Moreover, Arab nationalism (and Nasser himself) has been the subject of a continuous campaign to discredit it for more than three decades. No wonder that the key tenets of Nasserite Arab nationalism are increasingly seen as relics of the past rather than the way forward.

A civic, secular, nationalist frame of reference (devoid of any religious underpinnings) would face immense challenges in today's highly religious Egyptian society. Nasserite socialism also appears out of step with the era's consensus on capitalism. But more perilously, the Arab nationalist identity today is a highly fraught and complicated issue. Most observers claim that Egypt's dramatic change of political course, from being leader of the confrontational Arab nationalist project to a pliable ally of the United States, has diluted Egypt's standing in the Arab world. This is certainly true, but it is not the main reason. In the 1950s and 1960s, Nasser's call on Egyptians to rise beyond their local problems to meet the challenges of 'their nation' resonated with Egypt's historical experience. Egyptians, at the time, saw their country as the natural leader of the Arab world. The land of history, culture and sophistication had an almost missionary role in its region. And that message did not sound condescending to its non-Egyptian recipients. The Arabs of the Gulf, the Levant, North Africa and Sudan were appreciative of the qualities and qualifications of their 'older sister'. At that time, a grand Arabic project emanating from Cairo had credibility.

That is not true today. The relative standing of Egyptians (the country, the people and the culture) in the Arabic milieu has significantly declined. The major socio-economic challenges that ordinary Egyptians have struggled with for thirty-five years have exacted their price on the country's living standards, income levels, educational quality, as well as on the people's skills, aptitudes, behaviours and attitudes. Such deterioration was taking place while many Arab countries, especially in the Gulf (but also in the Levant), were improving their indices in all these areas. That dichotomy has changed how the average Arab views the average Egyptian – from a teacher and potential leader to a follower and lower-level worker; and how the average Egyptian ranks him- or herself in the Arab world. Cairo and Alexandria have lost their 'soft power' to Beirut, Dubai, Abu Dhabi and Bahrain. That change of perception also affected the traditionally revered 'Egyptian fighter' who led the 'Arab nation's' 1948, 1956, 1967 and 1973 wars, as well as volunteered in the wars to liberate Algeria and Yemen. In the 1980s and 1990s, however, thousands of Egyptians were forced conscripts and paid fighters constituting the bulk of Iraq's 200,000 reservoir in its war with Iran. The 'Egyptian fighter' was also absent from the Arabs' most important struggle against Israel in the last thirty years: the Israeli–Hezbollah wars in southern Lebanon. Also, today, an Arab nationalist identity based on the old premise of an Egyptian leadership does not match the reality of the developmental state of Egyptian society relative to its supposed constituency (the Arab world). The required characteristics of the implied Egyptian role within classic Nasserite Arab nationalism are lost. This situation results in foreign-policy blunders and troubles, and casts severe doubt on the adequacy of any form of classic Arab nationalism.

These challenges might doom Arab nationalism, making the old project too irrelevant to reinvent itself. It might remain in the intellectual comfort zone of its heritage: the 1950s to 1960s opposition to the West, antipathy to capitalism, stagnant definition of Arab nationalism and insistence on a socialist framework. Such an acceptance of political and intellectual mediocrity would mean gradually withdrawing from any serious political confrontation or debate; inhabiting a nostalgic corner of the Egyptian psyche that continues to remember the Nasserite experiment; and feeding on the sympathy and melancholy that comparisons between today's Egypt and 'the good old days of Nasser' evoke in the increasingly thin segment of grey-haired Egyptians who have lived through Nasser's times.

In that scenario, Arab nationalism's very existence as a political force in Egypt could be in question. Unlike political Islamism, Arab nationalism has no major following on the Egyptian streets. Unlike the regime's liberal capitalism, it lacks the state's resources and the might of the country's ultra-rich to impose itself on society. Nasserite Arab nationalism, failing to reinvent itself, could well become irrelevant as a result of the impending fight between political Islamism and liberal capitalism over the hearts and minds of young Egyptians. To a large extent, Arab nationalism's sole chance of reclaiming any political prominence in Egypt, and influencing the country's future, is a political reincarnation: the birth of another charismatic leader, who, building on the opportunities offering themselves and against the very low odds of overcoming the mighty political Islamism and the dominant liberal capitalism, propels it back into significance. Such an exercise would call upon a leader with immense intellect, a sense of history and charismatic appeal. The prospect may be difficult to imagine – but so was what happened in 1952, when a junior army officer, an ordinary *saiidi* (a man from poor, isolated Southern Egypt) without any claim to aristocracy or richness, became Egypt's twentieth-century hero.

CHAPTER 3

THE ISLAMISTS

MORE THAN A million mourners packed Cairo's streets in June 1998 in a display of grief for Sheikh Mohamed Metwalli Al-Sharaawi, Egypt's (and the Arab world's) most popular and successful Islamic preacher. Al-Azhar University erected a marquee to receive the huge crowds wishing to offer their condolences. It was a remarkable tribute to a man who illuminated the complex layers of religious sentiment and affiliation in Egypt.

Every Friday afternoon for almost three decades, millions of TV screens in Egypt would glow with the vivacious features of this elderly, amiable man. The Sheikh – by turn smiling, laughing, nodding, waving and wagging a finger to emphasize a point – would sit cross-legged under strong TV lights inside the grand hall of Al-Hussein Mosque, surrounded by dozens of his ardent followers, lecturing his audience in simple colloquial Arabic on the different interpretations of a Koranic verse.[1] But his reach went beyond Koranic interpretation and theology, and Sheikh Al-Sharaawi's fatwas carried even more authority among the people than Al-Azhar's. For example, Al-Sharaawi's opposition to conventional banking and support of 'Islamic money management' contrasted with – and overshadowed – Al-Azhar's repeated endorsement of the former, and greatly contributed to an exponential growth in the Islamic finance industry in the 1980s.

The Sheikh's following was particularly strong among the young. A few years before his death, Sheikh Al-Sharaawi disagreed with a decision made by the management of Al-Azhar concerning the university's theological curriculum. To avoid a backlash from the university's students, Al-Azhar's Grand Sheikh had to visit Al-Sharaawi to explain the rationale behind the management's decision and secure his blessings. The Sheikh's views shaped Egyptian society's agenda as well. Al-Sharaawi's fatwa that 'humans do not own their bodies' – and hence his prohibition of organ-transplant operations – was a key factor behind the Egyptian parliament's repeated blocking of legislation on the issue. His influence extended even to Egyptian cinema; he was one of the architects of the 'religious wave' among actresses in the 1990s who chose to shun the art, dropping out of the film business and 'reverting to God' as born-again Muslims.

Sheikh Al-Sharaawi's popularity and his status as one of the most prominent symbols of popular Egyptian culture in the last three decades make him the embodiment of the ascendance of religiosity in Egypt from the 1970s. Most observers trace the phenomenon to the missionary zeal of Saudi Wahhabism, fuelled by petrodollars in the wake of the oil shock of 1974–5. What makes this extension of reach and power so problematic is that the norms and traditions of Wahhabism were very different from Egypt's own.

For around two centuries (from the tenth to the twelfth centuries CE), Egypt was ruled by the Fatimids: an Ismaili Shi'ite dynasty that claimed descent from Fatima Al-Zahraa, the Prophet

Mohamed's daughter and the wife of Imam Ali, the Prophet's cousin and the first of the Shia Imams. The Fatimids had a lasting impact on Egypt: Cairo itself was founded under their rule in 969, as was Al-Azhar (whose name is derived from that of Al-Zahraa). The dynasty also inaugurated a large number of religious and social festivals, the most notable of which venerate Ahl Al-Bayt (Prophet Mohamed's descendants) and commemorate Al-Mwaled (the birthdays of the Prophet's descendants buried in Egypt, as well as those of saintly scholars).[2]

The Fatimid dynasty fell in 1171, when Saladin removed the last of its Caliphs and restored Egypt to the Sunni world; the Egyptian state became the most important province in the Abbasid Sunni Empire. But the society became characterized by a unique mix of Sunni theology and Shi'ite social traditions. Al-Azhar evolved and consolidated its unique status; and the people continued to honour the Prophet Mohamed's descendants (in many cases ascribing to them powers of divine and spiritual intercession), to celebrate Al-Mwaled and to embrace various Shi'ite traditions; even today, the country's social calendar is dominated by festivals and observances of clear Shi'ite origin.[3] This Sunni–Shi'ite mix made Egypt both hostile ground and a natural target for Wahhabism. Hostile, because the country's affinity to Shi'ism was at odds with this strict and purist form of Islam; Egyptians' veneration of the Prophet's descendants and of other 'holy men and women' offends the sensibilities of strict Wahhabis and other Orthodox groups, who insist that Islam does not revere any human or order; a natural target, because of Egyptians' piety and the dominant role of religion in their lives.

The place of religion in Egyptians' social lives had been changing in the Nasserite years of the 1950s and 1960s. Arab nationalism and its associated progressive ideologies pushed religion (Christianity as well as Islam) back into the private sphere of homes, mosques and churches, and away from the public arena of streets, schools and universities. The uncompromisingly civic nature of the Nasserite state relegated religion to the matter of a relationship between the person and his/her God. Religion became detached from national (Egyptian or Arab) identity, ceased to play a role in the era's grand projects and hardly featured in the country's active foreign policy of the time. This view could not be more different from that of Saudi Wahhabism, which bases political authority and state identity on religion; and that envelops any national project in religious colours and rhetoric.[4]

These substantial differences notwithstanding, the expansionist Wahhabi project found fertile ground in Egypt. Three indigenous factors contributed to its favourable reception. First, between 1974 and 1985, more than 3 million Egyptians migrated to the Gulf, with the majority settling in Saudi Arabia. Most of them hailed from Egypt's lower (and lower middle) classes, and had had limited exposure to Egypt's old glamour. In part as a result, they quickly absorbed the cultures of their new home; and more slowly, the dominant social and cultural milieu of the Gulf's most austere centre found its way to Egypt's Delta and Saeedi villages, and later to the heart of Cairo and Alexandria.

The change can be measured in the increase in the proportion of women in Egypt wearing the veil, from less than 30 per cent to more than 65 per cent in two decades; by the early 1990s, the veil was established as the dress code on the Egyptian street rather than as an occasional choice. In the less-privileged villages of the Nile Delta, as well as in Cairo's and Alexandria's poorest neighbourhoods, the veil became the natural step for girls as young as twelve.[5] There was also a general shift in the socially preferred pattern of gender roles, with the return to an emphasis on men's public role and women's domesticity.[6] At the same time, Cairo and other Egyptian cities witnessed a dramatic rise in the number of mosques. Thousands of prayer rooms (*Zawyas*) were established in garages and ground-floors in rich and poor neighbourhoods alike. In the mid-1980s there was a mosque for every 6,031 Egyptians, by the mid-2000s, there was a mosque for every 745 persons.[7] Even colloquial Egyptian changed: 'Good morning' (*'Naharak Saeed'*) and 'Good evening' (*'masaa al-kheir'*) were replaced by 'peace be upon you', Islam's greeting (*'al-salamu aleikom'*).

The politics of the 1970s were the second factor in this social shift. In his efforts to confront the Nasserite and socialist forces in Egypt, President Anwar Sadat unleashed Egypt's Islamic forces. He released thousands of the Muslim Brotherhood's leaders and members from jail (after years of imprisonment and prosecution under Nasser), and allowed the Brotherhood's old newspaper the *Call* (*Al-Dawaa*) to be reissued. He tried to assume the mantle of Islam by calling himself 'the guardian of the faith'; emphasized that his first name was 'Mohamed' not 'Anwar'; promoted religious schools; authorized a major increase in the budget of Al-Azhar and an expansion of its parallel educational system; opened the door for leading religious scholars and commentators to dominate the state-controlled media; introduced apostasy laws in Egypt after years of a highly liberal intellectual atmosphere; declared sharia law (Islamic jurisprudence) as the principal source for the Egyptian constitution (after decades during which religion was generally marginal to legislation with the exception of personal status laws); and declared himself the leader of 'an Islamic pious country'. In less than a decade the civic nature of the Egyptian state of the 1950s and 1960s was replaced by a quasi-Islamic one; and a liberal public atmosphere and discourse became predominantly religious and conservative.

In 1977, Sadat introduced the 'Shame Law' which gave the state wide powers to prosecute anyone 'who threatens the values of the society'; the values were defined as 'the genuine traditions of the Egyptian family'. The law also prosecuted those 'who propagate views that are not in step with divine religions'.

Third, the economic situation in the 1970s and 1980s also supported the rise of the religious movement. Open economic policies that Sadat introduced in the mid-1970s (*al-infitah*) put enormous pressures on Egypt's middle class, which witnessed a significant erosion in its purchasing power and its relative standing in society (especially with the rise of segments of the country's lower classes that had significantly benefited from the economic consequences of the migration to the Gulf); the result was a damaging reshuffling in its composition (discussed in Chapter 4). These pressures in turn provided an opportunity for the Muslim Brotherhood to re-establish its presence in Egyptian society.

The Brotherhood has had a turbulent history. The movement was established in 1928 in Ismailiya, one of the three main cities on the Suez Canal; its founder was Sheikh Hassan Al-Banna, a charismatic schoolteacher who had been highly influenced in turn by the ideas of Sheikh Mohammed Abdou (introduced in Chapter 1). The Brotherhood – concerned to bridge the gap between traditional religious thinking and the waves of modernity that Egypt witnessed in the first few decades of the twentieth century – won appeal thanks to Al-Banna's charisma, and soon became a countrywide political movement heavily involved in Egypt's struggle for independence against the British occupation, voicing the rights and grievances of Egypt's disenfranchised classes and advocating the establishment of a religious state and the imposition of sharia law. The group's growth was dramatic; in under fifteen years, the Brotherhood grew from a single room in Ismailiya to 3,000 branches across the whole of Egypt, and from a tiny cell round Sheikh Al-Banna to more than 450,000 active members.

The Brotherhood had complicated relationships with Egypt's key political powers of the time, the Palace and the Al-Wafd Party. Its intense and at times passionate pursuit of *al-dawaa* (the call to religion) led to confrontations with the regime, which culminated in the assassination of Hassan Al-Banna by the Egyptian police in 1949, under direct orders from the Egyptian prime minister. The tension continued after the 1952 coup that abolished the Egyptian monarchy. A number of the coup's leaders, including Nasser, had relationships with the Brotherhood. Some (but not Nasser) actually 'swore on the Koran and the sword' (pleaded allegiance to the group). But neither the Brotherhood's political nor its military leadership had any command of the group of officers who led the coup in July 1952.

In the second half of 1952 and early 1953, the Brotherhood tried – initially with success – to deepen its relationship with some of the coup's leaders, but it failed to form an alliance with Nasser. The Brotherhood gambled on the 'pious wings in the movement' (the words of Hassan Al-Tuhami, one of the closest members of the coup's leadership to the Brotherhood), and in so doing, positioned itself as a strategic opponent of Nasser (who at the time – the second half of 1953 – was sidelining all the coup's leaders who were not personally loyal to him). The chain of events led to a bitter confrontation between Nasser and the Brotherhood. In 1954 Nasser accused the Brotherhood's 'secret apparatus' of perpetrating an attempt on his life that had just taken place in Alexandria. Soon after, the Brotherhood was officially abolished, scores of its members were imprisoned and thousands were compelled to leave Egypt.

The diaspora proved highly beneficial to the Brotherhood. Thousands of its members found their way to the, then, sympathetic Saudi Arabia, where many managed to build vast fortunes. Others settled in Europe, especially in Switzerland, where new branches of the Brotherhood were created and were able to operate freely.[8]

Many of those who wrote about the Brotherhood's return to Egypt after Nasser's years of persecution and enforced exile focused on the group's political machinations, organizational structure, ability to propagate its messages, relationship with President Sadat and the characters of its successive 'general guides' in the 1970s and 1980s. But the factor that really cemented the Brotherhood's social re-emergence, and founded the Islamic movement's social base, was its highly efficient services infrastructure.

This included a range of provisions targeted at the poor and needy: affordable healthcare in the form of 'Islamic hospitals', 'non-corrupt' food-distribution centres in poor neighbourhoods, practical assistance in finding jobs (especially targeted at newly graduated Muslims), welfare benefits, innovative transport solutions in some of Cairo's and Alexandria's most crowded suburbs, accommodation for out-of-town students (in addition to lecture notes and study groups) and humanitarian activities in some of Egypt's most deprived areas. Through these vehicles the Brotherhood developed a matrix of social services that the Egyptian government, crushed by macro-economic burdens, was unable to provide. The Brotherhood's social infrastructure was both its most potent political instrument and its claim to legitimacy, especially after many years of absence from the Egyptian street. At a time when the socio-economic consequences of *al-infitah* were eroding the regime's legitimacy (a point discussed in Chapter 4), the Brotherhood was positioning itself to the majority of Egyptians as 'the provider', a role the regime was incapable of fulfilling.[9]

The Brotherhood's expanding social role was increasingly felt at the centres of Egypt's civic organizations too. Between 1992 and 2002, the Brotherhood repeatedly won the elections of the Lawyers', the Journalists', the Doctors' and the Engineers' Syndicates. In 1978–9, the Brotherhood won *all* the seats in the Cairo University Medical and Engineering Colleges' student unions, all but one seat in the Cairo University Law School's student union and around three-quarters of the Pharmacy College's union – a pattern that continued well into the 2000s.[10] The Egyptian media repeatedly presented the Brotherhood's successes as examples of the Brotherhood's disciplined organization as opposed to the regime's sloppy and corrupt machinations. That view ignored the strategic picture. By taking over some of the country's most important, and traditionally secular, groupings, the Brotherhood was gaining significant political power and actually realizing its objective of a cultural Islamization of society.[11] The victories were both clear proof of the power and allure of Egypt's Islamic movement, and an indication that the Brotherhood could challenge the regime's legitimacy in representing the country's middle class.

The rise of Islamism in Egypt in the late 1970s and 1980s coincided with a decline in Egyptian liberalism – civic and religious. Egyptian liberalism is typically presented as an odd combination of two arch enemies: monarchical (the liberal, Europe-oriented elite) and Nasserite (Arab nationalist, which despite an anti-Western political agenda is culturally drawn to London, Paris and New York). Indeed, these two groups were the pillars of Egypt's *cultural* liberalism in its golden age from the 1930s to the late 1960s, but by the 1970s and 1980s they were severely weakened: the first by its diaspora and loss of political and financial might during the Nasser era, the second by Sadat's successive assaults throughout the 1970s. In his 1971 'Corrective Revolution', Sadat imprisoned a number of Nasser's key lieutenants who were challenging his authority; he also sidelined a large number of

Nasserites from the 'Socialist Union', Nasser's key political vehicle. In the mid-1970s, especially after the first round of negotiations with Israel, the regime again chased the Nasserites, this time out of university student unions, professional syndicates and major newspapers. The Nasserites also featured heavily in the mass wave of incarceration in September 1981. But Egyptian liberalism's weakness was felt beyond those social segments. The reshuffling of Egypt's middle class has altered general societal values and tastes towards a mix of consumerism and religious conservatism – a new, ascendant cultural phenomenon.

The rising economic power and social presence of the Egyptians in the Gulf and their families at home, and the overall shift of orientation – especially in music, cinema and popular culture – from London and Paris towards Riyadh and Kuwait (at a time when those centres were much more conservative and inward-looking than they are today), led to a skin-deep form of modernization.[12] This meant exposure to the latest technology, familiarity with Western popular culture (from Hollywood films to the most successful American sitcoms) and accessibility (the newly affluent families sent their children to English and American schools; English was no longer a barrier). But that familiarity with Western products was compartmentalized; it did not – as its equivalent in an earlier era had – trigger 'an examination of the future of our culture' (Taha Hussein), 'a meeting of civilizations' (Al-Akkad) or a vast and productive wave of quality cultural productions. Rather, the society was wide open to popular Western culture at the very time when it was being drawn towards conservatism and increased religiosity. The Cairene and Alexandrian middle-class family would watch the afternoon lesson of Sheikh Al-Sharaawi only to switch channels later to watch the evening episode of *Dallas* or *Dynasty*, and later *Grey's Anatomy* or *Desperate Housewives*. As large segments of society became participants in the new consumerist waves,[13] they were also presented with archaic, debilitated views of 'a return to Islam'.

Here, it is important to highlight that the orientation away from Europe and to the Gulf was partly the result of Europe's policy of curbing migration, especially from North Africa. London, Paris, Vienna and Rome, which in the 1950s and 1960s welcomed cheap labour, were, by the 1980s and 1990s, restricting entry, and so were increasingly off-limits to the vast majority of young Egyptians searching for work opportunities abroad.

Sheikh Al-Sharaawi himself was one of the few commentators who found justification in maintaining that cultural compartmentalization when he argued that by using the West's technology and modernity – but without necessarily having the knowledge to master that technology, without being a productive agent in its world and era and without culturally interacting with it – God was enslaving the West to Muslims' interests.[14] That thinking was vastly different from attempts in the first half of the twentieth century to find a workable mix between 'the pillars of our rational religion' and the West's 'working schools of thinking'.[15] The 'modernization' of the 1970s and 1980s, by contrast, unintentionally blended plain Wahhabi Islamism with Western, especially American, popular culture, coexisting in an artificial comfort zone that numbed minds and discouraged courageous examination and intellectual scrutiny.

Not surprisingly, the liberal and creative Islamic thinking that had shaped the Islamic movement in the first half of the twentieth century – led by Sheikh Mohamed Abdou, Rachid Reda,[16] Taha Hussein and Abbas Mahmoud Al-Akkad – did not find its way into the Egyptian Islamism that emerged from the late 1970s onwards. In addition, many of the liberal Islamic voices that appeared in this generation (for example, Mohamed Saeed

Al-Ashmawi,[17] Mohamed Shahrour[18] and Rachid Al-Ghanoushi) were positioned as opponents, and in some cases 'enemies', of the Islamic movement, to be fought and suppressed, rather than engaged with. Even the weighty Salafist voices (for example, Mohamed Seleem Al-Awaa,[19] Mohamed Al-Ghazali,[20] Fahmi Howeidy[21] and Gamal Al-Banna[22]) were sidelined as 'too intellectual'. The dominant cultural force of the era suppressed even insightful and authoritative voices in the Islamic movement.

The country's literary and intellectual luminaries were marginalized in the same way. Naguib Mahfouz's[23] novels were no longer serialized in *Al-Ahram*. Tawfik Al-Hakeem's last two novels were published in Paris and Beirut, but not in Cairo. Ihsan Abdel Kodous, Egypt's foremost romance novelist, was branded a 'pornographer', and some of his publishers took it upon themselves to change the endings of some of his novels (without his knowledge) to suit the rising social conservatism. Egypt's leading (and genuinely independent) columnists were compelled to publish their work elsewhere (in London or in the more tolerant corners of the Arab world, mainly Beirut and Kuwait[24]) or in serious but low-circulation Egyptian publications. Even in art, the death of Umm Kulthoum and Abdel Haleem Hafez seemed ominous. Egyptian cinema and music went through a regrettable low period. Many observers blamed the deterioration in quality on the low production values of the time, induced by the withdrawal of some of Egypt's famed producers and the emergence of a new breed of 'parasites'.[25] The key liberal forces, religious as well as civic, that had dominated Egyptian society were gradually driven from its centre.

The rise of a strict form of Islamism in a traditionally peaceful, agricultural society like Egypt's should not necessarily have led to a strong wave of religious-inspired violence. But in the late 1970s, a number of trends in Egyptian society interacted with rising religiosity to yield dangerous outcomes. The *al-infitah* years produced dramatic levels of corruption and self-enrichment, and shocking gaps in income and living standards. This turbulence, occurring over a very short period of time, created undercurrents of anger that manifested themselves in outbursts of fury, such as the riots of 18–19 January 1977 (see Chapter 4) – and in Sadat's assassination in October 1981.

There were also deep and unhealed scars in the Egyptian psyche. Egypt's defeat in the 1967 war weakened the core of nationalist (and Egyptian) ideas; the intoxicating Nasserite wave with its grand dreams – and strictly secular framework – had been crushed. The retreat of the nationalist idea provoked an intellectual rejection of everything that had led to the humiliation. Society was also in an aggressive mood. More than a million young Egyptians had returned from the war front (*al-gabha*) to towns and villages all over Egypt. Less than a third of them had actually engaged in the hostilities of 1967 and the Ramadan/Yom Kippur War of October 1973, but a majority had spent more than six years (some almost a decade) in a harsh military environment, detached from the life of a changing society. The stressful military experience bred in many cases aggression and a predilection to violence, which were exacerbated by the wider social anger. Many of the returning soldiers described themselves as a 'defrauded generation': they claimed that 'the spoils of peace' had gone to the regime's cronies, not to the people or 'those who spent years away from home, under fire'. The anger sweeping society expressed itself in significantly rising crime rates and everyday violence.[26]

The tumultuous changes in Egypt's foreign policy at the time also played a role in redirecting aggression and rising violence – inwards. The Camp David Peace Accords between Egypt and Israel, signed by President Sadat and Israeli Prime Minister Menachem Begin in September 1978 and which laid the framework for the 1979 Egyptian–Israeli Peace Treaty, was supposed to herald an era of peace, but was regarded by millions as a 'sell-out' that 'betrayed the millions who died in Sinai' and represented a 'national humiliation and disgrace'. This is not to imply that the whole of Egyptian society opposed the Camp David accords. Many welcomed the treaty. Yet, the hostility that Camp David received from some of Egypt's most notable writers and commentators was so powerful that, for many, the treaty symbolized 'a betrayal'. Ahmad Fouad Nigm, Egypt's most popular satirist poet, wrote his most memorable (and scathing of Sadat) poems at that time. Nizar Kabbani, the Arab world's most famous poet over the last five decades, lamented the fall of Egypt, the Arab world's 'land of dignity', after 'the Great Nasser' in the hands of a 'slave' (Sadat). Ahmed Bahaa El-Din, ex-editor-in-chief of *Al-Ahram*, described his 'shock, disbelief, and pain' watching Sadat shake hands with Israel's leaders at Ben Gurion Airport in Jerusalem. And though Sadat had tried to mobilize the Islamic movement to defend the peace treaty from the attacks of Nasserites and Arab nationalists, that movement (and especially the Muslim Brotherhood) found it untenable to embrace a peace agreement with the 'Jews'.[27] The ideology of 'fighting the internal enemy who has sold out to the infidels' was born.[28]

But it was another event in the world of international relations that amplified the power and reach of violent religiosity in Egypt, and provided it with swaths of fanatical and experienced soldiers. This was the jihadist war against the Soviet army in Afghanistan after its invasion of December 1979.

After the invasion the US, supported by its leading Arab allies Saudi Arabia and Egypt, decided to turn Moscow's exercise in its then satrap into a war of attrition against its arch Cold-War rival. Islamic clerics declared it a religious obligation to aid the 'Islamic cause in Afghanistan', and tens of thousands of young Arabs –

including thousands from Egypt[29] – heeded the call to jihad against 'the atheist communist invaders'. These religious fighters (*mujahideen*) were motivated by a severe militant Islamism; their objective was the annihilation of 'God's enemies'. When that was achieved a decade later with the Soviet withdrawal, the fighters returned to their native countries with a belief that they could win over even mightier forces. The thousands of young men who 'fought for Islam' in faraway lands believed that their next mission was to install Al-Sharia and Islamic rule in their home-lands – using the means they were trained in and victoriously employed: violent guerrilla war.[30]

The Egyptian mujahideen had a rich experience in Afghanistan. Thousands of young Egyptian men lived in Al-Sindh and the Punjab regions, and among populations that cut through Pakistan and Afghanistan. Their interaction with the peoples of those regions, who are part of Islamic history and formed the core of the venerated Islamic Mughal Empire, exposed them to a different type of Islam. On the fringes of the Islamic Ummah, far from the centre of its successive empires, on the border with 'hostile' cultures such as the Hindus and 'the Muscovites', and not speaking Arabic (the Koran's language), the Punjabi and Al-Sindhi adhered to a strictly Islamic identity and a highly conservative modus vivendi; their geographic and historical conditions necessitated a vigilant and apprehensive way of looking at the world. The immersion in that culture, in the midst of a long war, left its mark not only on the mujahideen's thinking but also on their temperament.[31]

The Afghan War further helped to turn the wave of social anger in Egypt towards violence and militancy. Behind the phenomenon lay an intellectual framework that channelled frustration, filled the vacuum left by the retreat of civic and religious liberals and promoted the use of violence inside the country. Sayyid Qutb (1906–66) was the chief theorist of that framework.

Qutb, a teacher and novelist, hardly possessed the background, depth of knowledge or qualifications to become one of the grandees of Islamic thought in the land of Al-Azhar. But though he had not studied in that institution, he did revive the thinking of two respectable (if rejectionist) Islamic thinkers of mediaeval times, Ibn Hanbal and Ibn Taimiyah, and used their ideas as a focus for contemporary criticism of 'modernity and Westernization'.

Ahmed Ibn Hanbal (780–855) is considered one of the most rigorous scholars of 'Al-Hadith' (Prophet Mohamed's sayings and traditions); his book *Al-Masnad* is one of the key references on the subject. Ibn Hanbal's fame, however, was due to the school of thought that emanated from his teachings, and which came to be considered the purist and most conservative among Sunni Islam's four key schools of jurisprudence. The most intellectually intriguing episode in Ibn Hanbal's life was his fierce struggle with Al-Mutazillah, an isolationist school of Islamic philosophy that flourished in the eighth and ninth centuries in parts of Iraq and the Levant and which started with advocating the primacy of reasoning over tradition in interpreting the Koran and progressed into elaborate beliefs on the nature of God and the Koran that were very different from those of the Sunnis and the Shiis. Ibn Hanbal's struggle with Al-Mutazillah centred on the nature of the Koran and whether or not it was 'created'. Ibn Hanbal considered Al-Mutazillah's thinking heretical and vehemently attacked it, and as a result, he was subjected to severe torture by Caliph Al-Maamun, who believed in Al-Mutazillah's school of thought and was their grand backer. This story might appear irrelevant to the history of Islamism in Egypt over the past few decades. However, it was a milestone that led to the marginalization of the different schools of Islamic philosophy (*falsafah*); and it was that marginalization that paved the way for the emergence of the literalist movement of Koranic interpretations for the first time in the Muslim world. The dominance of this school in Baghdad, Damascus and later Cairo (especially after the fall of the Ayyubids and throughout the Mameluke period) stifled many creative movements and initiatives that could have enriched Islamic philosophy and jurisprudence over the centuries.

Ibn Taimiyah (1263–1328) was a rigorous disciple of Ibn Hanbal, yet, unlike his teacher, who lived in Baghdad at the height of the Islamic empire's power and grandeur, Ibn Taimiyah lived in an age when Islam was under attack, from the Crusaders coming from Europe and the Mongols attacking from the East. Being based between Damascus and Cairo (the centres of the 'jihad' at the time) helped radicalize his thinking. He saw creative, modernizing thinking as treason against the 'pure religion', and argued that all powers (intellectual and tangible), needed to be mobilized to defend the religion against 'its numerous enemies'. Ibn Taimiyah spent years hunting down any philosophical interpretation that appeared to deviate from the literalist, 'clear' interpretation of the Koran. He was especially scathing of the Sufis, the mystics of Islam, who, in earlier ages, had produced some of the most creative and refreshing insights in Islamic thought. Ibn Taimiyah's most famous book, *Politics in the Name of Divine Rule for Establishing Good Order in the Affairs of the Shepherd and the Flock*, called for strict imposition of the Sharia, set out the literalist interpretation of the Koran as the sole source and measure of law and rule, and criminalized the separation of power and authority from religious rule and jihad. Ibn Taimiyah's ideas had featured regularly, not only in Sayyid Qutb's writings, but in those of other jihadist theorists as well.

Qutb also drew on his own first-hand experience in the United States (as a graduate student specializing in education in

Colorado, 1948–50) to denounce Western society as a whole as a land of infidels; to argue that Egyptian society, like all Muslim societies at the time, was living in a *jahiliyah* (the days of ignorance before Islam was revealed to Prophet Mohamed); to depict nationalist leaders such as Nasser as apostates 'eradicating Islam from its lands'; to reject the notion of countries and states, arguing that they are 'idols' invented by man to replace God; and to contend that society needed a revolution to be accomplished by a 'new Koranic generation'. In that specific point, Qutb was influenced by Abu Al-Ala Al-Mawdudi, Pakistan's leading twentieth-century theological theorist, who introduced the concept of God's sovereignty (*Al-Hakimeyah Al-Ilaheya*), and argued that Western democracy, by empowering humans to 'rule', was antithetical to Islam's governing foundations which accept no ruling but that of God.

The intellectual grounding of Qutb's two main books – *Signposts on the Road* and *In the Shadows of the Koran* – is shaky in comparison to the work of Islamist thinkers such as Mohamed Abdou and Al-Akkad. But the religious (and increasingly violent) wave of the 1970s, which was detached from the insights of the canonical thinkers of the Egyptian Islamic movement of the early twentieth century, was inclined to promote simplistic voices that advocated hostility and resentment, rather than reflect on quieter ones that prioritized contemplation and rigorous reflection. Qutb's ideas also faced very limited competition. No rejectionist Islamic line of thought had emerged in the 1960s or early 1970s; when scores of angry young men later emerged and sought channels for their repudiation of society, Qutb's Islamist ideology was the only one available.

Qutb was a pure rejectionist. In the greater part of his work, he focused on denouncing the present as opposed to presenting an alternative (apart from the vague veneration of Islam's early society in Al-Medina, Prophet Mohamed's capital). He repeatedly informed his readers of what he considered *jahiliyah*, but rarely presented his 'ideal society' in contemporary hues. His views as well as his words were livid and irate. Even the greatest rejectionist (and arguably the most aggressive thinker) in Islamic history, Sheikh Hassan Al-Sabbah, the founder and legendary leader of the Assassins (the group that terrorized the Middle East in the eleventh century) situated his violent doctrine in a positivist philosophy that aimed 'to arrive at the pedestal of goodness'.[32]

Qutb was executed by hanging in 1966, having been accused with five other Brotherhood members of plotting to overthrow the regime and assassinate Nasser. His ideas had a life of their own, however. He emerged as the godfather of militant Islamism; and almost a decade after his death, his ideas became the theoretical platform for a number of militant groups terrorizing Egyptian society in the name of Islam.[33]

Egypt was to endure two difficult decades of severe armed struggle between the regime and groups seeking to overthrow it and inspire a socio-religious revolution. Most observers of militant Islamism in Egypt represent the phenomenon as the work of organized terrorist cells, with Al-Jamaa Al-Islamiya (The Islamic Group) typically presented as the most important. Al-Jamaa, which was set up in the mid-1970s, was certainly Egypt's largest militant Islamic group for twenty years from the late 1970s, and the key perpetrator of a large number of the attacks Egypt witnessed in that period.[34] The Egyptian Islamic Jihad was another major formation with a long record of violence.[35] But to view these as the grand masters of militant Islamism in Egypt is a Western-centric view rooted in the experience of dealing with groups such as the IRA in Ireland or ETA in Spain. In Egypt, those movements comprised hundreds of loosely connected, poorly organized and barely managed small cells of young

Muslims, who usually started out as members of the Muslim Brotherhood and who were later radicalized as a result of incarceration or exposure to militant ideology (or both). The cells were virtually independent; there was very little in terms of central planning, organizational nerve-centre or strict lines of command. The 1981 assassination of President Sadat is the perfect example of that flexible structure and decentralized modus operandi. The crime was undertaken by two groups (which, combined, comprised less than a dozen men) with limited technical capacity or hierarchy.[36] The real potency of militant Islamism in Egypt lay not in the organizational acumen of its militants; it was in the thousands of young Egyptian Muslims who embraced the violent doctrine of its radical groups and who were willing to die in order to terrorize their own society and rulers.

The work of Saad El Din Ibrahim[37] (of The American University in Cairo) and Hamdi Taha (of Al-Azhar University) cast light on some of the social frustrations behind the radicalization of thousands of young men (and women). But the several interviews that the Egyptian journalist Makram Mohamed Ahmed conducted with more than forty prisoners, all members of various groups (especially Al-Jamaa Al-Islamiya), and that were later published in the Cairene magazine *Al-Musawar*, delve into the reasons, justifications and rationale that led those young men to adopt such hostile doctrine. The story of Ayman Al-Zawahiri (in 2010 Al-Qaeda's deputy head), his transformation from a successful surgeon to a leader of a violent group, bent on the murder of thousands, is a perfect example of the radicalization of segments of the Egyptian middle class. Al-Zawahiri, the son of an upper middle-class family who had grown up in Al-Maadi, an affluent Cairene suburb, joined the Muslim Brotherhood at the age of fifteen right after the 1967 defeat. He quickly moved from the Brotherhood's ordinary ranks to join (and create) independent, highly radicalized cells. Though he had no links to the murder of Sadat, he was imprisoned in the major incarceration waves that followed the crime, and was sentenced to three years. Having served his prison sentence, he emigrated to Saudi Arabia, then soon afterwards to Afghanistan to join in the fight against the Soviets. It was during that time that he met Dr Abdullah Azzam, the Palestinian godfather of many militant Islamic groups and the founder of the Jihad Service Bureau, the vehicle that helped recruit thousands of Arabs to the Afghanistan War. Al-Zawahiri became a close friend and confidant of Azzam. After the Soviets' withdrawal from Afghanistan, he returned to Egypt where he became the effective leader of the Al-Jihad group. In 1992, Dr Al-Zawahiri joined his old Arab Afghan colleague, the Saudi multi-millionaire Osama bin Laden, in Sudan, and from there he continued to lead Al-Jihad, until its merger with Al-Qaeda in 1998. Dr Al-Zawahiri presented his thinking and rationale for 'jihad by all means' in his book *Knights under the Prophet's Banner*.[38]

From the late 1970s to the late 1990s, the militant Islamists carried out more than 700 attacks against various institutions and officials. Perhaps the bloodiest incident was the Luxor attack in 1997 in which Al-Jamaa Al-Islamiya killed fifty-eight tourists and four Egyptians outside a pharaonic temple. In the same year, an ambush near the Egyptian museum in downtown Cairo by the group took the lives of nine tourists. In 1995, eighteen Greek tourists had been killed close to the Pyramids. But the violence was not only directed at the 'infidel Westerners' (though they, and the tourism industry, were especially prized victims). Egyptians also suffered: between 1982 and 2000, more than 2,000 Egyptians died in terror attacks – from the speaker of parliament to a number of secular writers and commentators (for example, Farag Foda, a prominent and controversial writer, was assassinated in 1992, and in 1994 an assassination attempt was made against Egypt's Nobel Literature Laureate Naguib Mahfouz), to a series of senior police officers,[39] and children caught up in the blasts.[40]

Imbaba, a poor Cairene neighbourhood and for years a stronghold of some of the militants, was another scene of bloody face-offs. It was also one of the areas in the city hardest hit by the October 1992 earthquake. In the aftermath, the Islamic movement was active on the ground dispensing medicines, food and clothes. Between 1991 and 1993, the militants had virtually taken complete control of Imbaba, replacing the government as the social arbiter. The situation reached a climax in 1992 when the security forces decided to intervene. More than 12,000 troops in more than 100 armed cars descended on the neighbourhood (home to more than a million Cairenes) and sealed it off; by the end of a bloody, tense day, thousands were rounded up, including around 150 leaders of different militant groups. Khaled Yousef's *Hina Maysara* a voyeuristic, smash-hit film, produced in 2007, recounts of the story of Cairene slums – such as Imbaba – in which religious extremism blurred with aggression, drug use, child labour and abuse, the grey economy and prostitution.

Asyut, the largest city in Al-Saeed and a major centre of Egyptian Christians, was traumatized by an almost open war between the regime and militant Islamic groups. Indeed, Egyptian Christians were increasingly targeted. More than seventy attacks were directed at jewellery shops, video stores, small factories and various other establishments owned by Christians. In some neighbourhoods in Asyut and Cairo, Christians found it prudent to remove the pictures of Jesus and Virgin Mary from the walls of their shops. The high frequency of the attacks, the rising presence of militant Islamism in Egypt, and the environment of internal war led many commentators to whisper about the possibility of

Egypt falling for 'an Islamic revolution on the Nile'. Even some of militant Islamism's ardent intellectual opponents were pessimistic about the future. Judge Mohamed Saeed Al-Ashmawi told the *New York Times*: 'perhaps my murder is part of my mission'.

From the early 1990s, the Egyptian regime insisted that it was tackling the 'terror folder' – politically, economically and socially. In reality, the regime's approach focused almost solely on security. After the attempted assassination of President Mubarak in Addis Ababa in 1995 and the Luxor attack (the latter widely reported in the West as a serious indication of a regime unable to assert its control over the country and contain the threat), the Egyptian security forces launched a comprehensive campaign against the key militant groups in (and outside) the country: infiltrating the most important, targeting their key leaders, taking control of thousands of mosques, squeezing their financial sources, draining the weapons sources (especially in Al-Saeed) and stepping up the internal pressure with a series of arrests. In a very intelligent move, the government diverted the payment of Islamic alms (*zakat*) from the local committees and charities that traditionally had allocated it to government-controlled banks, depleting one of their key sources of internal funding. By the late 1990s, most of the militant groups operating in Egypt had declared a ceasefire, renounced violence or had been driven out of the country. The regime had handled the military threat successfully.[41] But the rise of Islamism as a social force was a different story.

Most of militant Islamism's leaders in Egypt, from the assassins of Sadat to latter-day chiefs such as Ayman Al-Zawahiri, portrayed their struggle with the regime as 'a war against Islam'. This stance did not measure up, however. There was a clear distinction between the militant groups and the other key players of Egyptian Islamism – from the Muslim Brotherhood to the various Salafist groups spread throughout the country, to leading preachers such as Sheikh Al-Sharaawi and to Al-Azhar.

The Muslim Brotherhood exploited that distinction. While the militants were embroiled in a vicious war with the regime (with hundreds of victims and thousands of prisoners), the Brotherhood extended its social reach and infrastructure into a much more developed political platform. In the late 1990s, the traditionally vague Muslim Brotherhood proposed a draft political manifesto, seen by many observers as the skeleton of an alternative constitution. It championed political reform, increased freedom and fair elections, all in the language of Egyptian political activism. The Brotherhood, for the first time since its rehabilitation in Egyptian politics, was positioning itself as a direct political competitor to the regime.

This became abundantly clear in the parliamentary elections of 2005 when the Brotherhood was virtually the sole competitor of the ruling National Democratic Party. It won eighty-eight seats, roughly one-fifth of the parliament; a number that could have been much higher but for the procedural and tactical interventions by the regime in the second and third rounds of the elections. In late 2005 and throughout 2006, a number of the movement's leaders stated that it was the Brotherhood's 'responsibility to lead reform and change in Egypt'. The Brotherhood also broached sensitive topics that were traditionally considered taboo. It put forward a framework outlining its belief in 'multiple loyalties', addressing an old suspicion about its belief in and loyalty to the 'Egyptian state' as opposed to a 'pan-Islamic nation'.[42] The Brotherhood also addressed the 'Coptic issue' in a way that went beyond the placatory tones of 'respecting rights' to arguing that Egyptian Christians' 'conditions' would be better 'under the Brotherhood group'. The Brotherhood declared Christian Egyptians to be 'full citizens', not *ahl-dhimma*. The group also insinuated that in power they would abolish the church building-permit system that had operated for decades.

In 2009, the Brotherhood went further by establishing its respect for the concept of transfer of power – something the Egyptian regime has not necessarily been in favour of. The eighty-year-old Mhedi Akef, the Brotherhood's general guide since 2004, announced his intention to resign and hand the leadership mantle to younger and more able leaders. A young Islamist blogger in Egypt wrote that 'the Brotherhood has given us freedom and a chance to express ourselves' – something very few Egyptians would say about the country's regime.[43]

The Brotherhood's new political momentum was also oriented to audiences outside the country. In the wake of its 2005 elections success, the Brotherhood sought to establish its credentials abroad and allay suspicions – especially among Western media and observers. It was the first time that the Brotherhood had directly positioned itself to Western decision-makers as well as public. The group launched an English-language website that linked to the online sites of many Western newspapers. In 2006, some of the group's leaders launched the 'Re-Introducing the Brotherhood to the West Initiative', listing and addressing many 'Western misconceptions about the Brotherhood'. The group's deputy general guide wrote an article for the London *Guardian* under the title 'No need to be afraid of us'; two senior members even composed an op-ed in the American Jewish newspaper the *Forward*.[44]

The charm offensive was complemented by the work of a number of Islamic intellectuals with strong links to the Egyptian Islamic movement in general and the Muslim Brotherhood in particular. Tariq Ramadan was the most famous of these. The grandson of Hassan Al-Banna and a scholar at Oxford University, he argued for a heterogeneous Islam that combined the religion's traditions with new aspects rooted in the experiences of Muslims living in the West. This approach represented a tendency of liberal, conciliatory Islamic thinking that helped present a burgeoning and assertive Islamism in an acceptable light in the West.[45]

But the stance of a potential interlocutor with whom the West could engage was also a grave strategic threat to a regime that had repeatedly portrayed the Islamists as radical ideologues bent on the Islamization of society and permanent conflict with the West. The Brotherhood's external appeals were to no avail at home; Egypt's government continued to round up its leaders in police raids, press them to adopt less confrontational positions and squeeze its finances. The regime also imposed a further restriction on religious parties (and independent parliamentary candidates), namely an amendment of Article 1 of the constitution to define Egypt as 'a state of citizenship' and remove the reference to Islam as 'the religion of the state'. The change in theory would have the effect of allowing women, and Christians, to run for any position, including the presidency. The ruling National Democratic Party (NDP) subtly challenged the Islamists to accept the change – and saw its tactic vindicated when, in a tense parliamentary session, all of the Brotherhood's lawmakers walked out of the legislative chamber rather than vote for or against the new version of the article.

The episode was a sad example of the deterioration of liberalism and tolerance in Egypt. In 1922, a committee was tasked with putting together the first draft of the 1923 constitution. The committee, which comprised five Christians, one Jew and six Muslims, instituted Article 1 (that Islam is the religion of the state) unanimously. And interestingly the five Christian committee members were the ones who rejected a clause, suggested by a Muslim, to have a minimum number of parliamentary seats and ministerial posts reserved for Christians. 'It would be a shame for Egyptian Christians to be appointed, not elected,' commented one of the Christian committee members. That was the era when a Christian politician such as Makram Ebeid Pasha, the legendary general secretary of Al-Wafd, was elected for six consecutive terms to the parliament in a constituency with virtually no Christians. Sadly, those were different times.[46]

In another incident following its 2005 electoral success, the Brotherhood's reckless attempt to assert its power by staging a militia-style march by masked Brotherhood students at Al-Azhar University was a feast for the state-controlled media, which reminded Egyptians of the banned group's 'history of violence'.

But the regime's main effort at stripping the Islamic movement, and especially the Brotherhood, from its emerging status as the representative of an emerging modern Islamism worthy of popular support centred on Al-Azhar. The regime wagered that the ancient institution, 'the Sunni world's seat of learning', the 'unrivalled beacon of progressive Islamism', would thwart the appeal of the Muslim Brotherhood (and all other Islamist players). In theory, that made sense. Al-Azhar, the alma mater of almost all of the key figures of Egyptian Islamism, should indeed have been Egypt's unrivalled Islamic force. But the Al-Azhar of the 1990s and 2000s was vastly different to that of earlier times. Little of the old veneration for the insitituion was left. It was increasingly perceived as part of the regime. Since Nasser's decision to abolish the tradition by which Al-Azhar's Grand Sheikh was elected by the institution's Council of Grand Scholars and instead have him appointed by a presidential decree, the venerated Grand Sheikh had become effectively a government employee. The perception was cemented when Sadat compelled scores of Al-Azhar's leaders to back the Camp David peace treaty on a 'religious basis' – to the horror of many religious scholars (many inside Al-Azhar). The university's unconditional support of the regime was extended, over the years, to other areas – from the compatibility of conventional banking with Islamic law to whether or not 'the disturbing writings' of opposition writers 'that spread rumours' are *haram* (religiously forbidden).

But it was not only Al-Azhar's lesser standing on the Egyptian streets that had diluted the institution's eminence. Al-Azhar had over several decades lost part of its authoritative intellectual fire-power. Several notable theologians emerged in Egypt (and else-where in the Sunni world) who had been trained by Al-Azhar yet later broke away from the institution's structure and became inde-pendent. Sheikh Yusuf Al-Qaradawi is the most prominent of these. The Qatar-based Egyptian sheikh, who had twice turned down the Muslim Brotherhood's general-guide position, became the foremost scholar on Islamic law and the face of Sunni Islamism in various international forums. He was, for example, the leading jurist of the Union of International Muslim Scholars and the European Council for Fatwa and Research; lead speaker and attendee at a number of conferences and permanent committees on the dialogue between the West and Islam; and – at least as import-antly – the star of one of Al-Jazeera's most popular television programmes, where he lectures and pronounces fatwas to millions of Muslims. Sheikh Al-Qaradawi's experience is similar to that of other scholars and jurists who have found Al-Azhar's closeness to the regime stifling. The defection of some of the institution's sharpest minds was telling, as the institution's own position on some of the region's most important issues (such as the Arab–Israeli struggle, or the emerging tension between Sunnis and Shiis) was barely audible relative to the stances of many independent sheikhs.

Al-Azhar was also undergoing a political dilemma. The insti-tution was trying to strike a balance between a conservative tone (to placate the mood of the increasingly religious, conservative masses) without embarrassing the regime as a result of its insufficient adherence to Al-Sharia. For example, Al-Azhar's quasi-silence during Israel's attack on Hamas in Gaza in December 2008–January 2009 was striking – in contrast to the incessant denunciations, fund-raising and lobbying led by the Muslim Brotherhood, the International Union of Islamic Scholars and others; and the fury among Egyptian citizens. The political manoeuvering of the old institution yielded confusion, awkwardness and equivocation.

Al-Azhar was seeking to tighten its grip on the more than 40,000 independent mosques in Egypt, gain more prime time on terrestrial TV and publish more books on theological studies. But the real momentum of the Islamic movement in Egypt was elsewhere – not in mosques, on state TV or in theology books. The more than 45 million Egyptians under thirty-five years of age were increasingly a digital generation – even in religion. New, charmingly young 'sheikhs' talking in Egyptian Arabic slang, delivering their sermons over the Internet, on private satellite channels and in sports clubs, were winning the day. Amr Khaled, the most successful of those young sheikhs, was described by the *New York Times* in 2006 as 'the world's most famous and influential Muslim television preacher'. The slick thirty-something preached about 'getting closer to God' without changing one's lifestyle; promoted the Islamic veil (*al-hijab*) while joking about dating and flirting; espoused entrepreneurialism and 'living a comfortable life'; and maintained a disciplined focus on the lives, issues and problems of the upper middle classes. The young sheikhs, though supposedly independent of any political ideology, were a strong reinforcement of the new liberal face of Egypt's Islamic movement. Through their reach and appeal, the movement gained valuable exposure to a social group that had traditionally been the stronghold of liberalism.

The rise of digital media preachers at the expense of Al-Azhar had a broad impact on the religious discourse in the country. Traditionally, Al-Azhar, drawing on its unrivalled reservoir of serious, profound religious scholars and driven by its long tradition of debate and intellectual curiosity, directed Islamic discourse in Egypt towards significant issues in Islamic history and jurisprudence. Such seriousness and weightiness were now replaced – at least in the most prominent and successful media outlets in the country and among millions of young Egyptian Muslims – by triviality and frivolity. In one of many examples, a serious study by Dr Mohamed Emara on Islam's view of Christianity (and the status of Christian minorities in Muslim-ruled countries) was brushed aside from prime-time religious programmes and time slots to give airtime to an Islamic version of Donald Trump's *The Apprentice*.

The success of the Islamic movement in thus broadening its appeal far beyond the poor and disadvantaged has been a function of other, non-economic variables. The evolving social mood was one. The 1980s, 1990s and 2000s lacked any Egyptian 'project', grand or small. The country's foreign policy at the time was monotonous, cautious and highly pragmatic (see Chapter 6). The domestic economy lacked inspiration or encouragement for the entrepreneurial and the daring. The vast majority of Egyptians were trapped in cycles of economic hardship, crushing living standards and humiliating daily lives. Survival was an objective in itself. The last national project (Arab nationalism) seemed to have been wandering in an intellectual and social wasteland for decades. The last moment of national momentum in recent history, the 1973 war, was more than three decades old. There was a sense of social emptiness, a large-scale brain-drain and an overarching feeling of social despair.

In these circumstances, Islam became the uncontested 'last resort'. The fall of loyalties and ideologies, the lack of national projects and the sense of humiliation as a result of successive decades of drift and what seemed to many as a series of historical defeats[47] left the society clinging to religion as its innermost identity, its only remaining shield and consolation.

The frustrations of the 'urban middle classes'[48] in a period of rapid change strengthened that despairing dependency. There was a major demographic boom in Egypt from the 1980s, in which the population almost doubled from around 45 million to 80 million, but there was also a notable increase in literacy and urbanization. The literacy rate in Egypt increased from around 45 per cent in the early 1970s to 65 per cent in the early 2000s, with the greatest improvement among those under thirty-five years of age (who were also the generation best equipped to engage with modern technology, from satellite channels to the Internet, to wireless communication). The demographic distribution of the country crammed the majority of those young Egyptians into Cairo, Alexandria and a few other urban centres where living conditions were increasingly difficult. The thwarted aspirations of these rela-tively educated youths, in a public environment dominated by corruption, patronage and authoritarian rule, was propitious for Islamism: the 'pure divine ideology' and the opposite of every-thing that might have contributed to current problems – from Nasser's Arab nationalism to Anwar Sadat's and Hosni Mubarak's westernization and pragmatism. Islamism was perceived as a posi-tivist form of rejection. Unlike the utter negativity and nihilism of terror,[49] 'a return to true Islam' seemed to offer a medicine for the social sickness – even if the nature of that Islamism was hardly defined and the medicine was utterly vague.

There have been serious attempts at defining what Islamism would mean in a modern society – for example, the writings of Mohamed Seleem Al-Awaa and Tariq Al-Bishri (a highly respectable Egyptian judge and Islamic philosopher) who presented multiple frameworks addressing the same topic. But, by and large, these attempts (and others) circulated in specialized journals. The vast majority of Egyptians, especially the young, have had no exposure to (and perhaps no interest in) these ideas. The dominant discourse has been, predominately, that of the Muslim Brotherhood. It was interesting that in a number of the constituents that the Brotherhood ended up carrying in the 2005 parliamentary elections, the voters had very limited knowledge not only of the candidates' programmes, but even of their names. The winning slogan was 'Islam is the solution'.

The rise of the 'new Gulf' has also contributed to the appeal of Islamism across different segments of Egyptian society – including the upper middle classes and the rich. The Gulf region has undergone impressive development at the same time as Egypt has stagnated – in terms of economic growth, living standards, internationalization and of becoming an attractive destination for world-class expatriates. This has given credence in the Arab world to the notion that development and progress need not be associated with Western lifestyles, schools of thought and social frameworks. No longer, it seems, do successful professionals, professors, social commentators, entrepreneurs and politicians need to be Anglo- or Francophiles extracted from successful careers in London, New York and Paris and planted in Cairo; Saudi-, Kuwaiti- and Dubai-philes were emerging.[50] The consequences have included a subtle reduction in the gap between modernity/progress and Islamism in the Egyptian psyche.

With this too came the rise of Islamism in the country's economic life, as Islamic finance gained ground in multiple ways and across different social levels. Islam was no stranger to the Egyptian finance scene. The story of 'Islamic money management companies', and especially Al-Ryan, is one of the most interesting in the Egyptian economy of the 1980s. Started in

1977 as a *hiwala* (an informal system of money transfer through a series of intermediaries) house focused on the Egyptian market, Al-Ryan managed, within a few years, to expand from Saudi Arabia to Egypt. Using mass-market advertising and heavily promoting its 'halal trading' business, as opposed to 'conventional banks' usury', in 1986 Al-Ryan Money Management Company amassed assets under management in excess of 5 billion Egyptian pounds (at the time circa US$1.3 billion). A few years later, the entire company collapsed, and with it one of the most active segments in the Egyptian economy in that decade.[51]

The *hiwala* has been in use in the Middle East for centuries, and between the Gulf and Egypt for decades. It was especially popular and effective among poorer emigrants to the Gulf who worked there in low-paying jobs and lacked the ability or the knowledge to use the standard banking system in sending remittances back home. The *hiwala*'s expansion in the 1980s and 1990s, when hundreds of offices were set up across Egypt, was exponential. In a few years, the *halal hiwala* became the main (sometimes the only) interface through which hundreds of thousands of families were receiving their livelihood from absent fathers and brothers.

At higher levels too, Islamic banking was gaining ground. By the mid-2000s, Islamic banks operating in Egypt controlled around 10 per cent of the commercial deposits in the country's banking system; and a number of the world's leading banks (from Citigroup to HSBC) were heavily promoting their 'Islamic arms'. The economic aspect of Islamism penetrated a number of the economy's industrial and service sectors. For example, eight of the twenty richest families in Egypt throughout the 1990s and 2000s, with vast and interconnected equity stakes across the country's private sector, had direct links to either the Muslim Brotherhood or other Salafist groups.[52] More recently, Islamic mortgaging has emerged as the key player in one of the country's most strategic and growing industries. By the 2000s, Islamism was establishing itself at the high end of the Egyptian social ladder.

In the mid-2000s, a leading Egyptian government minister said of Islamism: 'Give me five years of high growth, and I bet you, it would go away.' This was an oversimplification, at best. The Islamic movement's ability to establish itself as the country's most potent social force was rooted in a number of social, economic and political factors, and no one was more cognizant of that fact than the Islamic movement itself. The Brotherhood's increased political assertiveness and engagement with the world derived from a confident understanding of the power of these factors.

But the Brotherhood was not the only Islamic political group with that understanding. The Centrist Party (*Hizb Al-Wasat*), a breakaway faction of the Brotherhood led by three respectable Islamic figures, represented a refreshing development in the dynamics of political Islamism in the country. The new party, impelled partly by frustration over the Brotherhood's continuing illegal status, was launched (unofficially) in 1996. It attempted to bridge the gap between the Islamic movement and other trends in Egypt's political terrain, the ideologies and programmes of which were not opposed to 'Islam as a framework', but which would not endorse 'Islam as a government'. The party included a number of leading liberals and a few Egyptian Christians; it was portrayed by many observers as a form of 'moderate and liberal Islamism'. Over subsequent years the party's influence remained limited, but the experiment showed the potential of sections of the broader Islamic movement to reach out to some of the country's liberal forces and courageously adopt civic political frameworks.

But the minister's 'economistic' comment represented a dominant strand of thinking within the regime's upper echelons, reflected in the launch of a number of socio-economic initiatives and development programmes that aimed to alleviate some of the severe economic suffering of most Egyptians – and at the same time, prove that it can and deserves to lead the country, unlike the Islamists who 'offer nothing but verbal programmes and vague slogans'. But if the analysis is simplistic, the larger point is that, despite all of the regime's sticks and carrots, the Islamic movement's main challenges today are internal.

Over the past few decades, the Islamic movement was everything to everyone: an alternative social provider to the poor masses; an angry platform for the disillusioned young; a loud trumpet-call announcing 'a return to the pure religion' to those seeking an identity; a 'progressive, moderate religious platform' for the affluent and liberal; an increasingly civic interlocutor with Egyptian Christians and the West – and at the extremes, a violent vehicle for rejectionists and radicals. That flexibility of intellectual and political identity is increasingly unsustainable. It dilutes the focus, message and integrity of the movement. Nowhere is this clearer than in the movement's (and especially the Brotherhood's) relationships with the regime and with major international players. For a period, especially in the mid-2000s, Islamism led by the Brotherhood was asserting its role in internal politics. The Brotherhood parliamentary block took its responsibilities very seriously, and quickly emerged as the only real opposition group in the parliament. The Brotherhood's parliamentary programme addressed some of the country's most pressing political issues: ending the quarter-of-a-century imposition of emergency law; promoting the independence of unions and universities; stressing the need for much higher transparency in government transactions; freeing many of the country's political prisoners; and cracking down on corruption. The Brotherhood's most notable parliamentary coup, however, was the respect it showed for the constitution and the 'secular' parliament. In 2006, Mohamed Habib, the deputy general guide, declared that 'should the People's Assembly (the parliament) propose a law that violates Al-Sharia, the legislature should have the ultimate jurisdiction in deciding upon the matter'.

The group also challenged the regime a number of times, especially when it felt the regime's policies were widely at odds with feelings on 'the street' (for example, during the 2008 Gaza War, the Brotherhood mobilized more than 50,000 on to the streets of Alexandria to protest about the regime's political stance and actions, especially the closure of the Rafah border crossing). Yet, in many other situations, the Brotherhood seemed to miss (or avoid) confrontations that any serious political challenger would relish. The Brotherhood distanced itself from Kefaya – arguably the country's most vocal and inspiring grassroots opposition group in the 2000s (examined in detail in Chapter 4). The Brotherhood was also absent from the wave of industrial protests that Egypt experienced between 2005 and 2008 (which managed, in a number of cases, to corner the regime and extract rights from it). Even inside the Brotherhood, a current has emerged advocating a disengagement from politics, and a return to *al-dawaa*, arguing that politics has brought the group nothing but grief.

The same apparent indecisiveness is conspicuous in the Brotherhood's interaction with key international players, most notably the United States. After the group's parliamentary victory of 2005, the Brotherhood sought to position itself as an interlocutor and a potential partner of the West, and especially the United States. But that outreach runs against the Brotherhood's attempt to placate its support base, the millions of pious – and at times very angry – young Egyptians who strenuously oppose Washington's foreign policies and almost invariably associate the

United States both with Israel and the region's dictatorial regimes. It was, for example, notable that despite some encouraging comments from a number of the Brotherhood's leaders regarding President Obama's visit to Cairo in June 2009, the Brotherhood's public line was hardly welcoming. 'The visit would be useless unless it is preceded by real change in the policies of the US Administration . . . the US is trying to recruit all Arab States in favour of Israel,' the group's website said. The Brotherhood also, after a number of conciliatory engagements and interactions with the West, retreated into its comfort zone of inflammatory rhetoric intended for local consumption: all suicide-bombers are 'martyrs'; 'Israel' regularly became 'the Jews'; even its theological discourse became more confrontational and oriented to social conservatism.

The group's intellectual dilemma goes deeper. The Brotherhood is torn: between the conservative (and often rejectionist) ideas on which it was founded;[53] the progressive arguments of some of its foster children (such as Tariq Ramadan) who see room for cooperation with the West; and the views of those – less intellectual but perhaps more influential inside Egypt – who engage in vibrant discussions on many Islamist Internet blogs, exploring ideas in often daringly creative ways. The resulting confusion and fragmentation exact their price on the group's standing. The Brotherhood is increasingly excluded from discussions in areas where it could have made a contribution and found a hearing, such as strategies to counter terrorism and the renewed American role in the Middle East after the election of President Obama.

The confusion collides with the Islamic movement's other internal challenge: a leadership deficit. The Brotherhood seems to lack the determination to maintain its strategic position, and unable to make the evolution from a strong opposition group to a political challenger. And as the December 2009 general-guide election showed, there is not only a clear lack of talent at the

Brotherhood's top levels, but also a conspicuous disconnection between the political *savoir faire* of the upper echelon and the fiery enthusiasm of the grassroot members. Other potential candidates for the movement's leadership seem unprepared – or unwilling. The Al-Wasat Party remains small, unorganized and trapped in a marionette game controlled by the regime; more than thirteen years after it was first formed, the group is still waiting for the verdict of multiple parliamentary committees.[54] The young sheikhs seem happily confined to the realm of lucrative TV shows targeting the upper middle class; and none of them has shown the talent or depth, let alone the charisma, required to evolve into a social phenomenon of the like of Sheikh Sharaawi. The serious intellectuals (whether inside or outside the country) address the impotent internal intelligentsia and/or curious global observers; in all cases, they fail to communicate with the segments that really count: the country's middle class and young. The different Salafist movements are scattered with close to no political power or ambition.

In the next few years will the Egyptian Islamic movement (including the Muslim Brotherhood) manage to graduate to become a genuine political challenger, or descend to the status of a permanently weak opposition group? The most important variable in answering that question is the choices of young Egyptians (the topic of Chapter 7). In turn, the subtle struggle between the regime's liberal capitalists and the Islamists for that group's loyalty will be decisive for the outcome.

1 The Nile was revered by ancient Egyptians as a giver of life, second only to the Sun. Life in Egypt remains an oasis on the Nile banks, in the midst of vast deserts.

2 The opening of the Suez Canal on 17 November 1869 by French Empress Eugenie and Khedive Ismael.

3 Ismael Pasha carried on his grandfather Mohamed Ali's developmental project, and aimed to create a 'Paris on the Nile'.

4 Egypt's last reigning king, Farouk, who ruled Egypt from 1936 to 1952, when the 'Free Officers' forced him to abdicate to his infant son and leave the country.

5 A walk through central Cairo reveals the hundreds of Paris-, Rome- and Vienna-inspired buildings, boulevards and squares – the architectural product of Egypt's liberal experiment in the first half of the twentieth century.

6 President Gamal Abdel Nasser in the later years of his reign.

7 More than five million mourners crowded Cairo's streets for Nasser's funeral on 1 October 1970.

8 Al-Azhar Mosque: the Sunni world's seat of learning.

9 President Anwar Sadat (centre) with Israel's Prime Minister Menachem Begin (left) on
Sadat's first iconic visit to Israel in 1977.

10 The largest city in Africa, the Middle East, and the Arab world, Greater Cairo spreads over 480 square kilometres and is home to 16 million people.

11 Cairo's City of the Dead, home to more than four million Cairenes.

12 Gamal Mubarak, the Head of the National Democratic Party's Policies Committee.

13 President Hosni Mubarak (right) with US President George Bush in 1990.

14 Anti-riot police facing protestors near a Cairo court where pro-reform judges were being questioned by a disciplinary tribunal, in May 2006.

15 President Mubarak (right) and US President Barack Obama during the latter's visit to Egypt in June 2009.

16 Running along the city's seafront, Alexandria's Corniche is a magnificent shore promenade.

CHAPTER 4
THE RISE OF LIBERAL CAPITALISM

THROUGHOUT 2008, THE Egyptian parliament debated the reasons behind the double-digit inflation from which Egypt was suffering at the time. The parliamentary committees assessing the situation comprised a score of the country's largest business tycoons and some of the key beneficiaries of the rising prices, most of whom were also leading members of the ruling National Democratic Party (NDP).

That bizarre situation is one example among many of the dominance of the alliance between Egypt's regime and the country's main economic and financial powers. The picture is clear: more than 40 per cent of the country's wealth (real and semi-liquid assets) is controlled by the richest 5 per cent of the population. The top ten companies in the Egyptian stock exchange, which commands more than 45 per cent of the market's total capitalization, are controlled by less than twenty families. Almost 40 per cent of the country's credit supply goes to the thirty largest private companies in the economy.[1] And, most importantly, the 2004 government (the 'reform government' as it was dubbed by the

NDP) includes a number of leading businessmen and scions of prominent families: a major shareholder of one of Egypt's largest consumer-goods empires is the trade minister, the country's most successful healthcare entrepreneur is the health minister and the country's most prominent wheat trader is the agriculture minister.

The regime's alliance with Egypt's capitalists may be profound, but its relationship with Egypt's people is troubled. The country witnessed more than 150 demonstrations and strikes in 2007–8. Some were violent and required heavy deployment of the security forces. The most notable episode, though still only one among many, saw riots erupt at a state-owned weaving factory in Al-Mahla Al-Kobra, which led to the death of at least two workers, the wounding of more than 100 and the arrest of over 300. The police and security forces have also frequently sealed off Cairo University's campus amid violent clashes with students; thousands of alleged sympathizers of the Islamic movement have been detained without trial under the emergency and terrorism laws; and even more than thirty bloggers – most of them university students writing from their bedrooms – have been arrested. A number of activists called for 'An Egyptian Intifadah' against 'oppression and suppression'. The Egyptian Organization for Human Rights estimates that as many as 18,000 people remain in detention without charge or trial, with many held in horrific conditions.

The escalation in such demonstrations of anger, and increasing violence in the relationship between regime and people, is partly a result of the very difficult living conditions of most Egyptians. The people are expressing their rejection of how they are ruled – and who is ruling them. But it is also linked to the tight nexus of power in the political-economic elite.

The alliance of politics and economics goes back to Anwar Sadat's *al-infitah* (literally 'the opening up'), the policy that began in 1974 and aimed to open the economy to freer trade, foreign investments and market economics. Sadat, who ascended to the presidency after Nasser's death in 1970, was an untested man with limited influence, no popularity and few supporters. Though he was a member of the 1952 Revolution's leadership, he was not a key pillar of Nasser's regime during the 1950s and 1960s. Arguably, he retained his position at the regime's upper strata, albeit without real power, because he was never perceived to be a threat. His ascension to the presidency was primarily a result of the power vacuum following Nasser's sudden death. And yet he managed to come out of his predecessor's shadow when he led Egypt's attack on Israel in October 1973, which most Egyptians considered a strategic victory for the country. (The Egyptian army crossed the Suez Canal, despite very heavy fortifications, and annihilated Israel's defensive Bar-Lev Line; the Egyptian rocket shield proved highly effective at neutralising Israel's air force; and Israel suffered significant losses. Millions of Egyptians believe that were it not for the 23,000 tons of supplies and weaponry that the United States shipped to Israel in the two weeks following the onslaught, enabling the Jewish state to mount a major counter-offensive, Israeli losses would have been much higher.)

Al-infitah was in origin a political rather than an economic strategy. After the 1973 war, Sadat had both the political capital and the courage to break with Nasserism and preach a whole new political strategy to Egyptians.

Sadat had come to detest the warmongering mentality that had dominated the Egyptian political-economic discourse in the 1950s and 1960s, and believed that the just-concluded war had to be the last between Egypt and Israel. He also had a realistic view of power dynamics in the Middle East (many of his detractors believe his view went beyond the 'realistic' to the 'defeatist'). Sadat decided to seek what he believed to be a realistic objective – a viable peace between Egypt and the Jewish state; to transform Egypt from the base of Nasserite Arab nationalism to one of the United States' key allies in the region; and to promote prosperity (*rakhaa*) that would spread over Egypt as a result of a massive reduction in the military budget, and the transformation of the country from a stalwart of the Arab 'solidarity front' into a regional investment destination open for business, trade, commerce and high finance.

Sadat's vision was an integrated political and economic strategy for the country. Opening up the economy and establishing a capitalist system were seen as crucial to getting American commitment to supporting Egypt; the expected prosperity was supposed to win over the majority of Egyptians to the new geo-strategic direction; the economic changes were expected to disseminate power from the state, the government, the military establishment and the public sector to a newly emerging private sector. Sadat imagined *al-infitah* as laying the seeds of a democratic, capitalist, Western-oriented Egypt.

But not during his period in office; he was, of course, to remain an absolute leader. Ahmed Bahaa El-Din, ex-editor-in-chief of *Al-Ahram*, recounts in *My Conversations with Sadat* the broad and sweeping effects that Sadat envisaged would materialize as a result of *al-infitah*. Yet those changes were intended for the future; 'Nasser and I are the last pharaohs,' he told Bahaa El-Din.[2]

But theory and practice did not converge. The implementation of *al-infitah* was flawed. The regime used the new economic opportunities to build its own power base, to reward its cronies and allies and to create a capitalist class whose loyalties were not to free markets and open economies – and certainly not to democracy – but rather to the regime itself. From concessions on land, goods and commodities to mandates and contracts, to agencies and dealerships, the regime (through the government and the different arms of the security apparatus) exerted immense influence on who was winning and who was losing. In many cases, it directly controlled the allocation of those economic mandates and interests.[3]

The development of the tourism industry in southern Sinai is a good example. After the withdrawal of the Israeli troops from Sinai, the region underwent a major transformation from a war front to a tourist paradise. The pristine beaches of Sharm Al-Sheikh and Noeibah, the diving spots (with some of the world's richest coral reefs) of Dahab and the serene mountains of St Catherine were high-potential assets waiting to be monetized. Suddenly, a significant percentage of the prime locations for the new hotels and resorts, and the multitude of economic interests that emerged, were in the hands of ex-military and intelligence officers, the friends and family of leading regime figures and a select group of companies with connections to the regime. By the 1990s, southern Sinai was the jewel of the Egyptian tourism industry;[4] but its development had been a conspicuous example of the blurring of the lines between power and wealth in the country.

The same dynamics were visible in the burgeoning real-estate industry. The more than a million young men who returned from the war front and army reserve to their cities after the 1973 war were promised prosperity and rapid development under the new economic model. The opening of the country to waves of capital set off rapid growth in the real estate and property markets. Entire new neighbourhoods sprang up in east and west Cairo,[5] on the desert borders of Alexandria and around (and within) the Delta's agricultural land. A major prize was up for grabs. The selling price of a square metre in a 'cordoned' (that is, approved for development) area on the periphery of Cairo tripled in less than six years. But it was the state that managed the distribution of the spoils. The awarding of the newly cordoned land, the allocation of tenders and contracts, the issue of licences and approvals, and the provisioning of financing – all were controlled and managed by the government and its different vehicles, with conspicuous roles for the different security apparatuses. And as was the case with the tourism industry, a significant number of the beneficiaries were friends of the regime. In Al'Asher Min Ramadan (a satellite city on the eastern edges of Cairo), most of the 'cordoned' land was allocated to a select group of companies, many of which were owned by investors with various connections to leading members of the NDP and other factions of the regime. One of Ismailiya's prime beaches came to be known as 'The Ministers' Bay', in reference to the politically thrusting among its owners. In Alexandria, President Sadat entrusted a few business tycoons with the lion's share of the city's development work.

Al-infitah's major social impact, however, was its transformation of the *structure* of the country's middle class. At the time of the fall of the Egyptian monarchy in the early 1950s, the Egyptian middle class comprised roughly 4 million people (in a population of 21 million, of which 17 million were considered lower class and poor, and less than half a million upper class and rich[6]). Landownership was the decisive factor. Nasser changed that. Land reform, the major assets-confiscation programme, the dramatic growth in university education, the expansion in industry and services and the creation of a dominating public sector flattened the social curve; millions of previously poor Egyptians, through education and jobs in the public sector, joined the middle class. The nature of one's job replaced landownership as the key social determinant. Doctors, engineers, teachers, lawyers, journalists, army and police officers and the millions working in the public sector's administrative structure constituted the bulk of the swelling middle class.

Al-infitah introduced different forces of change. The rise of the private sector and foreign direct investments,[7] and the corresponding decline in the role (and status) of the public sector in the 1970s and 1980s, led to substantial income gaps between workers of both sectors. The public sector's top talent and elite university graduates moved to much better paying (and more prestigious) jobs in the private sector; a young marketer in the Cairo branch of, say, an international consumer-goods company could earn more than five times the salary of a senior public-sector executive. But millions of government employees, the bulk of Egypt's middle class at the time, were left stuck in the increasingly marginalized, stagnant and low-paying public sector.

The story of the public sector in Egypt remains untold. For more than three decades it was the backbone of the Egyptian economy and almost the sole production arm serving the country's military efforts. The changes that *al-infitah* brought deprived the sector of vital investments and, to a large extent, worsened its many administrative and incentivization problems. However, it remained until the early 2000s the key pillar of the Egyptian economy. In a series of long TV interviews with the Egyptian journalist Emad-el-Din Adeeb, Dr Aziz Siddqui, one of the key architects of Nasser's economic policy, discussed the factors that 'necessitated the creation of the public sector'; he did not examine, however, the development – or the deterioration – of the sector. The views of other key people, unfortunately, were not recorded.[8]

The massive population growth in the 1950s and 1960s, and the skewed nature of Egypt's educational system, exacerbated the gap between the public and private sectors. Every year from the mid-1970s onwards, a few thousand skilled graduates joined the large, successful private-sector companies, while hundreds of thousands more were relegated, through the hapless

Public Employment Office, to the increasingly desolate public sector.

At the same time, at the height of the first oil boom in the late 1970s, millions of Egyptians were lured to the Gulf States (and Iraq) to fill jobs in construction, infrastructure, agriculture and to some extent in teaching and the new administrative structures. Between 1974 and 1985, more than 3 million Egyptians (construction workers, labourers, mechanics, plumbers, electricians as well as young teachers and accountants) migrated to the region. Their remittances increasingly allowed families back at home to buy refrigerators, TV sets, video recorders, cars and flats.[9] Their social mobility was supported not by higher educational or professional standing, nor by an overall socio-economic equalization – as had been effected by Nasser's policies – but by an exponential increase in domestic purchasing power. Membership of the middle class was now a function of disposable income.

The bulk of Egypt's traditional middle class, however, witnessed a parallel erosion of its purchasing power. Inflation ran at around 14 per cent from 1975 to 1982. The government slowly but steadily withdrew its social safety net. The expansion in services (education, healthcare, retail and housing) was led by the private sector and mainly targeted at the newly affluent. Public-sector salaries and non-trading revenues (the earnings of the vast majority of Egyptian farmers, for example) declined in real terms. Those at the periphery of the economy with the least marketable skills, pensioners and the vast majority of low-level government employees among them, were effectively falling into poverty.

At the centre of *al-infitah*'s new elite, closest to the regime, were former military and intelligence officers – many of whom were simultaneously playing a number of roles (as associates of influential security organizations, leaders of semi-governmental companies, businessmen and entrepreneurs, members of parliament). But there were others in the new power elite, including old, monarchical-era families, who siphoned their capital to Europe in the first few years of Nasser's era and managed to multiply that capital abroad.[10] Many such families, sensing the change as a result of *al-infitah*, returned to Egypt with various ambitions – and business plans. The result was many business partnerships between scions of aristocratic families and ex-military and intelligence men who, a few years earlier, had been ardent socialists and Nasserites.

The blurring of the lines between power and money took place at lower levels as well. The relatively low wages of the public sector, the economic pressures on the country's middle class, the overall sense of opportunism that accompanied *al-infitah* and the emergence of numerous economic and financial power centres had baleful effects in terms of the corruption of large sectors of the Egyptian bureaucracy, a glaring increase in dubious economic practices and the emergence of parasitic links between sections of the public sector and private capital.[11] The rise to riches of a dock worker in the port of Alexandria who in 1974 was earning 35 piasters a day (less than 20 US cents) and within a few years had become a prominent member of the NDP's Alexandria branch is exemplary. By the time he was investigated by the general prosecutor, his wealth had reached $200 million – the result of drug trafficking, smuggling, monopolizing a number of industries and expropriation of state-owned lands. It was but one example of the corruption of the public sector and executive system in that era.[12]

Sadat's promises of prosperity came after more than thirty years of continuous wars, struggles and overly ambitious developmental programmes that took an enormous collective toll on Egyptians. The prosperity (*rakhaa*) of *al-infitah* was supposed to be the people's reward. But the excesses of the 1970s; the pressures on the middle class; the emergence of a new upper class of merchants, middlemen, brokers and shady liaisons; and the unabashed alliance between power and money – all were turning Sadat's vision into an empty promise. Millions of Egyptians felt cheated, that their reward was instead being reaped by a privileged elite floating over them.

Al-infitah's fusion of power and wealth was especially shocking because it was the exact opposite of the principles of the Nasserite socialist experiment. It seemed to revoke almost all of Nasser's major policies, from free education to social equality, reform to abolition of feudalism, nationalization to progressive taxation, the public sector to active income redistribution, and the severing of the relationship between capital and power. The dreams of equality and social justice that animated the 1960s were dissolving, and the fruits of the replacement were hard to see.

Sadat's image as the hero of the 1973 war began to fall apart; his status as 'the family's patriarch' crumbled; his credibility disintegrated. A number of political opponents, from Arab nationalists and Nasserites to new Islamic groups, came to the fore. More ominously, Egyptians were becoming increasingly angry and resentful. The uprising of 18–19 January 1977 in which millions took to the streets of Cairo burning, looting and cursing the regime – and Sadat – was only the most extreme incident.[13]

Sadat's apologists lay the blame for the poor undertaking of *al-infitah* on Egypt's substandard administrative system and widespread low-level corruption. They argue too that the tumultuous upheavals of the negotiations with Israel that consumed the better part of the 1970s – followed by Sadat's premature death in 1981 (only six years after launching *al-infitah*) – cut the programme short. Sadat's detractors, by contrast, claim that his 'vision' was nothing but a sales pitch intended to rally popular support for *al-infitah*, which was from the outset a programme of self-enrichment, corruption and crony capitalism.

But *al-infitah*'s main fault was that it was over ambitious. It failed to recognize the complexities of Egypt's socio-economic conditions – especially after the dramatic social shift that had taken place in earlier years. It ignored the limitations of the country's administrative system and the power of the military establishment. It was slow in responding to the social dynamics of the time, mainly the emigration to the Gulf and the mismatch between the skills of the Egyptian middle class and the various economic opportunities springing up as a result. It didn't empower the judicial and regulatory authorities to rein in the excesses that were certain to materialize. It also reflected Sadat's escapist and evasive tendencies. As such, it was an unrealistically rapid developmental programme that was doomed to fail.[14]

Even from the micro perspective, *al-infitah* failed. It enriched many of the leading figures of the regime, their cronies and scores of their political allies and friends, but Egyptian society – the people – did not prosper, as Sadat had promised. It lifted restrictions on importing, exporting and travel; it removed prohibitions on many commercial activities. But it did not overhaul the foundations of the economy. The public sector remained the largest economic player in the country. The regime did not dare to touch the Nasserite land reform. And despite the dramatic rise of the private sector, the state continued to be by far the country's largest employer. At the fall of Egyptian monarchy in 1952 roughly 2 per cent of the Egyptian population were working for the state; at the height of the socialist Nasserite era, the percentage was 3.8 per cent; by the early 1980s (after the full thrust of *al-infitah*), 10 per cent of all Egyptians were working for the public sector – circa 35 per cent of the the country's entire labour force. In 1952, the state's contribution to the formation of investment capital in the country was 28 per cent; in the mid-1960s, it was circa 72 per cent; the percentage had barely moved by the end of the 1970s.[15]

Indeed, by the late 1970s the regime seemed to be abandoning its free-market slogans in favour of a completely different message and tone. Sadat was returning to a 1960s repertoire to soothe the tension on the street. The motto of his political baby, the National Democratic Party (established in July 1978), was 'food for every mouth and a house for every citizen': hardly the slogan of free, unobstructed market forces. Sadly, such failure took place despite significant windfalls[16] and direct assistance (especially from the Gulf[17] and the United States) that poured into the economy and the state's coffers throughout the 1970s and early 1980s.

Ambassador Hermann Eilts was one of Henry Kissinger's assistants in his shuttle-diplomacy efforts in the mid-1970s, a key participant in the negotiations that led to the Camp David accords and subsequently the US ambassador to Egypt and Saudi Arabia. His memoir describes in detail the US–Egyptian negotiations that resulted in the different US aid programmes to Egypt. It seems that some of those discussions were thorny. He describes the attitudes and expectations of some of his Egyptian counterparts as 'bringing to mind pharaonic friezes showing subject peoples bringing tribute to Egyptian rulers'. Western aid to Egypt, and especially American aid, was provided within a political rather than an economic framework. A brusque report by the US General Accounting Office, presented to Congress in 1989, stated that 'if aid to Egypt were considered purely on economic or developmental grounds, Egypt would have received annual obligations of not more than US$100–200 million'. At the time, US aid to Egypt was more than US$800 million per year in economic terms and US$1.3 billion in military assistance.[18] Egypt was reaping the benefits of the strategic change of direction in its foreign policy – from a close Soviet friend to a pillar of the United States' Middle East strategy (discussed in chapter 6).

But *al-infitah* was not all doom and gloom. It did open up the Egyptian economy to trade and financial liberalization. It upgraded the country's job market – even if at the beginning only for a fraction of the labour force. It created momentum and triggered growth in a number of industries. And it ushered in the private sector, which in the following three decades evolved to become the leading economic player in the country. Taking a long-term view (it being more than three decades since it was launched), *al-infitah*'s story has had a number of bright spots. Its immediate outcomes, however, were vastly disappointing.[19]

But *al-infitah*'s cardinal sin (and political failure) was that it severely diluted the Egyptian regime's legitimacy. Since the 1952 revolution, the regime had based its legitimacy on popular consent. Electoral mandates, in classic pharaonic style, were seen as rubber stamps, used only for appearances; religious mandates were untenable given the country's two faiths. Only the people's consent, their approval to be ruled, was the basis for governing. *Al-infitah* cracked that basis. The regime appeared to have abandoned its solidarity with the poor (a founding principle of the 1952 revolution) and to have allied itself with the rich. This had fatal political consequences.

Hosni Mubarak was propelled into the presidency by Anwar Sadat's assassination in October 1981 – an assassination carried out by 'his' army in front of 'his' people, live on TV.[20] Mubarak, who as vice-president was sitting beside Sadat, received a bullet in the wrist – and a clear message in the head. He needed to stabilize Egypt, 'grab hold of the country' as Jehan Sadat (the dead leader's widow) advised him at his inauguration. Most observers expected Mubarak to distance himself from the 1970s alliance of power and money, and to amend the regime's relationship with the people. He was considered a fresh face, neither an insider of Sadat's clique nor implicated in any of *al-infitah*'s scandalous corruption cases. A number of observers saw the Mubarak presidency as the military establishment 'grabbing hold' of an Egypt on the brink of social unrest.

But Mubarak decided against a radical move away from his predecessor's stance. He ignored the political failure of *al-infitah* and concentrated on its economic side. He championed the notion that economic, rather than political, reform was the priority and that change could be very disruptive, unless the country's economic foundations were strong and solid.[21] Unlike Sadat, he did not aim for any major political transformation. He had no interest in any substantial change in the country's power dynamics. The original vision that lay behind *al-infitah* was shelved. The NDP retained its solid grip on the government and the parliament; the regime continued its avid struggle against Islamism; the military establishment retained – and in certain aspects increased – its influence; power and money were getting closer and more intimate; the regime continued to contain the most important social institutions (Al-Azhar, the Church, the universities and the professional syndicates); and the state-controlled media maintained their adulatory tone.

President Mubarak's reforms were in the economic sphere. Like Sadat before him, Mubarak bet that an improvement in economic conditions would win over the people and soothe the discontent on the street. He launched a programme of structural adjustments to enhance the sources of foreign currency (one of the major pressures on the Egyptian economy at the time), improve living conditions, expand high-employment sectors and reduce poverty. President Mubarak and his advisors realized that the five key sources of foreign capital in the country (oil revenues, Suez Canal dues, remittances of Egyptians abroad, tourism and foreign aid) were largely independent of the economy's productivity. For example, in 1982 (Mubarak's first year in office) oil revenues were equal to circa 75 per cent of Egypt's total merchandise export (the main output of the economy). This bred an inherent unpredictability and reliance on external forces. His first two governments led an ambitious programme of Keynesian-style investments in key infrastructure sectors.[22] The infrastructure investments were followed by an overhaul of the fiscal and monetary foundations of the Egyptian economy.[23]

A government headed by the economist Atef Siddqui was tasked with leading a major restructuring programme. In nine long and difficult years, his government managed to reduce substantially the ratio of servicing external debt, devise a more effective system for allocating subsidies,[24] increase revenues and cut administrative waste. The government also entered into long negotiations with the World Bank and the International Monetary Fund,[25] with the objective of rescheduling Egypt's external debt. The negotiations were parallel to the agreement that was reached with the Paris Club in 1991 to reduce Egypt's debts to seventeen of the Club's members by US$19 billion. And for the first time since *al-infitah*, the government took privatization seriously. More than 300 of the largest public-sector companies were put up for sale.

There is a widespread view in Egypt that the country's privatization programme in the 1990s was a failure – a lethargic process with negligible yield. In reality, the programme was a relative success (if compared to other programmes in South America or even in East Asia). In around ten years, the government sold controlling stakes in 118 companies and minority stakes in sixteen companies. Roughly 50 per cent of all of the programme's proceeds went to the Ministry of Finance to reduce the budget deficit; 30 per cent of the proceeds went to settle the debts of the privatized companies with local commercial banks; and circa 17 per cent were allocated to finance early retirement schemes to affected employees. The IMF ranked the Egyptian privatization programme the fourth most successful in the world.[26] The government established a new ministry to stream-line the entire public sector. The finance ministry undertook a sweeping restructuring of the country's colossal pension system. In the 2000s, the regime pushed the monetary restructuring further, especially with the floatation of the Egyptian pound, a complete liberalization of the country's money markets, a reform of the tax system and strategic reductions in governmental social spending.

The restructuring programme (especially the adjustments in the monetary and fiscal systems) resulted in staggering hardships for the majority of the people. True, the expansion of the country's infrastructure increased the overall availability of elec-tricity and drinkable water, and improved transportation and telecommunications. There was a notable increase in foreign direct investments. Egyptian capital markets prospered. And, as discussed in Chapter 7, a number of Egyptian companies managed to grow into regional heavyweights with impressive success stories. But Egyptians' social suffering intensified. Many observers saw the successive restructuring programmes of the 1990s and 2000s as the regime's 'disengagement' from its social obligations. But the regime was engaged; its programmes, however, were lacking. In a visit to Egypt in 2007, a managing director of the World Bank noted that 'economic reforms in Egypt would take at least a generation to show results. And even in the best case scenario, Egypt is only five to ten years into this process.' Unemployment was rising (an effective rate of 18–21 per cent in the 24–54 age group, the core of the country's labour force). Housing was becoming a social challenge. As a consequence, marriage became harder for young people; it became common to have a family of six or seven living together in a single room; tens of millions of Egyptians were experiencing 'social suffocation'.[27]

Inflation, in double digits for half of the 1990s and 2000s, degraded the living standards of poor Egyptians and sizable sections of the middle class. The World Food Programme estimated that the cost of living for an average Egyptian household had risen by more than 75 per cent between the mid-1990s and the mid-2000s. The higher prices of bread and basic food staples led to violent clashes in long lines for government-subsidised loaves; in 2008 at least ten people died in one such incident. In spring 2008, Cairo's and Alexandria's doctors went on strike; their spokesman was seen shouting at the TV screens: 'Egypt's doctors are suffering.' Soon it was the academics' turn, as university professors across the country demonstrated in only the second recorded instance of a teachers' strike in the country's history.[28]

Islamic medical clinics were gradually becoming the main healthcare providers for Egypt's poor, and for millions of middle-class families. Severe poverty led to a thriving black-market in the sale of organs, whereby the poor were turned into 'spare parts for the rich'. An energetic social worker in one of Cairo's poorest slums reported that in summer 2007 kidneys and livers were 'the currency of choice, fetching around $7,500 per piece'. Economic want in Egypt seemed to have reached painful extremes. Sahar Al-Gaara, a feminist and journalist, put it succinctly: 'The Egyptian family used to complain for decades of the increasing fees of private tutoring, now they complain of the price of bread, sugar and tea.' A leading Egyptian psychologist estimated in 2007 that at least 17 million Egyptians (around 20 per cent of the population) were suffering from serious depression. Mubarak's bet, like that of Sadat before him, seemed to have been lost. And the legitimacy problem was becoming ever thornier. The regime was increasingly seen as reneging on another tenet of the 1952 revolution: subsidizing the people's basic needs and enabling a 'dignified life'.

President Sadat is reported to have joked that 'those who will not make money in Egypt during my reign will never make money'. The privatization programme of the 1990s and the swelling role of the private sector in the economy proved him wrong. The long campaign against 'biases' in the Egyptian banking sector by the leading Egyptian magazine *Rose-al-Yousef* noted that more than 40 per cent of all outstanding banking credit in Egypt in 1995 was extended to less than 100 businessmen or families, many with complex (if at times obscure) connections to various parts of the regime. A number of strategic industries in the economy suffered shocking levels of ownership concentration; in certain situations, almost half the production of an entire industry (valued at billions of US dollars) was controlled by a single family with conspicuous political connections, and at times prominent positions in the ruling party . . . .

It would be wrong to claim that all key economic and financial powers in the 1990s and 2000s were allies of the regime. There were also cases of genuine entrepreneurialism: businessmen (and women) who made independent use of the expansionist policies, the waves of foreign direct investments that poured into Egypt, and the privatization programme. For example, the significant participation of the local private sector (as opposed to international capital) in the privatization programme and the significant growth of the sector during the 1990s were typically presented, in local media, as a major corruption story. And, indeed, corruption was abundant. Yet the major role of the local private sector was a result of two factors. Egypt in the late 1980s and early 1990s did not have major financial and/or institutional investors that could have acted as pioneering investors in the privatization programme and the subsequent economic growth. The major insurance companies and the largest commercial banks were traditional, conservative players – and mostly state controlled, and as such not mandated to participate in privatization transactions. There was also a dire lack of investment funds or heavily capitalized investment banks. At the same time, Egypt was an undesirable destination for foreign direct investments – mainly because the Asian financial crisis in the late 1990s turned large institutional investors away from all emerging markets, especially shaky ones (such as Egypt at the time); and also because the deadly attacks on tourists in Egypt (culminating in the disastrous Luxor attack in November 1997) exacerbated the negative positioning of the country.

Local private capital was one of the few options available – and it was ready and eager. There were also people who took the initiative to develop new value-adding businesses in industries that had witnessed significant growth: real estate, entertainment, healthcare, tourism, home appliances and food and beverages. Some were just in the right place, at the right time and with the right people. For example, the owner of a (at the time medium-sized) Egyptian manufacturing business was introduced in 1990 through a senior contact at the Egyptian Chamber of Commerce to a Russian importer with a vast distribution network in Russia who was visiting Egypt to assess potential business opportunities. The chemistry between the two men evolved into a partnership that, in few years (at a time of dramatic pricing differential opportunities in the Russian market) blossomed into the business of manufacturing, packaging and distributing Egyptian-made products in Russia. Success breeds success; the Egyptian businessman, by now an expert on the Russian market, diversified into different sectors. And by the early 2000s, the medium-sized manufacturing business was transformed into an economic empire in four industrial verticals, all focusing on sales in Russia, the CIS countries and Eastern Europe. But, in general, power and money continued to mix, their relationship became increasingly intimate and the lines continued to blur.

An additional factor transformed the relationship of the regime with the country's leading capitalist forces: the meteoric rise of Gamal Mubarak, the president's son. By the early 2000s, President Mubarak was clearly ageing. He continued to rule supreme with unrivalled power and authority, but the once super-active president was less visible and less engaged. He increasingly delegated decisions to members of his inner clique – the stalwarts of his administration for more than two decades. But many of the leading members of that old group were themselves ageing, some were embroiled in high-profile corruption cases and some were very unpopular and became liabilities for the regime and the president himself. Gamal Mubarak, the fresh face with no legacies and baggage, quickly became his father's main advisor, and increasingly his right-hand man.

Mubarak junior also had a break. Egypt's economic leadership was vacant. Atef Siddqui, the long-serving prime minister who had led the major restructuring reform of the 1990s, retired on grounds of poor health. His successors were hardly popular or admired. The talented economists inside the NDP, such as Mahmoud Moheideen, were developing strategies and writing plans[29] away from the limelight and the party's power centre. Gamal Mubarak saw the vacant leadership position and the opportunity.[30]

He led an energetic exercise within the NDP.[31] The policy committee that he founded and headed quickly became the party's new engine: the centre for designing, structuring and debating policies, programmes and law proposals (part of that work also took place at the Egyptian Centre for Economic Studies, one of the country's leading – and low-profile – think tanks, whose members include Gamal Mubarak as well as a select number of Egypt's most prominent capitalists). He gathered around him a group of successful businessmen, economists and public-relations professionals, who gradually became the centre of gravity within the party. He chose the chief members of that elite new group from among the same capitalist class that had come to dominate Egypt's economy from the mid-1990s.

In creating circles of economic powers around him, Gamal Mubarak was to a large extent repeating the work of Anwar Sadat in the late 1970s. Yet, unlike the tribalism and provincialism that characterized Sadat's approach, Gamal's style was more systematic and modern. He imposed a structure within the NDP through which he promoted his trusted elite, channelled ideas and projects and found roles (and government positions) for the favoured capitalists. Also unlike Sadat – and even his father – Gamal Mubarak did not rely on the military and the intelligence establishment; his allies, almost without exception, came from the upper business echelons.

The new power base was modern, Western-oriented and in tune with the age. Its leading members were educated at top Western universities, fluent in English or French (or both) and comfortable with their counterparts in Europe, the United States and the Gulf. They represented an impressive facade for the 'new thinking' that Gamal Mubarak was promoting. And unlike in *al-infitah*, with the emphasis on 'making it' and creating wealth, the message of the 2000s was all about development, national growth rates, GDP per capita, 'the economic tiger on the Nile', fighting poverty and social mobility.

In less than ten years, a mesh was formed between the regime (in which Gamal Mubarak became the unrivalled strongman, second only to his father) and some Egyptian business and finance tycoons. The framework was a further evolution of the webs of interconnecting interests that had been forged and extended since *al-infitah*. The mesh comprised the most important vehicles of the NDP (especially the highly influential policy committee); the key secretariats and committees of parliament (also controlled by the NDP); some of the largest and most important economic sectors in the economy; the entire banking sector; some of the most active civic and charity organizations in Egypt; and of course the government itself. The new power group also had a close relationship with Egypt's leading Christian economic powers (as well as the immensely influential Church), which – sensing the peril of political Islam – have developed over the past two decades a tacit alliance with the regime (discussed in Chapter 5).

By the mid-2000s, Gamal Mubarak and his close associates within the NDP were concerned about the regime's political positioning. The George W. Bush administration, after the overthrow of Saddam Hussein's regime in Iraq and in its aggressive democracy promotion campaign in the Middle East, was putting significant pressure on President Mubarak to enact political reforms. These pressures significantly affected the personal relationship between Presidents Mubarak and Bush. President Mubarak stopped his traditional annual spring trips to Washington. And, interestingly, at the May 2008 World Economic Forum – Middle East Division – in Sharm Al-Sheikh, President Mubarak walked out of the main conference hall at the beginning of President Bush's speech.

The regime was also facing increasing ideological challenges and political insurgencies at home. The 2003–5 period was particularly perilous. A large group of civil-society activists, supported by professional associations and syndicates, came together to form

Kefaya ('Enough') – more formally the Egyptian Movement for Change. The group quickly became a platform for protests against hereditary rule; political corruption and stagnation; the blurring of the lines between power and wealth; and the regime's cruelty, coercion and disregard for human rights. A domino effect was created. The Judges Club launched a disciplined campaign to ratify the elections law; some of its members published a manifesto urging Egyptians to 'withdraw their consent to be ruled'.[32] Student groups organized protests and demonstrations in the heart of Cairo. A large number of feminists (from Islamic as well as civic groups) came together and established We Are Watching You (*Shayfenkom*) to monitor the increasing harassment and intimidation of women in demonstrations. The tone of the Nasserites became increasingly loud. The regime looked weak, and Egypt seemed to be once more on the verge of change.[33]

The real danger for the regime, however, was a perceptible change in the strategy of its arch rival, the Islamic movement. The movement was increasingly targeting the middle and upper middle classes in Egypt, with a strong focus on university students and young professionals. The soft and intellectual strands of the Islamic movement were establishing themselves as formidable opponents in the war for the hearts and minds of the Egyptian middle class and affluent youths. The style of the movement was modern and forward-looking, unlike the traditionally Salafist Islamists; it embraced technology (satellite channels, the Internet, blogs and even music video clips), and was in step with the capitalist tone of the era. Wealth was touted as a force for good; entrepreneurialism was encouraged.[34] The regime had a dilemma: it needed to confront the increasing external pressures (especially from Washington) and to distinguish its doctrine from that of the Islamists – and capitalism per se was no longer a differentiating factor.

A vaguely defined liberalism became the regime's cultural doctrine: under its umbrella gathered active promotion of women's rights, somewhat more daring cultural products (especially in cinema and on TV)[35], a recollection of the values of Egypt's liberal age from the 1930s to the 1960s, a revival in the interest in pharaonic Egypt and more engagement with the West (especially Europe). For example, the Culture Ministry launched a number of initiatives to preserve Cairo's and Alexandria's *belle époque* central areas. Some of the old monarchical palaces were opened to the public, most notably the Abdeen and Montazah Palaces (a reminder of the glamour of Egypt's liberal age). Egypt was the co-founder (alongside France) of the Euro-Mediterranean Partnership for Development (established in 2008). It was the only Arab shareholder in the European Bank for Reconstruction and Development. More films were produced in cooperation with the European Union's Media Programme. And increasingly the Egyptian government focused on trading agreements with European countries.

The other innovative factor was an emphasis on competence. Gamal Mubarak's mantra was: 'We are doing, while others just preach theoretical programmes.' The 2004 government, and behind it the NDP, undertook a number of (mostly economic) initiatives to prove that it was serious about change. The restructuring of the Egyptian banking sector is arguably the most notable example of the effort. The 2004–7 period witnessed a breakthrough in the elimination of weak banks, mainly through 'forced' mergers, sound recapitalizations, the privatization of a select number of banks[36] and modernizing and upgrading the country's monetary policy through a complete overhaul of the central bank.[37]

Most Egyptians did not grasp the details of the banking reform, nor of the other economic initiatives that the NDP and its allies undertook; but most noticed that the new government had a different approach. The message was evident in the assured delivery and sharp and fluent expositions on policies of such politicians as trade minister Rachid Mohamed Rachid, finance minister Yousef Boutrus Ghali and investment minister Mahmoud Moheieldeen – and even in the relatively balanced discussions in the parliament among the NDP's heavyweight industrialists and financiers. The liberal capitalist camp was positioning itself as a confident, competent and poised force for change in the country. The message was not 'we can sort out the banking sector or work out economic policies', but 'we can and deserve to rule'.

There is a major problem, however, with the 'deserve' part. Liberal capitalism in Egypt lacks legitimacy. As a political force, this current remains a confined, detached, elitist movement. Unlike Islamism or Arab nationalism, it does not have any constituency on the Egyptian street. Its leader, Gamal Mubarak, embodies that legitimacy dilemma. He comes across as being at least as confident and sharp as any of his economic and financial lieutenants; his work at the NDP shows leadership skills and a rigorous work ethic; and his ability to subvert internal party opponents and to crystallize a solid power elite around him all reveal determination, intelligence and political resolve. Yet he remains a top-down figure, and it will be very difficult for him to gain a popular mandate from the people.

Gamal Mubarak grew up in the 1970s and 1980s as the vice-president's and then the president's son. His life experience has been vastly different from that of his contemporaries; he has not experienced any of the challenges that most Egyptians face in terms of education, transportation, accommodation, health care, the job market, dealing with the country's administrative system or with the security apparatus; he spent his formative years at

The American University in Cairo, then in the City of London (as an investment banker and later a private-equity professional), before returning to Egypt to work with and advise his father at the country's highest (and most detached) level. But if there is nothing in his personal experience that enables him to connect with ordinary Egyptians, unlike most politicians he has never claimed to *represent* the people. It was telling that in an interview with *Middle East Quarterly*, Gamal Mubarak emphasized his (and his party's) persistence in adopting unpopular policies. He genuinely advocates what he believes to be 'the right strategies for Egypt' (and they could well be). His approach, however, is that of a technocratic politician who is not concerned about gaining an electoral mandate to remain in power. His public persona aggravates that problem, for Gamal Mubarak comes across as detached, elitist, condescending – and westernized. Despite the many assets he brings to the liberal capitalist current in Egypt, Gamal Mubarak is also its main liability. That would be especially true in a fair election.

The legitimacy problem is compounded by the fact that most Egyptians of the lower and middle classes have a major trust problem regarding the country's rich and political elite. A key ingredient in this is a pervasive feeling that successive waves of 'enrichment' have been the result of fraud, sleaze and the suspect fusion of political authority and economic interests. This trust issue has been aggravated by numerous cases of extreme profiteering and abuse of power – many of which have been extensively covered in opposition media as well as visible in everyday life.

In Egypt, corruption is about large-scale transactions *and* small-scale deals – from using privatization to generate illicit wealth to paying a low-level government employee a few dollars to expedite a bureaucratic procedure. In its 2005 Corruption

Perceptions Index, Berlin-based Transparency International ranked Egypt 70th out of 158 countries (the lower the ranking, the more perceived corruption there is). In the 2008 report Egypt came 115th out of 180 countries – a significant deterioration. Corruption in Egypt is an institutionalized phenomenon that pervades almost every aspect of the country's socio-economic life. There are many highly publicized accounts of corruption in ministries and government agencies, cases of political influence exerted to gain government contracts and mandates and situations of pure disregard for the law. In a score of such cases, the accused were notable members of the ruling NDP. In one specific case in which more than a thousand Egyptians died after a ferry sank in the Red Sea, the court acquitted the accused in a decision that the national prosecutor announced his decision to appeal on grounds of 'violations in documented records, corruption in investigations, shortcomings in validation, and arbitrary conclusions'.[38]

Egypt's liberal capitalism is plagued by profligacy as well as corruption. Egypt has always been a country of severe inequality, but the 2000s took that phenomenon to new extremes. The impact of the demographic boom in the country was a factor in its suddenly greater visibility. Cairo metamorphosed into a city of 18 million people, in which vastly wealthy neighbourhoods are minutes away from alleys of crushing poverty. The haves and have-nots were no longer able to sneak past each other, interact briefly then retreat to their seclusion; in an increasingly crowded capital, they rubbed against one another. In her essay 'Pyramids and Alleys' (in *Cairo Cosmopolitan*), Petra Kuppinger describes the disconcerting inequality between deprived villages in Giza lacking running water and electricity and the next door Pyramid area, the location of major investments in luxurious hotels, new affluent and secluded residential compounds and a world-class museum. Cairo, and to a lesser extent Alexandria, crammed together a high proportion of Egypt's population into a tiny space – Zamalek's swanky nightspots next to dilapidated public housing; Mohandeseen's shiny boutiques next to deprived Meit Okba; a Porsche Cayenne cruising next to a minibus containing twenty people packed together in the burning heat.

At a time when inflation on basic products (bread, sugar, tea, tobacco and fuel) was running in double digits, and with more than 40 per cent of the population under the international line of poverty, the Egyptian stock exchange registered the world's largest index appreciation in 2005; pricings of high-end real-estate developments skyrocketed by more than 20 per cent per annum – reaching levels comparable to those in West London; at a time when more than 2 million pensioners were facing an annual depreciation in the worth of their savings close to 8 per cent (a frightening prospect given that for many families, those pensioners were the bread winners!), the country was spending close to US$1 billion per annum on voting SMSs on music shows on satellite channels. Symbols of luxury and lavishness were popping up under the shocked eyes of the masses. Increasingly, the 'rich' were abandoning the centres of the cities (especially Cairo) for gated communities and compounds in distant new leafy suburbs – while the old corners of the cities crumbled under an over-used, ageing infrastructure. From transportation to health care, to education and in almost all basic constituents of daily life, a clear, vast distinction between the lives of the thin layer of the rich and that of the rest was emerging – and becoming more obtrusive. Inflation was running out of control, and the middle class was increasingly squashed under its heavy and taxing burdens. Repeated scenes of anger (some of which ended in violent demonstrations) took place in different universities, factories and public spaces across the country. The accepted wisdom became that the top 5 per cent of the population were the engine of the country's purchasing power for almost all sectors other than the basic needs of living.

In principle, inequality could have been seen as a natural by-product of a growing economy where some social strata (typically because of privileged background or education) manage to exploit the emerging opportunities, while other and far larger ones lose out. It could have also been seen as a temporary phase in a long, protracted route towards development. This, as it were theoretical, view had elements of the truth. But it could not disguise a stronger undercurrent of feeling among millions of Egyptians that the elite, the upper crust, the wealthy, the haves, the capitalists are undeservedly so. The point is illustrated by a scene in a popular Egyptian film of 2005. The leading character waves his hands in protest about being labelled a thief and shouts at the expensively dressed people around him at a plush golf resort: 'But *they* are all thieves!' Many Egyptian cinema audiences erupted in clapping at the line.

Liberal capitalism has made significant strides in Egypt. Its internal demons, however, are haunting it. It also continues to face a still potent Islamic movement. What, though, of Egypt's other major religious community, its Christians?

CHAPTER 5
EGYPTIAN CHRISTIANS

'WITH STEPS SUCH as this, your majesty's wisdom and vision would take Egypt to lead modernity in the East,' said Nubar Pasha, a senior civil servant – later Egypt's first prime minister – whose family had settled in Egypt in the early nineteenth century. He was addressing Khedive Ismael, and the occasion was the inauguration of the Cairo Opera House in 1869 – only the fifth in the world, and the first anywhere in the Middle East, Africa and Asia. Nubar Pasha, the obsequiousness to a ruler aside, was not exaggerating. As discussed in Chapter 1, the era was one of great social progress in Egypt, marked by the establishment of new educational institutions, factories, publishers that translated foreign books and cultural bodies. Nubar was among those who pioneered this wave of modernity; one of the small army of visionaries, business and community leaders and officials who had helped the ruling Mohamed Ali family take Egypt forward. Nubar, like many of these luminaries, was Christian; in his case of Armenian origin.[1]

Egyptian Christians, in the second half of the nineteenth century and the first half of the twentieth, were at the forefront of the renaissance that propelled the country towards a cultural and economic resurgence. The Christian Takla family, in 1875, founded *Al-Ahram*, Egypt's pre-eminent daily newspaper. George Abyad was the creative force behind the birth of the Egyptian theatre. Ya'acoub Artin guided the transformation from a religion-based teaching doctrine towards a civic educational system. Christians who were close to the experiment of the Levant's House of Wisdom (*Dar Al-Hikma*) were among the leading figures that founded Fuad I University (later Cairo University), the first Western-styled educational institution in the Arab world. Acia and other Christian producers and directors led the growth of Egyptian cinema. The first banking, translation and automated manufacturing facilities in the country were introduced by Egyptian Christian entrepreneurs and businessmen. Some of the most visible figures in the history of the Egyptian economy over the past century and a half were Christians, especially from Al-Saeed's leading families.

Egyptian Christians' endeavours and enterprise were not only part of the country's liberal renaissance but contributed greatly to the formulation of its identity and historical role. The presence of Christians in Egyptian society was at the heart of the evolution of Egyptianism into a rich fabric comprising different heritages, legacies and religions; a unique cultural blend that made Egypt more than just another province of any of the region's Islamic empires. The existence of two religions in the same land – the rich agricultural valley that for centuries valued stability, tranquillity and perpetual cycles of giving and yielding, centred on the great Nile – shaped Egyptian society's tolerant view of itself as a mixture of blood, a sanctuary of peacefulness and constancy and a partnership between 'one people worshipping the same God in two different ways', a phrase repeated by Patriarch Kyrillos VI (Patriarch from 1959 to 1971).

That internal view generated a virtuous cycle. When the Levant was suffering from socio-political tensions (such as the massacres of the 1860s between the Druze and the Maronites) or Ottoman oppression, when the Arabian peninsula was backward-looking, and when Iraq (then, as it is now) was embroiled in sectarian strain, Egypt became a refuge for the talented and the ambitious. The country became a destination for swaths of Levantines, North Africans, Iraqis, Arabs from the peninsula as well as Armenians, Greeks and Jews. Cairo and Alexandria ruled supreme as the cultural, commercial, financial and political centres of the region. That diversity, and the richness it had fostered, was behind Egypt's 'soft power' in the first decades of the twentieth century, which became the main pillar of the Egyptian project discussed in Chapter 2.

The Christians' role in society was also Egypt's cultural bridge to Europe. Several courageous thinkers – such as Saad Zaghloul (Al-Wafd's godfather), Taha Hussein and even Islamists such as Al-Tahtawi and Mohamed Abdou – had spearheaded the drive towards modernity and progress. But an equal momentum came from the tens of thousands of families that decided to send their daughters to school; from the thousands that insisted on teaching their children English and French; from the major transformations of the educational, administrative and judicial systems into modern, Europeanized ones; and from the social change towards modern clothing, art and tastes. Christian families were pioneers on all of those fronts.

The outstanding role of Egyptian Christians in formulating Egyptianism stemmed from their solid status as an integral component of Egypt's social fabric – not a marginal minority in a Muslim society. Egypt was, in Christian doctrine, the Holy Family's early host; the Virgin Mary, Joseph and baby Jesus fled to the country to avoid the turmoil in Palestine in the early years of the first century. Most scholars believe the family resided in Egypt for a few years, although nothing is really known about their time in the country.

Christianity proper came to Egypt in 43 CE when St Mark visited the country and bestowed the priesthood on Hananya, a Jewish Egyptian who would later play a primary role in leading a number of missionary efforts in the country. St Mark visited again in 65 CE; by that time, Egyptian Christians were a sizable community, and increasingly under pressure from the Romans. A number of scholars believe Mark wrote his gospel during that visit, shortly before his assassination at Serapis temple in Alexandria. St Mark's remains were buried in Alexandria until Venetian merchants and soldiers smuggled them back to their city state. Those remains would later become the base for the world-famous cathedral, today at the centre of Piazza San Marco in Venice, which was later named 'the Republic of St Mark'.

Over the following few centuries, Christianity enjoyed tremendous growth throughout Egypt, and quickly became the country's main religion. Christianity's peacefulness corresponded with the Nile valley's serenity and quiet farming life; and by the fourth century, Christianity was the religion of almost all Egyptians from Alexandria in the north to the deep Saeedi south. There are a number of studies on the early years of Christianity in Egypt, and the reasons the new religion proved highly successful in the country. On one side, Christian theology resembled many aspects of old Egyptian religions: the holy trinity of a father, mother and son-god; the virgin birth; and the resurrection from death. But perhaps more importantly, Egyptians saw in the new humane religion a reprieve from the oppression of the pagan Romans, and a solid socio-political catalyst for differentiating themselves from their occupiers.[2]

The embryonic Egyptian Church (the Seat of St Mark) grew from a repressed, isolated organization (in its early days in the first and second centuries) into the state's nerve centre, and later, into one of the main schools of thought and theological philosophy within Eastern Christianity. Origen, one of the leading thinkers on Christian divinity and the originator of the analogical interpretation of Christ's life, was among its graduates. The Church also played a crucial role during the Arian crisis – the debate on whether Jesus was equal to or created by God the Father. Under the leadership of the charismatic Patriarch (later, Saint) Athanasius, the Church played a prominent role in fighting the Arian doctrine, and upheld the majority's decision taken at the Council of Nicaea. Alexandria, Rome and Antioch were the only three patriarchates in the Christian world;[3] and the 'Alexandria school' was considered 'the seat of learning' in that world. The Egyptian Church also managed to retain its independence, especially after the schism between the Western and Eastern churches;[4] there were a few attempts to unite the Egyptian Church (and other Eastern churches) with the Western one in Rome, but Egyptian Christians insisted on their independence.[5] The Church's independence, theologically as well as operationally from any international influence, allowed it to evolve into a governing and administrative body – at times in direct (and violent) confrontations with the ruling Romans. A number of historians believe that the hostility between the Romans and the Egyptians fundamentally arose from religious reasons. While the Romans were increasingly oriented towards the doctrines that were to evolve into Catholicism, Egyptians believed in Monophysitism (the belief that Christ had a divine nature only, rather than both a divine and a human one), a concept that Rome vehemently discredited. Rome later excommunicated Dioscurus, one of the founding fathers of the

Egyptian Church and a successor to St Cyril of Alexandria, a historic hero to Egyptian Christians.[6]

Even the advent of Islam in Egypt did not change Christianity's dominance over the country and society. For more than four centuries following Islam's conquest of Egypt (in 640 CE), the vast majority of Egyptians remained Christian. Islam's conquest of Egypt has always been a historical puzzle: a weak army of around 4,000 warriors taking over a huge country such as Egypt and defeating its strong Roman garrison. One reasonable explanation is that the Egyptian population, antagonistic towards the Roman rulers, threw their lot in with the Arab invaders, seeing them as political liberators, rather than the heralds of a new divine revelation. It was only the establishment of Arabic as the state's official language at the beginning of the eighth century that compelled Egyptian Christians to start learning Arabic in order to keep their jobs in government and administrative offices, and that presaged a wave of conversions to Islam.[7] Christians, however, remained more than 40 per cent of the country's population until the mid-sixteenth century. In the next century, Egypt was on the receiving end of two major migration waves from the Arabian peninsula,[8] and in addition saw many Christians convert to Islam (in part as a result of sustained Ottoman efforts across the key provinces of the empire).[9] By 1700, Muslims accounted for around 75 per cent of the population.

The period of Ottoman rule over Egypt witnessed a notable regression in Christians' role in the country's public life. Under the Ottomans, Egypt was a mere colony, not the base of an empire as it had been under the Fatimids, the Ayyubids and the Mamelukes. The Ottomans were thus unconcerned with the country's national unity or with mobilizing Christians' cultural role in connecting Egypt with Europe. Despite its economic importance to the Ottomans (as a crucial base in international

trade routes linking the Mediterranean with the Indian sub-
continent, as well as its geo-strategic weight within the empire),
Egypt had attracted subprime Ottoman viceroys; the position was
'the customary fate for dismissed chief eunuchs'.[10] The Ottomans'
strict and hierarchal administrative system also favoured the
Turkish-bred janissaries over any other group in any province –
especially non-Muslim ones.

The picture changed with Mohamed Ali and his successors, an
era that lasted from the beginning of the nineteenth century
until the beginning of the 1950s. Christians were then at the
forefront of the national endeavours – from the political to the
economic to the artistic. The role of one person best exemplifies
Egyptian Christians' place in the society: Makram Ebeid Pasha,
the legendary secretary general of Al-Wafd, and the long-term
finance minister in every Wafd government from the 1920s
to the 1940s. He controlled the nerve centre of the party and
ensured its command of an unrivalled majority in the country; he
was the era's fiercest member of parliament, elected more than
six times from a constituency with a negligible Christian presence. Ebeid, the Saeedi who had completed his studies at Oxford
and the Christian who memorized the whole of the Koran,
represented the intellectual meeting between classic Egyptian
values and Western modernity, as well as between Islam and
Christianity. In his role, influence and social standing – and not
least in his long and complicated relationship with Mustafa
Al-Nahas Pasha (Al-Wafd's leader from the 1930s to the 1950s),[11]
Makram Ebeid embodied the significance of the Christian
presence at the heart both of Egypt and of Egyptianism, with
its tolerant, relaxed, liberal and secular view of society and
national identity.

That definition of Egyptianism has almost disappeared.
Egyptian Christians increasingly withdrew from society in the

second half of the twentieth century. The country did not have another Makram Ebeid in these years. The general consensus is that the ascent of Islamism from the mid-1970s was responsible for the retreat. True, Islamism was a transformative factor in making society more religious, conservative, anti-secular and an agent of the attachment of religion to national identity – and thus in many ways was perceived as hostile to Egyptian Christians. But the rise of Islamism was not the sole culprit; three other factors contributed to the retreat of Christians and the dilution of their role in Egyptian society – even before the ascent of Islamism.

The first and most important was economics. Between 1880 and 1953, more than 40 of the 100 families with the largest landownership in Egypt were Christian; in Al-Saeed, the ratio was much higher. Christians owned some of the country's most important manufacturing facilities, retail empires, shipping companies, insurance and banking entities, and were invariably represented in key business associations. Economic power in a relatively relaxed and liberal social environment was the route to social prestige, glamour and influence across various socio-economic domains – politics, journalism and the arts. All that ended in the 1950s and early 1960s. Land reform and the subsequent socialist laws implemented by the Nasserite regime stripped those families of their power and effectively blocked them from all avenues of engagement with society. A significant majority of those families, after decades of economic indulgence and sumptuous lifestyles, were too westernized, too detached, to remain in a changing country and to start afresh. The result was a notable wave of Christian emigration from Egypt, comprising those families that, a few years earlier, had been social luminaries in the country.

The second factor was political and cultural, for Nasser's transformations altered these structures too. The drive towards

Arab nationalism was comprehensive in both areas. It produced an Arabic identity that supplanted (for a time) the Egyptian one that had been dominant throughout the country's liberal experiment, and changed the mood of Egyptian society. The westernization and Europeanization that characterized Egypt's liberal experiment were replaced by an Arabization, the outward features of which were secular and liberal, but the cultural depth of which was rooted in Islamic history and civilization.

The Nasserite regime, in its attempt to forge a macro-Arabic project, was aware of the sensitivities that such Arabization could evoke – not only among Egyptian Christians, but also in places such as Lebanon where Christians were traditionally society's leaders. The regime's cultural machinations worked on positioning the Arabized society as a secular and national rather than religious, one. Al-Azhar's role was muted; Nasser developed an amicable relationship with Patriarch Kyrillos VI (1959–71); the state media's rhetoric glorified the people, the nation, 'our Arabic history' and steered away from any religious language or symbolism. Even history was doctored; as mentioned in Chapter 2, the regime's take on Saladin (in the 1963 smash-hit film *Saladin the Victorious*) turned the Kurdish Muslim fighter chasing the Crusaders into an Arab leader fighting the Westerners. But that positioning could not alter the fact that immersing Egypt, politically and culturally, in the Arab world, and shaping its national identity in uncompromising Arabic colours, entailed a thorough redirection of society towards the Islamic culture that had ruled the Arabs' historical heartland for fourteen centuries.

Many Egyptian Christians were keenly aware of these changes. The Church saw that as the Egyptian (and mainly Muslim) middle class was becoming engulfed in the dynamic Arab nationalist project, sectors of the Christian middle class were undergoing an intellectual revision of their own status within the new, post-1952 Egypt. Some felt that the reorientation would in the long term corrode Egypt's Christian heritage and dilute the role of Christians in the country: the Arabist 'turn' was, according to this way of thinking, destined to propel society towards Islamism. The emigration of rich Egyptian Christian families exacerbated those concerns. This sentiment was especially strong among young middle-class Christians, many of whom in the 1960s opted out of their academic or business careers to become priests. The 'migration to the Church' was part of an 'internal revolution' that sought to transform the ancient institution into a dynamic platform that could match the pace of social change and pressure.[12]

In effect, the trend marked the beginning of the politicization of the Church, a new phenomenon in modern Egypt. Throughout the nineteenth and twentieth century, the Church had remained detached from the vagaries of politics. The new approach aimed to mitigate the danger it perceived to Christians' role and interests in the country by asserting its social as well as spiritual role. Patriarch (later Pope)[13] Shenouda III, consecrated in November 1971, championed those efforts. The Egyptian Church too expanded its role from being the 'historical home' and 'the theological guide' of Egyptian Christians to a major provider of social services. Through diverse associations, social groups and parishes, the Church increasingly supported large numbers of poor Christian families, young graduates and the unemployed, the elderly and students. There was also a very noticeable swelling in the role of Sunday schools, which became the key social gatherings for many young Egyptian Christians. The secluded schools became places where Christian doctors, engineers, teachers, civil servants, merchants, businessmen, journalists and professors could find refuge from the spreading Islamism and carve out their own social space.

The same crystallization occurred among various Christian social groups, and resulted in the emergence of Christian clusters: companies that predominantly hire Christians, university faculties with a significant over-representation of Christian young professors and *keiretsu*-like business enclaves with intermingled dependencies, ownership, and interests and which act in concerted patterns. The 1980s and 1990s also witnessed a major drive in building churches,[14] especially in areas where the Muslim Brotherhood was increasingly gaining prominence. The Sunday schools and the business webs were efficient fund-raising networks for that purpose. 'Christian media' also proliferated: this included *Watani*, the key publication of the Egyptian Church, new Christian satellite channels and a plethora of Internet sites.

The Church was also increasingly adopting its own, independent political stance – at times in defiance of the regime. Throughout the 1970s (the period when President Sadat espoused Islamism in his efforts to suppress Nasserism), Pope Shenouda led a restrained but determined opposition to Sadat's Islamizing policies. He repeatedly refused to make compromises that he deemed unacceptable to Egyptian Christians, and took positions unambiguously defiant of Sadat – such as over the latter's pressure to allow Egyptian Christians to make Easter pilgrimages to Jerusalem. In 1981, after a number of highly intense confrontations, the Pope paid the price when President Sadat deposed and exiled him. President Mubarak ended the exile in January 1985 after a lengthy and complicated legal process. The relationship with the regime changed during the Mubarak era. The Church's politicization adapted to a subtle understanding with the regime by which the institution's concerns over the rise of political and militant Islamism were accommodated. In return the Church was expected to nudge its constituents to vote for the NDP, toe the line of the regime on all sensitive issues and moderate escalating international criticism of the 'violence' against or 'persecution' of Christians in Egypt, as vigorously expressed in particular by Christian Egyptian–American groups.

The violence against Christians was the third factor behind their social withdrawal. Egypt witnessed cycles of violent sectarianism, and Christians were positioned as a victimized minority.[15] In 2005, a DVD of the performance of a play mounted at the historical Mar Girgis Church[16] in Cairo – purportedly denigrating Islamic beliefs as well as the Prophet Mohamed – was widely distributed. A large mob besieged the church, where at the time more than 150 Christian girls were attending a religious lesson. There was panic, stone-throwing and near disaster. A few months later, at the same church, a group of young Muslims outraged at alleged anti-Islam slurs at a summer festival again attacked the church; for a second time, forceful police action prevented tragedy.

In other areas, such as the village of Al-Kosheh in Al-Saeed, repeated waves of violence left around twenty Christians and two Muslims dead; some churches were burned in Asyut and other attempts in northern Al-Saeed and the Delta were foiled. Even in Cairo and Alexandria, there were many attacks on churches, some involving Molotov cocktails, and Christians' properties (especially jewellery shops) were attacked. There were also assaults by militant Islamists (mainly Al-Jamaa Al-Islamiya) that left dozens of Christians dead, sometimes as a result of refusing to pay protection money.

The violence, the dilution of economic power in the 1950s and 1960s, the move towards Arabism and, inherently with it, embracing Islamic history and culture, and the rise of Islamism led to Christian withdrawal and retreat – whether to the different social enclaves that had emerged in the country's socio-economic life, or physically through emigration. Credible figures are extremely hard to come by, but a number of independent sources reporting on Egyptian demographics in the 1990s and 2000s (as well as the testimonies of a number of Egyptian community leaders abroad) reveal a significant upswing in Christian emigration from Egypt. There was a widespread feeling that society was increasingly 'Islamic'; that religion had replaced nationalism as the pillar of identity in Egyptian society; that there was an increasing entrenchment of Islamism, not only in politics, 'but in social attitudes, behaviours, even discourse'; and that though there was no systematic discrimination against Christians, there were numerous cases of unfairness in daily life. These could not be reduced to dry social trends or perceived easily by outsiders; to those affected they were real and personal. Nevine, an educated, upper middle-class mother of three who is considering emigrating to the United States or Canada, was 'not only worried, but also sad': 'When I go to Heliopolis [a prestigious Cairene social and sports club] my boys tend to play together; it's my daughter who breaks my heart when she comes with a sad face and says that nobody wants to play with her because her name is Mary,' she said.[17]

Almost a century before Nevine uttered her frustrations, Lord Cromer (Britain's consul-general in Egypt between 1883 and 1907) commented that it was impossible to distinguish between Christians and Muslims in the country. In the 2000s, this has become a much easier task. A certain sectarianism has taken its toll on the fabric of Egyptian society. It is felt in the Christians' withdrawal into economic enclaves, the emergence of Christian neighbourhoods, in clearer dividing lines in university classrooms and professional syndicates, in the near impossibility of any Christian politician winning an election in any constituency with a Muslim majority, in job advertisements 'for Muslims only', in dress codes (especially after the exponential increase in the number of veiled women in Egypt), even in slang.

The situation was becoming alarming; and by the early 1990s the regime was compelled to intervene. A number of albeit toothless ministries – emigration and environment – became the preserve of Christians; some senior, yet marginal, positions in the interior ministry were allocated to heavily vetted Christian officers; the president consistently assigned the majority of the ten parliamentary seats he has the right to appoint to Christian politicians (thus avoiding the embarrassment of a Christian-free parliament); the Eastern Christmas (7 January) and Easter became national holidays.

The regime also sought to use Egyptian Christians and the country's civic heritage in its struggle with political Islam. It was keen to emphasize that the Islamic project denies both the social composition of the country and its historical experience of two religions on the same land. President Mubarak refused to allow the creation of religion-based political parties; his regime led a fierce campaign against political and militant Islamism, labelling them 'un-Egyptian'. But, unlike Nasser's strictly secular course, the Mubarak regime's attempts wavered. Throughout the 1980s and 1990s – the high tide of the years of confrontation – it retained an Islamic facade. Mubarak did not form an alliance with political Islam, as Sadat had done; yet his regime continued to use Al-Azhar and various factions of the Islamic movement to discredit and contain political Islam, especially the Muslim Brotherhood.

The regime's endorsement of Christianism also lacked a context. Unlike Nasser's, the Mubarak regime had no grand political project, and this made its use of Egyptian Christians' role seem opportunistic and tactical, rather than as part of a comprehensive programme. Egyptian Christians were aware of this. It was notable, for example, that when Farouk Hosni, an influential minister in the Mubarak regime for more than twenty years, made some offhand comments on the ubiquity of the Islamic veil, he was harshly criticized not only by the Muslim Brotherhood and the Salafist movement, but also by prominent members of the ruling National Democratic Party as well as by a number of government ministers.[18]

Society's civic forces had less ambivalence about its relationship with Egyptian Christians. There was a widespread feeling that the increasing social divide in Egypt between Muslims and Christians, the withdrawal of Egyptian Christians and emerging sectarianism have all been eating into the essence of Egyptianism, corroding the mix upon which society has been formed for centuries. The Egyptian middle class felt caught between the regime's authoritarian rule on one side and political Islam on the other. Moreover, without necessarily being able to articulate the crucial role of Egyptian Christians, some elements of the Egyptian middle class began slowly to champion Christian concerns as a form of holding onto a past for which they felt an aching nostalgia – and out of fear of the future. In a number of universities, and despite the strong presence of political Islam, 'student fronts' advocated non-religious student unions; the active feminists of the We Are Watching You group (*Shayfenkom*) combined Muslim and Christian women, and adamantly stuck to a nationalist repertoire; the hyperactive journalists' syndicate and parts of the media made determined efforts to highlight the 'Christian role' in the various protests that the country had witnessed in the 2000s, and to emphasize that political Islamism is not Egypt's sole opposition – that 'Egypt, as a whole, is united, under the same sufferings'. Egyptian cinema and literature followed the same theme: from *The Terrorist* (*Al-Irhabi*, a hit of the late 1990s) and Omar Sharif's latest film *Hassan and Morcos* (2008) to the work of a number of leading writers (for example Usama Anwar Ukasha's *Al-Masraweya* ('The Egyptians') and Bahaa Taher's *Khalti Safeya wa-el-Dir* ('My Aunt Safeya and the Monastery')),[19] there was an emphasis on the experiences shared between Egyptian Muslims and Christians.

Even political Islam increasingly recognized the enduring value of the Christian role in Egyptian society. The Muslim Brotherhood accepted the concept of 'citizenship' and 'equal rights for all Egyptians' and promised to relax the rules governing the building of churches; the Islamist Al-Wasat party invited distinguished Christian activists to the membership of some of its most senior committees; a number of leading Islamist thinkers (most notably Gamal Al-Banna) unequivocally called for a civic governing system;[20] and all political Islam's leaders condemned the waves of violence carried out in its name. With the failure of jihadism in Egypt and the waning of political Islamism, the wiser Islamic leaders realized the need for a fresh approach that transcends sectarianism and focuses on economic and social development. But will political Islam, and not just in rhetoric, be able and willing to abandon its strictly Islamic definition of society and move towards an Egyptian (secular, liberal) definition?[21]

Much of the answer to that question depends on the evolving dynamics within the Egyptian Christian community. The role of the Church over the coming years will be crucial. Despite its immense influence, alliance with the regime and various resources, the Church has recoiled from confronting the causes (and the effects) of the rising Islamism. Apart from the electoral support it routinely gave to the regime (typically subtle and economic, rather than obvious and political), and despite the different facets of Christianism that it had championed in the 1980s and 1990s (the expansion of the Sunday schools as well as the major social mandate), the Church, and with it the most powerful Christian forces in the country, have shied away from shouldering with the regime the burden of fighting political Islamism. The Church has also refrained from showing any conspicuous support to any of the country's civic forces (whether in the professional syndicates or in the universities).[22] The Church, after the strenuous confrontations between President Sadat and Pope Shenouda at the end of the 1970s, was unwilling to engage in a tough political fight – and especially against a mighty opponent such as political Islam. The Church was also acutely aware that, with a few wrong decisions, such a contest could backfire; instead of supporting the regime in its efforts to contain and confront political Islamism, it could inflame the feelings of the Muslim middle class, risking a damaging counter-reaction. The Church was also reluctant to back any civic social force since almost all of these were active opponents of the regime.

That strategy, however, could change. The politicization of the Church could result in a more independent (from the regime) and assertive stance against the Islamization of society; it could even – under a new leadership, after the elderly Pope Shenouda III leaves the scene – take the lead in defining a new form of Egyptianism that responds to the liberal sparks glimmering among young Egyptians today (see Chapter 7).

Egyptian Christian forces outside the Church are highly influential in Egyptian society. The capitalist wave since the early 1990s has created vast economic interests, many of them led by Egyptian Christians – including Egypt's largest telecoms-holding company, the country's most successful construction conglomerate, its largest car maker, and a score of major investors in the pharmaceuticals, consumer goods, hospitality and tourism, real estate and food and beverages industries. These interests are too large to ignore, too entrenched to emigrate – and some of their figureheads are determined to make a difference. Some of them are already trying to affect how the cultural contest between the regime's liberal capitalism and Islamism influences the hearts and minds of young Egyptians. For example, a number of powerful Christian economic interests have invested in satellite TV channels, digital radio channels and websites, through which they try subtly and intelligently to advance liberalism and Egyptianism – as opposed to the Islamism and conservatism prevalent elsewhere. A number of prominent Christian intellectuals are also promoting serious discussion of sensitive issues, such as Muslims' conversion to Christianity; the extent to which Egyptian law is (or should be) governed by Islamic jurisprudence; and the allocation of parliamentary seats to Christians on a proportional basis. There has also been a revival in defining Egyptianism not in Arab nationalist terms but in the context of a Mediterranean-ism that situates the country in a wider (more tolerant, liberal and socially lenient) sphere as part of its search for the sources of future progress and development.

Some Christians are playing more conspicuous political roles. George Ishak, a Christian activist, was the effective leader of Kefaya, the country's most vocal civil opposition group in the 2000s. The fact that a Christian led a diverse group of Egyptian figures (including notable Islamic thinkers such as Abdelwahab Al-Messeiry) and civic organizations (the Journalists' and the Engineers' Syndicates, and the Judges' Club) was highly symbolic.

At the same time, there are worrying trends within the Egyptian Christian community. Egyptian Christians comprised roughly 14–16 per cent of the population in the 1960s and 1970s; by the mid-2000s, the Christians' lower birth rate and the impact of emigration had reduced this to 9–10 per cent. The trend is most discernible in the country's middle class, where Egyptian Christians' leadership since the 1970s has declined in private enterprises (from 35 to 25 per cent), university professorships (from 25 to 15 per cent) and jobs such as medical doctors and engineers (from 30 to 15–20 per cent).[23] This has been reinforced by extensive human and capital expatriation. Hundreds of thousands applied for (and many received) Canadian, Australian and New Zealand passports; hundreds of Christian businessmen quietly shifted their key revenue streams out of the country; and, increasingly, a large number of Egyptian Christians believe that Egypt's liberal experiment from the 1920s to the 1950s, and with it the ultra-prominent role of Egyptian Christians, was destined to oblivion.[24]

A few social efforts from within the community have harmed its public reputation or otherwise presented new challenges. In the 2000s there has been an increase in missionary campaigns by groups of Egyptian Christians targeting very poor Muslims, especially in Al-Saeed, but also among rich and westernized youths in Cairo and Alexandria. A number of satellite channels have also attacked Islam in coarse language, creating tensions that flare up in aggressive mutual denunciation. The politicized campaigning of activist Egyptian Christian groups abroad can also heighten tension in the Egyptian environment in circumstances which can easily be depicted as part of a wider effort to impose change from the outside. For example, repeated demonstrations took place in London and Paris 'protesting against the conditions of Christians in Egypt'. In Sydney, thousands marched 'to draw attention to the plight of Egyptian Christians'. The United Copts of Britain published a number of papers and reports petitioning against the 'ill-treatment' of Christians in the country. And in the United States, there were a number of vociferous Egyptian Christian voices in the background of George W. Bush's democratization 'crusade' in the Middle East.

The evolution of Egyptian Christians and whether the positive dynamics or the ones raising concern will stand out will depend greatly on how young people in the community come to perceive their status in their country and society – and how they interact with political Islam, including its new liberal voices. Christianity's long history in the country, Christians' compelling presence in Egypt's renaissance in the late nineteenth and early twentieth century, the capitalist wave that Egypt is currently witnessing and the Egyptian middle class's apprehension about rising sectarianism and the social divide are all factors that argue for more active engagement by young Christians with their society. The rising Islamism, however, especially as a social identity, and the sense of 'historical depression'[25] that many Egyptian Christians feel will push these young people to emigration, withdrawal and seclusion. The interaction between those dynamics will help define tomorrow's Egypt.

CHAPTER 6
THE MUBARAK YEARS

THE ARGUMENT OF Jonathan Fenby's insightful book *France on the Brink*[1] – that the character, style and personal experience of a country's president can strongly influence its political system – is of central relevance to Egypt's experience. The absolutist nature of Egypt's presidency since the inception of the republic in 1953 makes the nature and outlook of the ruler a matter of vital importance to his subjects.

Gamal Abdel Nasser's Egypt was dynamic and revolutionary. It grabbed the political landscape of the region via a thunderous coup that abolished monarchism; installed republicanism; transformed the country's socio-economic fabric; eliminated entire social strata and created others; built whole industries; introduced ground-breaking political systems; created new political forces; entered into wars (close and far away); and triggered the regional political tsunami of Arab nationalism. In culture, too, the new era opened the way for an intoxicating artistic ambience where literature, films and plays vibrantly reflected and expressed the wider tumult. Nasser's ambition, energy and intelligence were indispensable to Egypt's self-invention in the 1950s and 1960s. Nasser was not only a grandly ambitious leader, but also a man with varied interests ranging from art, cinema, photography, literature and music to the study of history and biography. Nasser's fans paint him as a larger than life figure comparable to Otto von Bismarck, Nehru or Charles de Gaulle.

Anwar Sadat, too, led Egypt through an era of change. The new president's leadership – following the war against Israel in 1973 – represented in effect a counter-coup against Nasser's model, incorporating a series of *bouleversements*: Sadat broke with the USSR to make Egypt a staunch ally of the United States, initiated the peace process with Israel by his dramatic flight to Jerusalem in 1977 and led Egypt away from socialist-style central planning towards what was intended to be free-market capitalism. His policies brought about major changes in the composition of the country's middle class. Sadat may have lacked Nasser's charisma, but he did cultivate a fatherly, leader-of-the-tribe persona that secured him considerable popular appeal. In contrast to Nasser, who interacted with his people as a missionary figure charting a path to national glory and redemption, Sadat was the village chief (*oumda*): a traditionally dressed, honoured, pious and modest guest at weddings, funerals and regional celebrations, ready to engage in discussions on matters of day-to-day concern.

Hosni Mubarak's Egypt has been a very different story. The man possesses neither Nasser's grandeur nor Sadat's appeal. A leading Egyptian publication once described Mubarak as severely lacking in the leadership department but excelling in executing tasks and delivering policies. At the time of Mubarak's sudden accession after Sadat's assassination in October 1981, some argued that such a profile perfectly suited the new occupant of the presidential office, on the grounds that Egypt and the

Egyptians needed a tranquillizer to relieve the pain. Indeed, it was plausible to suggest that after the tumultuous changes of the previous three decades – from Arab nationalism to Islamism, Nasser's political mobilizations to Sadat's frenetic upheavals, from frequent conflicts to relentless social and economic change – the country needed a period of calm. Mubarak, with his relaxed demeanour and a gravitas rooted in his impressive military experience,[2] offered the hope of an Egypt restored to balance and given the time to nourish its weakened self-confidence.

For much of his first term in the 1980s, Mubarak undertook this mission with considerable domestic success. A number of controversial laws that Sadat had introduced in his later years were quietly shelved; thousands of prisoners were freed; censorship of the press was relaxed, to the extent that it was able to criticize any senior regime member – though the president remained off-limits.[3] Civil associations proliferated. Professional syndicates were allowed to play an increasingly visible political role (especially in demanding civil liberties). The regime also reached out to different political forces in the country. For example, a number of parliamentary elections were conducted under a new 'list system', which allowed opposition parties to aggregate votes that otherwise would have been distributed in constituencies controlled by the National Democratic Party.

The new president also dropped many of Sadat's power pretensions: the pharaonic stick that Sadat had insisted on carrying, the Pierre Cardin-designed military uniform that his predecessor had commissioned, the incessant moves between palaces and rest houses. Mubarak's tone was also different. The gist of his speeches, his choice of words, the way he described himself and his vision for the country's future suggested a man who was concerned less with his legacy or with how he was viewed as a leader and more with his capacity to deliver.

Mubarak seemed pragmatic, wholly concerned with Egypt's immediate economic problems, the inheritance of *al-infitah*.

The 1980s witnessed a plethora of economic initiatives and programmes, most devoted to upgrading the country's ailing infrastructure. Egyptians even joked that in between inaugurating a new bridge and a new tunnel . . . President Mubarak would inaugurate a new bridge.

But these programmes never extended to the 'structural reforms' that the International Monetary Fund (IMF) had repeatedly pushed for. Mubarak's pragmatic focus and his deep concern to maintain stability made him cautious about the potentially disruptive consequences of any far-reaching economic-reform programme – especially one that would have a negative impact on the living standards of lower income groups. In the end, however, Mubarak had no choice. The fall of oil prices in the mid- and late 1980s meant that the jobs of hundreds of thousands of Egyptian migrant workers in the Gulf evaporated; there were also significant reductions in foreign direct investments and a fall in revenues from Suez Canal trade. The Egyptian regime suddenly had an acute need for short-term financial help, and in 1991 was obliged to accept IMF prescriptions.

This reversal might not have mattered had a decade of treatment by tranquillizer been followed by the long-term effect associated with curative medicine. That did not happen. Rather, the IMF's structural reforms, which cut deep into the welfare system, pensions and key subsidies, exposed the fact that for the first time in many decades, Egypt (and the Egyptians) had no national project of its (and their) own – neither a Europe-inspired modernization programme, a vibrant liberal experiment aiming to liberate Egypt from the occupier, a grand Arab nationalist dream, nor a major political or economic transformation. All that seemed on offer were painful steps to meet economic and financial milestones in various restructuring programmes and a sluggish movement to fulfil the requirements of successive five-year development plans.

The lack of political reform was clear; the ruling NDP was still controlled by the same acolytes, including ministers appointed in the early 1980s who continued to govern into the 2000s. The indolent pace of economic development, with little tangible improvement of people's living standards, did not help. As the tranquillizer's effect began to appear numbing, President Mubarak's style became associated with lethargy, stillness and lack of imagination.

A large part of the problem was that President Mubarak was unable or unwilling to connect with his people in a more 'personal' way. Even today, after being ruled by him for almost thirty years, Egyptians know very little about Hosni Mubarak as an individual. His persona remains associated with state ceremonies and public events; while the thoughts, feelings and dispositions behind the facade are a mystery to the people. Egyptians hear that he is a fan and a good player of squash, and enjoys traditional Egyptian folk music; but he has never played the sport or displayed such affection in public.

Perhaps more surprisingly, and fundamentally, Mubarak differs from all his modern predecessors in that he has not left his own stamp on Egyptian society. Such detachment between ruler and society is a novel departure from a pattern whereby the tastes as well as the vision of Egyptian leaders have shaped the country's evolution. Modern Egypt (and especially Cairo and Alexandria) has been shaped not only by the vision, but also the taste, of Khedive Ismael. King Farouk's liberalism, infatuation with Europe and even licentiousness played up the society's tolerance and open-mindedness in the 1940s. Nasser's morality and integrity inspired the grandeur and stateliness of the 1950s and 1960s. Sadat's piety and unpredictability triggered the waves of religiosity and the tumultuous changes that the society underwent in the 1970s. Mubarak's imprint is missing; while Nasserism and Sadat-ism evoke impassioned feelings (whether of endorsement and admiration or rejection and denunciation), their successor remains without a 'following'; he stirs no passion or excitement. Despite the millions of words and images that the state-controlled Egyptian media has devoted to Mubarak's deeds and presence since 1981, Egyptians do not know him.

This outcome is all the more striking given the fact that the circumstances of his accession to power presented Mubarak with a great opportunity to become a major leader. In particular, militant Islamism offered him and the Egyptian regime a potentially defining project. Militant Islamism was a true peril; it challenged the regime's authority and the security and peace of the whole society – and Egyptians realized that. Although political Islamism was growing in popularity and influence, the vast majority of Egyptians were inherently opposed to militants killing and looting in the name of religion, and condoned the regime's attempts to combat them. Egyptians (from those who had directly suffered because of the dwindling tourism revenues to those who abhorred the existence of any militant group in the country) supported the regime's efforts, even the use of violence; these efforts seemed entirely legitimate (something not very common in Egypt's modern history). But, despite the lack of a national project, the mediocre (and sometimes outright failure) of the different economic reform programmes of the 1980s and 1990s, and despite the increasingly lacklustre positioning of the regime, the Mubarak regime shunned the opportunity to rally its people behind a larger cause. Instead, it defined the issue as a security one, lacking in social and developmental dimensions and surprisingly without exploiting the people's support and backing.

The regime's fight with militant Islamism in Egypt took place at the same time as nearby Algeria was undergoing frightening levels of social violence and unrest in a similar war between radical Islamism and the regime. The vast majority of Egyptians were horrified by the idea of Egypt following Algeria into chaos and quasi-civil war. And yet it was left to a few films and TV series to portray the 'problem of terrorism' as one that revealed deeper tensions in Egyptian society. The chance to elevate the campaign against militant Islamism into a positive, constructive national endeavour around which the whole nation would coalesce was lost.

President Mubarak's modus operandi, especially in the 1980s, contributed to this outcome. Despite the fraught beginnings of his presidency, Mubarak faced no threat from within the regime comparable to Nasser's or Sadat's entanglements with the supporters of their predecessors. Nasser had to contend with the 'revolution's enemies' – mainly the remnants of monarchical Egypt and later the Muslim Brotherhood – for at least the first three years after the revolution; Sadat, in 1970 and 1971 (the first two years of his period in power), was engaged in a severe polit-ical struggle with some of Nasser's most senior aides. Mubarak, however, could firmly rely on the internal-security apparatuses he had inherited to sustain control. And in his early years in power, Mubarak greatly expanded the Egyptian FBI (Mabaheth-Amn-Al-Dolah) and the 'central security' (anti-riot and containment forces). Moreover, Mubarak, again unlike his predecessors, had set his confidence and trust, not on his visible entourage, not on his leading ministers and not on senior advisors or leading intel-lectuals; he had no independent advisors to rely on: no Mohamed Hassanein Heikal (Nasser's closest advisor), Osman Ahmed Osman (Sadat's confidante)[4] or any other public figure who commanded wide appeal. Mubarak's trust lay with his security chiefs – various interior ministers, army commanders, and the heads of the ultra-influential intelligence services.

The experience of seeing Sadat assassinated right in front of him had instilled in President Mubarak a focus on and absorption with security. President Mubarak was a fully 'militarized' man. Again unlike Nasser or Sadat, who abandoned their military career at an early stage, Mubarak's service in the Egyptian army stretched from young officer to field-marshal and reflected his commitment to a command and control mindset. Indeed, this security mentality actually shaped Mubarak's lenient approach towards his opponents in the 1980s. The opening up of electoral opportunities to a number of opposition parties, the relatively free press and the relaxation of some restrictions on the professional syndicates were tenuous measures designed to contain an agitated country but never intended to extend into substantial political reform and a sophisticated structure of checks and balances. The various players who were increasingly empowered (from the syndicates to the press, to the multitude of political parties) were not supposed to evolve into viable opposition or real agents of change; they were pawns in a game controlled by the regime. The 'relaxation' was one of the tactics of governance, a marginal tune in a broader, security-led composition.

Mubarak's style shaped his approach in foreign affairs too. The Iraqi invasion of Kuwait in 1990 was a prime example of an opportunity for leadership not taken. The event – the first time in modern history that an Arab country had invaded another, in turn laying bare the Arab world's division and the impotence of many regional players – triggered panic and confusion. Egypt had been welcomed back into the Arab 'family' after being ostracized for years following the signing of the peace treaty with Israel, but was a long way from the influence it had exerted in the 1950s to the 1970s. The scene was empty, the contenders for regional leadership compromised; Iraq was the main culprit of the disaster; Saudi Arabia embroiled in it and fearful of its implications, Jordan and the Palestinian Liberation Organization confused and politically paralyzed. But Egyptian foreign policy did not assume the mantle of leadership, and opted to play a subordinate role: it followed the Saudis' lead in allowing the United States to become the key defender of the Arabs against Saddam Hussein. The Egyptian regime was offered an opportunity to resuscitate Egypt's influence and assert its special place in the Arab world. But it was unable (or unwilling) to exploit the opportunity; it failed to formulate a spirited, influential and purposeful policy out of it. Cairo's political purposelessness was reflected in what became its key objective in the fiasco: convincing the Gulf States and the United States to cancel billions of dollars of its foreign debt.[5]

The project-less pragmatism of the Mubarak regime extended to traditional areas of Egyptian influence in the region. In the Levant its role diminished from a leading player with immense influence on the region's orientation to that of a supporter of the Saudi agenda; in the Maghreb, where Egypt in the 1950s and 1960s enjoyed immense political and cultural influence, it became virtually non-existent; in the Gulf, it had changed from leader and teacher to follower and émigré worker.

Such retreat was a novelty in Egyptian foreign policy. Egypt under Mubarak was no longer the political powerhouse of the region, the base for fighting invaders, the cultural and artistic soft power, the Arab nationalist centre of gravity, the regional trend-setter. These roles had been at various times necessities both to the country's political positioning and to its view of itself. Egypt, with its long historical experience, was cognizant that, alone within its own borders, it was a poor country with crippling problems and limited potential; in its roles as the political hub and the cultural axis of the region, Egypt was able to transcend its challenges and exponentially enhance its powers and potential. And even if they were unable to articulate it, ordinary Egyptian peasants (*fellahin*), with their rich and varied historical experience, were aware of the need for that regional role.

The writings of many Egyptian historians, theorists and opinion leaders have ensconced Egypt's special place in its wider region in the country's national psyche. Taha Hussein and Tawfik Al-Hakeem marked out 'Egypt: the bridge between the East and Europe' and emphasized the country's 'missionary role' in the region. Ahmed Shawki, the country's leading poet, hailed 'Egypt, the crown of the East' and paved the way for the eastern-ist school of thought that saw Egypt's future in an increasingly prominent role in the Levant, Iraq and the Arabian peninsula. A number of Islamist thinkers blurred the Egyptian project with the 'Islamic identity', depicting the country's long history of wars in the Levant as 'Egypt's jihadi obligation'.

The Arab nationalist view of Egypt as the pillar of a pan-Arabic project, and especially the writings of Mohamed Hassanein Heikal, was, arguably, the clearest, most voluminous and, certainly, the most impassioned Egyptian (and Arab) take on that role.[6] Away from literature, jihad, politics and international relations, the writings of Gamal Hemdan (Egypt's most famous geography professor), and especially his book *Egypt's Identity: A Study in the Genius of the Place*, provided the most comprehensive view of the basis and rationale of the Egyptian project. Hemdan delved into the historical, geographic and identity 'imperatives' that have 'dictated' Egypt's role in the region. He positioned the country's 'destiny' in its wider regional role. Even in classic Egyptian art, from Umm Kulthoum's songs to Farid Al-Attrash's films, the country placed its identity squarely in a broad Arabic format. For millions of Egyptians, Egypt's missionary role in the

Arab world was the country's sole route not only to retaining significance, but also to defining itself.

President Mubarak's supporters repeatedly emphasized that the president's 'internal focus on Egypt' was 'courageous and pragmatic': he was the first pharaoh to confront his country's problems without an escapist embrace of unrealistic ambitions in the wider region; he did not seek glory and adulation by punching above Egypt's weight; he was 'wise' in not dragging Egypt into struggles that it could ill afford even to win; and, crucially, unlike Nasser and Sadat, his calculated and methodical diplomacy, even if it had not led to dramatic successes, had not resulted in any grand failures.

But the country, in great part precisely because of the absence of any Egyptian project, and as a result of the new, overly pragmatic doctrine, neither solved its internal problems nor avoided major strategic losses. Mubarak's detractors lament the corrosion of Egypt's standing, positioning and influence on the Arab street, especially when compared with that in Nasser's days. But this dissatisfaction is merely nostalgic, and that corrosion is just a symptom. With the disappearance of Egypt's uniting and leading role in the Arab world, other valuable things were buried: the notion that the Arab world has common objectives and challenges that could only be addressed together; that individually Arab countries face significant challenges and have, on their own, limited potential, while collectively they garner a synergy, the potential of which is much larger than the sum of the individual components; and that Egypt's best contribution lies in a constructive role in its wider region. Egypt's foreign policy had served that notion many times in its history: from Al-Azhar's historic role in the Arab and Islamic worlds across the ages to Egypt's role as the region's power base in confronting the crusaders as well as the Mongols, to the country's cultural role during the nineteenth century and the first half of the twentieth century, and, of course, to leading the Arab nationalist project during Nasser's 1950s and 1960s. Even Anwar Sadat's reorientation from Arab nationalism towards an alliance with the United States was based on Egypt's indispensable role in the Middle East and its ability to 'deliver' in the Arab world.[7]

The remission from the Egyptian project left others to gain prominence. Saudi Arabia, bankrolled by its oil fortunes and fuelled by its Wahhabi ideology, was expounding a theocratic view that fused Islamism, capitalism and political absolutism in search of objectives very different from anything in Egypt's political inheritance. Whereas the Egyptian project was civic, Arabic and (at least in theory) based on a bottom-up mobilization of the ordinary, poor Arab masses, the Saudi project was theocratic, exclusively Islamic and extended its authority from alliances with world powers (mainly the United States), rather than the Arab masses. Israel also sought a pan-regional role; after the Madrid peace conference of 1991 that was part of the diplomatic repositioning in the wake of the war over Kuwait, it engaged in a lengthy peace process that led to the signing in 1993 of the Oslo Peace Accords: a framework for future negotiations between Israel and the Palestine Liberation Organization, which led to the creation of the Palestinian Authority in Gaza and parts of the West Bank.

It was an opportune moment. At the Madrid peace conference, Israel saw its strategic ally, the United States, dictating the terms of engagement to all Arab states. The USSR, represented in the conference by Mikhail Gorbachev, behaved as a pliable subordinate to the United States. Israel's political elite saw the opportunity to lead a 'new Middle-Eastern order' that would include – but transcend – the Arabs (with the Turks involved too). The Israeli 'Middle-Eastern project' did not have any qualms about its contexts and aspirations. It saw itself as a much more able and sophisticated successor to the Egyptian equivalent. In 1994, Israel's then foreign minister, Shimon Peres, is reported to have told a regional economic summit in Casablanca: 'Egypt led the Middle East for forty years and brought it to the abyss; you will see the region's economic situation improve when Israel takes the reins of leadership in the region.'[8]

* * *

The failure of these 'rival' projects may be seen as fate's further generosity to Egypt and to the Mubarak regime. The Saudi project conjured up more of the region's many demons (mainly militant Islamism), and failed to douse others (chiefly the Islamic revolution in Iran); Islamism was too powerful a notion to be tamed by the Saudi/Wahhabi strictures; soon enough the Iranian Shi'ite and the militant Islamism challenges were frustrating the Saudi project and forcing it not only to curtail its expansionist Wahhabisism, but also to curb it, even within Saudi Arabia itself. The Israeli project was crushed by the intransigent realities of the endemic Palestinian–Israeli conflict. The Israeli mood itself was changing. Yitzhak Rabin (Israel's prime minister and 'peace hero') was assassinated by a young Jewish Israeli in what appeared to be a dramatic psychological dilemma brought about by the idea of peace with the Arabs, a dilemma confronting the whole of Israeli society. Shimon Peres was sidelined; and Benjamin Netanyahu, an 'Israeli hawk', came to power with a very different Israeli view, based not on an economic integration in the Middle East under Israeli leadership (Rabin's and Peres's objective), but on a forceful foreign policy aiming to impose Israel's objectives on its neighbours – using military power if needed.[9]

But true to form, the Egyptian regime failed to gain leverage from the fallout: it engaged in repeated and futile efforts throughout the 1990s and 2000s to mediate between Israelis and Palestinians (and later in intra-Palestinian disputes); half-hearted meddling in Sudan's various troubles; repeated diplomatic tussles with Iran; petty squabbles with Qatar; helping French president Nicolas Sarkozy to promote an ill-defined 'Mediterranean partnership'; and stubborn insistence on punishing the region's radicals, especially militia groups such as Hamas and Hezbollah. Egyptian foreign policy came across as a series of tactical moves, intended to extract tiny rewards from minor engagements. Most Egyptians followed their country's reactive and inchoate foreign policy with bewilderment and nostalgia.

President Mubarak did not lack the energy or courage to follow through on the traditional Egyptian project; nor did he fail to understand the project's premises and dimensions. Instead he opted out of it, deciding to view Egypt's strategic orientation as part of a grand *Pax Americana* in the Middle East, in direct opposition to Iran, at times Syria, and radical movements such as Hezbollah and Hamas.

A number of factors triggered Mubarak's approach. The end of the Cold War and demise of the USSR turned the Middle East's Arab–Israeli conflict from one of the defining features of the Cold War, and a major stage in the strategic confrontation between the US and the USSR, into a mere regional struggle. The United States had already won the 'race to the Middle East'; the conflict was no longer of immense strategic importance in the grand international geopolitical game. The loss of urgency and the dilution of significance reduced Egypt's international importance.[10]

This was compounded by the Arabs' clear indication that 'peace was their strategic choice'. The Palestinians' recognition of Israel and the beginning of the Palestinian–Israeli peace talks (with the blessings and encouragement of Egypt and the financial backing of all Gulf States), the Israeli–Jordanian peace treaty, the increasingly open channels between Israel and a number of Gulf States, the sidelining and demilitarization of Iraq, in addition to the already cemented Israeli–Egyptian peace accord, meant that the Arab–Israeli conflict was not prone to sudden eruptions that could destabilize – or even threaten – American interests in the region. Israel's superiority – militarily, technologically and scientifically – relative to all Arab states buttressed that situation. The Arabs seemed unable (and unwilling) to challenge US or Israeli interests in the region. In view of this, Egypt's traditional role of leading Arabic opposition to foreign influences in the region was increasingly perceived to be redundant.

Mubarak's opting out was, paradoxically, an attempt at finding a role for Egypt amid these new developments. The Mubarak regime rode the wave for peace in the Middle East. It helped bring about the 1991 Madrid peace conference, and crucially the rapprochement between Palestinian and Israeli negotiating positions. It was a major supporter of Yasser Arafat's decision to sign the Oslo accords in 1993 – despite ferocious Syrian criticism and even Saudi coolness towards the whole process. In the absence of the country's traditional role, promoting the peace process, opposing any confrontational force (from Hamas to Hezbollah to Iran) and championing a new Middle East based on economic integration under the Pax Americana became the chief function of Egyptian foreign policy.

Mubarak's approach built upon Sadat's peace accord with Israel, but, more importantly, on what appeared to be the realities of the time. In the late 1980s and 1990s, Egypt was feeling the full effects of the painful economic reform programme and the different developmental plans that were proving ill equipped to lessen the people's suffering – and the pressure on the regime. In the same period, the United States – with the advent of the Internet, the economic boom of the 1990s, the rise of the Anglo-

Saxon capitalist wave and the vibrancy of the Clinton years – was not only crowned as the world's sole superpower, but increasingly viewed as the harbinger of the world's triumphant socio-economic model. America's 'soft power' was at its zenith, and Egypt, like many other developing countries with failed socialist experiments, wanted to be part of the seemingly omnipotent American camp. Clinging to 'obsolete ways of thinking' and 'yesterday's conflicts', and abandoning the 'new world order' and the 'focus on economics' seemed foolish. The Egyptian regime's media was singing the praises of 'the end of history' while decrying 'the clash of civilizations'. Adhering to Egypt's traditionally confrontational role seemed a relic from the past while the Pax Americana in the region was deemed the shape of the future.

The Pax Americana was also an attractive option. Throughout the 1980s and 1990s, Egypt continued to receive billions of US dollars in American aid. Successive American administrations, one after the other, extolled President Mubarak's 'wisdom' and dealt him the respect due to 'one of the US's most important allies in the Middle East'. The Egyptian–US joint military exercises ('Bright Star') evolved into one of the most important strategic operations in the Middle East. Increasingly, the United States gave Egypt preferred trading and exporting status, especially in the vital textiles industry.

Indeed, Mubarak realized that, given the unbridgeable gap that had opened up between the United States and the Islamic Revolution in Iran, Lebanon's collapse into the quagmire of civil war and the continuously troubled situation in Pakistan and Afghanistan, the United States was in desperate need of stability in the Middle East. A supportive Egypt, as opposed to irksome Syria, hostile Iran and hesitant Saudi Arabia, became an important pillar of support in the region.

Throughout the 1990s, state-directed Egyptian media reminded Egyptians that Palestinians and Jordanians now negotiating with Israel and anxiously waiting for invitations to the White House were following the 'courageous and visionary' Egyptian strategy initiated by President Sadat in the late 1970s, and developed by President Mubarak since then. The 'war on terror' and America's ferociousness after 9/11 gave momentum to the Egyptian regime's pragmatist approach. America's 'shock and awe' in Afghanistan and Iraq, its uncompromising attitude towards the dissident regimes of Libya and Yemen and its sidelining of the traditionally Arab-sympathetic voices in 'old Europe' left the Egyptian regime with no illusions about the need to confirm its allegiance. Egypt was a key participant in the CIA-led international intelligence war against 'terror'. The Egyptian 'religious leadership' was mobilized in the 'war of ideas'. The American military had relatively easy access to some vital Egyptian assets, notably the Suez Canal, despite Egypt's public opposition to the invasion of Iraq. Also, subtly and inconspicuously, Egyptian security agencies played leading roles in supporting the United States in building viable and sustainable security systems and platforms in Iraq.

President Mubarak's decision to 'opt out' of the Egyptian project resonated with some parts of the Egyptian psyche. Egypt's pharaonic past has always been a source of national pride and a distinction from the neighbouring Arabs and the Islamic world. The heritage of 'the world's oldest civilization', as most Egyptian history books refer to ancient Egypt, conferred on the country uniqueness and a feeling of individuality, and at times made Egyptians reluctant to adhere to any identity framework other than 'Egyptian-ness'. The people's confinement in the narrow Nile River valley, with vast deserts separating them from their neighbours, cultivated a tendency towards isolationism. The valley's dependence on the Nile, which originated from 'far away lands' (the source plateaus in East and Central Africa), the self-sufficiency that agriculture had previously allowed, and the minor role that trading had played in the country's history, instilled in Egyptians a propensity for looking inwards and insularity. Also state-sponsored media, for many years, emphasized 'Egypt's sacrifices' for the Arab nation, and the 'heavy cost' that the country had paid 'for defending the Arabs', which led many Egyptians to believe that the country's 'limited resources' needed to be directed towards 'our interests', not 'the struggles of others'.

The priorities of Egyptian foreign policy changed. Egypt accordingly began to work towards a region where greater security was founded on American guarantees and regional economic integration. In return, Egypt would be rewarded with increased foreign direct investment, a leading place in an emerging system and continued international support; its success in the effort would be measured by investment dollars, trade surpluses and regime continuity rather than any true internal regeneration, the achievement of long-term strategic objectives or sense of historic fulfilment.[11]

But ordinary Egyptians never supported that foreign-policy doctrine. In the 1980s and 1990s, challenging economic conditions forced the Egyptian middle class to direct their energy and momentum towards meeting the basic needs of living. Unlike during Nasser's period when the country's foreign policy had been based on legitimatising bottom-up impetus, now foreign policy became removed from the street, a top-down imposition on the country. Politics retreated to the shadows of the society's life and economics took centre stage. The cut off between the country's new foreign policy and the people denied the new doctrine popular backing

The absence of major events in which Egypt's own strategic interests were challenged reinforced that separation between people and foreign policy. From the mid-1970s until the 2000s,

Middle Eastern wars, conflicts and confrontations took place in the Persian Gulf, on the Israeli–Lebanese border and in Iraq, far from Egypt. Egyptian society was neither challenged, nor incentivized.

And yet the Egyptian street's hostility to the new foreign policy doctrine was building up. Most Egyptians perceived the United States-led sanctions programme against Iraq following the 1991 Gulf War as 'cruelty against our brothers' and a deliberate attempt to weaken Iraq, 'a pan-Arab nationalist power'. There was strong sympathy for the Palestinian intifada that erupted in 2000 following Ariel Sharon's visit to Temple Mount. Egyptian students at Cairo, Ain-Shams and Al-Azhar universities repeatedly demonstrated in the wake of Israel's war against Lebanon in July–August 2006. The Egyptian regime's equivocation in all of these situations did not resonate with the street's discontent. But it was Israel's siege of Gaza, following Hamas's victory in the legislative election of 2006 there, that flared up the feelings of most Egyptians.

Hamas refused to acknowledge Israel's right to exist and adamantly stuck to a jihadist repertoire. It took a defiant stance against the Palestinian–Israeli peace process and the 2002 Arab Summit's peace initiative, which declared 'negotiated peace' to be the Arabs' 'strategic choice'. Its military wings undertook acts of violence against Israel, in contrast to the Palestinian Authority's insistence on a 'negotiated solution to the conflict'.

The differences between Hamas and the Palestinian Authority deteriorated to a quasi-civil war, and eventually into a division of the Palestinian community and land: the Palestinian Authority controlled the areas in the West Bank that were not under direct Israeli occupation, while Hamas ruled over Gaza, one of the world's most densely populated areas and the home of more than 1.5 million people.

To suffocate Hamas and punish the people who voted it into power, Israel began a tight siege over the entire strip, stopping the movement of people, goods and supplies in and out of the region. The siege resulted in an acute humanitarian crisis. Gaza witnessed severe shortages in food, medicines and basic supplies. A March 2008 report published by Care International UK, Amnesty International, Oxfam and Save the Children UK stated that 80 per cent of Palestinians in Gaza relied on humanitarian assistance and that around 70 per cent of households earned less than US$1.20 per day. In that dire situation, Gaza's border with Egypt, notably at Rafah, was the sole route for allowing food, medicines and crucial supplies into the strip. The Rafah border crossing became Gaza's only breathing space.

Throughout 2006, the crossing was selectively open for goods and supplies, but in June 2007, after Hamas took complete control over Gaza, the Egyptian regime decided to close the border crossing completely with very rare openings only for severe humanitarian cases. Most international observers explain Egypt's decision in light of the regime's alliance with the United States. True, Egypt's new foreign-policy doctrine inherently opposed Hamas's confrontational and jihadist approach. But other reasons were at play here. Egyptian diplomacy led a number of initiatives to bridge the gap between the Palestinian Authority and Hamas, with a strong focus on softening Hamas's position and nudging it towards an engaged role in the peace process with Israel. But Hamas, which continued to regard the peace process with scepticism and cynicism, repeatedly rebuffed that effort, and in so doing, antagonized a large number of senior figures in the Egyptian regime.

Unlike the Palestinian Authority, Hamas was not a nationalist movement, but a religious one. Hamas traced its roots to the Egyptian Muslim Brotherhood; its 1988 charter called for the creation of 'an Islamic state in Palestine'; its socio-political programme was conspicuously Islamic; its 'historical leadership', from Sheikh Ahmed Yassin (whom Israel assassinated in 2004) to Khaled Mashaal, the Damascus-based Head of its Political Bureau, boasted religious credentials. The existence of such a political-Islamic movement on Egypt's borders undermined the Egyptian regime's internal fight against political Islamism, and especially the Muslim Brotherhood.

Hamas's rule over Gaza also became a security nuisance to Egypt. In addition to food, medicine and basic supplies, many Hamas-linked groups inside Gaza used the border with Egypt, and tunnels they dug in the area, to smuggle weapons and explosives into the region. Following its painful struggle with violent Islamism inside Egypt, the Egyptian regime was not keen on entertaining a religiously oriented militant movement using its borders to smuggle weapons. The regime was therefore sympathetic to any containment or weakening of Hamas.

But if the regime's decision to continue closing off the Rafah border crossing was highly unpopular in Egypt, Israel's war against Hamas rule in Gaza in December 2008–January 2009 ignited anger on the street. On 27 December 2008, the first day of the war, more than 85 Israeli war planes dropped more than 100 tons of targeted explosives, rockets and 'intelligent bombs' on an area less than 140 square kilometres. The devastation was dramatic. More than 250 people died on the first day of the war and by 18 January 2009, when Israel declared a unilateral cease-fire, more than 1,200 Palestinians were dead.

The Egyptian regime's foreign-policy doctrine faced a serious challenge. President Mubarak had met (then) Israeli foreign minister Tzipi Livni on the eve of the attack. His now-famous handshake with her on that day was widely interpreted as Egypt's tacit approval of the onslaught. Many observers speculated that President Mubarak gave Israel his blessing 'to destroy Hamas'.

Egyptians vehemently denounced the bombing and destruction, and the many demonstrations extended beyond voicing opposition to 'Israeli aggression' to scorn for the regime's stance. In Alexandria, more than 50,000 protestors forced back anti-riot police while chanting songs and slogans hostile to the regime and the president; in Cairo, the police were forced to close down transport hubs (including a metro station named after President Mubarak) to secure control. The widespread anger extended to civil groups (some of which organized 'solidarity convoys' to Gaza, demanding that the Rafah border crossing be opened), university students and teachers, journalists, Muslim Brotherhood members and workers (including in the public sector). There were also strikes and riots, for example by textile-spinning and weaving workers in Al-Mahala Al-Kobra. The Egyptian street clearly voiced its dislike of Egypt's foreign-policy doctrine.

At a deeper level, the lack of a national project was interacting with socio-economic frustrations to create a perilous mixture. The crushing socio-economic conditions, the widespread corruption and the devastating gaps between the haves and have-nots fuelled the anger that vast swaths of Egyptians felt towards their regime. The rise of political Islamism significantly radicalized large sections of ordinary people, who increasingly saw their regime not only as 'mistaken' or even 'corrupt', but also as 'working with "the Jews" against our brothers and sisters in Palestine'. Egyptians' suffering under a coercive political climate had diluted their sense of belonging, their appreciation of their country's identity, role and dignity, and their perception of themselves. Sensing the deterioration of their country's (and their own) standing both in and outside the nation, the people's perception of what their country (and they) stood for was increasingly muddled and perplexed. Egypt was no longer an Arab nationalist champion; it was not the custodian of a grand Arab dream, nor the fighter for 'Arabic rights and dignity'; but also, it was not, at least in the people's minds, a US ally, a follower of Saudi Arabia or a friend of Israel.[12]

This anger and frustration created feelings of discontent, restlessness and resentment. The regime's judgement and the people's feelings inhabited different worlds, and a significant part of Egyptians' disappointment was targeted at the president himself. By his third decade in office, the only leader most of them had ever known was held responsible for many of their daily sufferings and resentments. The classic Egyptian jokes at the expense of their presidents, and the heated sighs of frustration, were turning into waves of demonstrations – and, at times, violent manifestations of hatred. The 2005–9 period witnessed hundreds of riots, in which demonstrators often tore down billboard images of the president. Many writers, whether prominent in leading opposition newspapers or anonymous in student magazines across the country, accused him of being the cause of 'our backwardness' and 'the protector of the powerful and corrupt'. 'Mubarak's Egypt is his, not ours,' said one demonstrator furiously. 'He doesn't care about us,' shouted hundreds. The repeated and bitter mantra was 'He has failed us'.

A popular explanation of 'what has brought us here' was that the regime was 'getting old': an 'older sister' who was waiting at home, not doing much, living off the kindness of foreigners (and the remittances of family members abroad) and sidelined by her younger and richer siblings (in the modernizing Gulf, rising Lebanon and Jordan, or the new Morocco). There was an endemic sense of wasted energy and unused potential, of a young population held back by a tired regime. Mohamed Hassanein Heikal summarized that view succinctly when he commented that 'the problem is that of an authority ageing in its positions' as compared with the youthful population.

There was a missing link in this argument: namely that, although the president himself and his cronies represented an elderly generation that governed according to centralizing instincts and lived at a great social distance from their people (increasingly, President Mubarak was also at a great physical distance from his people, spending a significant percentage of time in Sharm Al-Sheikh, away from polluted, crowded and arguably dangerous Cairo), in other respects the Egyptian regime was actually getting younger. The inclusion of Gamal Mubarak and his group of young, well-educated, liberal capitalists represented a form of internal rejuvenation.

But this development also only underscored the truth of the protesters' depiction of a regime mired in profound debility. The ills that Gamal Mubarak and his clique inherited were overwhelming. Not only had there been enormous damage to the regime's relationship with the people, but also the key vehicles and instruments that the regime had traditionally used to assert its authority had suffered consistently over the past few decades.

This was especially true of the institution of the presidency itself, which, especially under the continuous jurisdiction of the emergency law, has been by far the country's most influential political player, with no supervision over its actions. By the 2000s, it had long ceased to be (as under Nasser and Sadat) a vibrant nerve centre of governance, full of notable advisors and intellectuals, with links to most of the country's think tanks, and acting as a laboratory of ideas; instead it became a mere administrative structure around the president. That dilution could have been welcomed had it been combined with a strengthening of democratically elected institutions (mainly the parliament) and a new balance between presidency and government. What happened in Egypt instead was that the (undemocratic) parliament, the government and the presidency had become varied representations of the president's will – executive bodies, rather than the pillars of a balanced political system.

The extent to which the regime revolved round the president became clear after the 1995 assassination attempt on President Mubarak in Addis Ababa, Ethiopia. Panic gripped the entire country. Even some of President Mubarak's ardent opponents expressed great anxiety about 'what could have happened' had the assassination attempt succeeded. Less than a month after the attempt, President Mubarak himself addressed the issue by stating that though he remained unwilling to appoint a vice-president, the processes of government control and power transfer are dictated by the Egyptian constitution. Amr Hamzawi, at the Carnegie Endowment for International Peace in Washington, has written a number of articles on the 'potential instability' that President Mubarak's disappearance could create. Less scholarly, but perhaps more engaging, were the televized interviews that followed the attack with scores of Egyptian commentators and ordinary citizens who didn't 'comprehend what alternatives there are to the President'.

The same decay was true of most other state institutions. The government's administrative structures and the public sector remained mired in lethargy and corruption, and, with the rise of the private sector, were increasingly losing their relevance.[13] Even the armed forces and the intelligence services, arguably the regime's most sophisticated and well-developed organizations, had strict reporting lines to the president alone. In this respect, the formation of a new power circle around Gamal Mubarak could not be expected to use the regime's waning institutions as instruments of a genuine renewal.

The next generation thus faced a dual dilemma: their ability to use the power they aspired to for progressive ends was limited by the instruments available to them, and any move in a democratic direction would almost certainly bring them into conflict with an impatient and disaffected people. The new power elite was acutely aware that in any free elections the people would chose to throw them out. To some extent, their dilemma was reminiscent of that of the National Party of South Africa in 1993–4: resort to free elections and the judgement of the people's will and lose the election (and power); or tighten the hold over power and relegate the game of free politics to another day (in the future, when the programme would have achieved its objectives and the people would be willing to vote for it and its leaders). Of course, the National Democratic Party in Egypt did not face a pressing ethical dilemma as with the issue of apartheid or an opponent of the calibre and moral integrity of Nelson Mandela, and it did not have a leader with the strategic vision of F.W. de Klerk.

But those differences aside, there is no doubt in Egypt's political circles that the relationship between the regime and the people is suffering – even the serious thinkers within the ruling NDP do not dispute that. The definition of that suffering varies, however. Key members of the NDP's Policies Committee and stalwarts of the party's 'new thinking' argue that the problem lies in the regime's tendency to complicate its messages to the people – messages that ought to be simplified and popularized, for example explaining that Egypt's stance in the Gaza War of 2008–9 was not siding with Israel, but a reaction to Hamas's insistence on provocations and an antagonistic course of action against Egyptian national interests. They also argue that the regime's 'economic achievements' are dwarfed by the suffocating population growth. On the other hand, the ferocious writings of many of the regime's opponents, for example in *Al-Dostour* and

Al-Arabi newspapers, argue that the regime's problem with the people transcends rhetoric and marketing; that the people's trust in the regime has evaporated, and that the relationship is increasingly highly confrontational – between an oppressor and the oppressed.

The new ruling elite has more reasons to be hesitant about disrupting the existing modus operandi. Given that the lines separating power and wealth in the new power circles in Egypt are blurred, losing power (or even sharing it with new forces) would mean jeopardizing immense economic interests. In this situation, shared by the old regime Gamal Mubarak and his colleagues wished to inherit, Egypt's leaders were caught between strategies of containment, coercion and confrontation.

The containment lay in launching a number of economic development and investment programmes aimed at alleviating some of the pressures of Egyptians' daily lives, and winning some goodwill among young and middle-class Egyptians in particular. These included elements of 'sham democracy' (the *Economist* newspaper's description), at the same time as iron control was exerted by the exclusion of the Muslim Brotherhood and the maintenance of permitted political parties as mere platforms. The facade of elections, a multi-party political environment and the existence of upper and lower houses of parliament allowed the regime to claim progress and some political development, and to diffuse some of the masses' anger. The 'sham democracy' was never a threat to the regime. Even Mahmoud Abaza, the then head of the Al-Wafd party, in 2009 described his party's role in Egyptian politics as 'stirring debate' – not as participation in decision-making, let alone seeking to govern the country; and Nader Fergany, a prominent Egyptian academic and the lead author of the United Nations Human Development Report on the Arab world, denounced all opposition forces in the country as 'corpses'.

The coercion lay in the state's suppression of any potential challenge. This was most evident in the crushing of public disorder and in strict controls on civic organizations and universities. It also manifested itself in the endemic use of torture, with some cases reported by human-rights organizations and bloggers in the country. The Egyptian Organization for Human Rights estimated that in 2003–7, severe mistreatment had caused more than 167 deaths in Egyptian prisons. The group contends that crimes of torture 'occur in Egyptian streets in broad daylight, at police checkpoints, and in people's homes in flagrant violation of the people's dignity and freedom'.[14]

The confrontation lay in curbing the spread of any new political initiative from within Egyptian society. The Kefaya movement, which in the mid-2000s quickly became a lively vehicle of opposition, employed creative tactics (before the 2005 presidential election, for example, it organized a candlelit freedom vigil in front of the mausoleum of Saad Zaghloul Pasha, an icon of Egypt's struggle against British colonialism and of Egyptian independence). The group also set up and directed a number of activist opposition groupings across key professions, for example 'Journalists for Change', 'Doctors for Change' and 'Workers for Change'. The state responded by the routine hassling, beating and arresting of its members[15] (one activist said: 'the regime's sticks and thugs trumped our words and rhetoric'). The same tactics were employed against the more traditional enemy, the Muslim Brotherhood. And though the Brotherhood was repeatedly unable to stage a compelling political campaign, the regime time and again confronted the Brotherhood's electoral successes or political initiatives with widespread arrests and assertions of forcefulness.

The regime also expanded its instruments of control by implanting groups of agents in a sort of 'viceroy' role among different sectors of society, charged at various times with controlling, placating and subjugating their constituents. The approach was particularly clear in professional unions, media circles, the sprawling public sector and universities (where assessment by security agencies was often the vital criterion in the appointment of senior faculty members and officials). Allegiance to the regime, personal political views, history of political activism and willingness to cooperate were significantly more important than academic excellence or leadership qualities. Instead of trying to widen its support, in many cases, the regime imposed viceroys whose sole legitimacy was their support from the top (and whose personal incentives were closely linked to the regime's approval of their performance).

This was a new approach for the Egyptian regime. In Nasser's time, and aside from maintaining and enriching the president's links with ordinary people, the regime had relied on building quasi-corporate structures designed to encompass almost all of society (from the Socialist Union, to which almost all labourers belonged, to Al-Tanzeem Al-Taleei, the most comprehensive organization Egyptian universities had witnessed). During Sadat's era, and in his efforts to purge Nasserism and Arab nationalism from national politics, he tried to dismantle these Nasserite structures, and replace them with laissez-faire social dynamics in a free capitalist society. The Mubarak regime's reliance on such viceroys, however, was a notable degeneration in terms of how the regime interacts with society; where previous regimes had used structures (Nasser) or transformations (Sadat) to secure loyalty, the Mubarak model is based on individuals' incentivization and preferment. Serious damage was being done to the relationship between the regime and society. Increasingly, the key links between vast swaths of society and the regime were either avoiding coercion or maximizing gains. This was no way to ensure the legitimacy that the system desperately needed.

The Mubarak regime's use of such methods entrenches its predicament. The longer time passes, the bigger its 'disconnect' from society, and the more entrenched the trust and legitimacy problem becomes. Economic development, the key lever of the new dynamo of the regime, is proving to be a double-edged sword. While improvements in living conditions (which are yet to materialize) *could* lessen the masses' disatisfaction, the newly empowered businessmen (and women) springing up in different sectors are increasingly demanding a bigger say in how their economy (and country) is governed (this point is discussed in detail in Chapter 7). Demographics also complicate the picture. In the early 1990s, around 50 per cent of Egyptians were under thirty-five years of age. By the end of the first decade of the twenty-first century, that ratio had jumped to circa 75 per cent. The various demands, ambitions and restlessness of a young population could well compel the regime to rely more on force – confrontation and coercion much more than containment.

That is already happening. While there have not been mass Tehran-style demonstrations led by young activists on the Egyptian streets, many Egyptian civil organizations, for example universities, have been enraged by the country's deteriorating socio-economic conditions, and the prevalent political stagnation. Several violent confrontations have taken place at some of the country's universities. Increasingly, student (and professors') groups complain of intense and regular interference by security forces on campuses in all aspects of academic life. At the universities in Cairo and Alexandria, campuses are policed by interior ministry forces that have no link to the academic institutions in which they work and that are not answerable to them. In November 2008, the Cairo Administrative Court issued a ruling that bans the presence of police officers at Cairo University's campus. And though the ruling pertains to Cairo University, a number of activist groups assert that it should be applicable to Egypt's eighteen government-run universities. At Helwan University, there were a number of legal complaints from students against police officers accusing them of regular and repeated assaults. Egyptian blogs are full of stories of students being 'kidnapped' by the police forces. New media (from satellite channels to the Internet) also complicate the situation for the regime. Not only are young Egyptians able to follow the election of a black man whose middle name is Hussein as America's new president, or the repeated humiliation of British politicians because of expenses irregularities, they closely track free elections in neighbouring and comparable countries, such as Lebanon and Turkey. Moreover, the regime's clique of viceroys is increasingly thin, and not necessarily dependable in controlling their constituents (a point discussed in Chapter 8).

The pressures and resistance of society suggest that the regime's tactics – whether of containment, coercion or confrontation – are reaching a limit. The country's internal security agencies now number almost 2 million people – roughly twice the number of soldiers mobilized in all Egypt's wars – and yet the people's anger and resentment are growing. The regime is potentially close to a tipping point after which it could lose control of the increasingly unstable situation. President Mubarak's age (he turned eighty-two in 2010) also aggravates the problem; he remains the regime's key security valve, and he (and not the liberal capitalist elite) commands the gravitas that the military establishment reveres. Dr Yehya Al-Gammal, Egypt's foremost expert on constitutional law, has recently raised alarm bells by stating, live on TV, that 'the country could be moving towards a disaster'. The question that many observers are asking (privately) is whether the leading forces within the regime (and especially Gamal Mubarak) have the strategic vision to confront the disturbing reality that their modus operandi in the past decade could well crumble at any moment. The regime, at least for its own survival, let alone for the country's good, is being forced to think of a new basis for its relationship with society – especially in the period post-President Mubarak.

The question of legitimacy is fundamental. It is one that has been faced by states elsewhere in the region that Egyptian leaders might benefit from studying: among them Morocco, Bahrain and even Turkey. In Morocco, King Mohamed VI has explicitly distinguished his rule (which he claimed would be based on openness and respect for democracy and human rights) from that of his deceased father, King Hassan II (which was highly autocratic and at times terrifying). The same dynamics, though to lesser extents, took place in Bahrain when King Hammad took over after the death of his father, King Eissa. In Turkey, the AK Party, under Recep Tayyib Erdogan, has been meticulously bridging the gap between Turkish society's increasing religiosity and the establishment's (and the army's) strict secularism. Sadly, the Egyptian regime does not appear to be taking note. Rather, it seems to be isolating itself, relying more heavily on the security apparatuses and insisting that solutions to the country's many quandaries can be found exclusively in economic reform without any true political change. The huge gulf between it and the people endures, and stands in the way of Egyptian progress and regeneration.

CHAPTER 7
YOUNG EGYPTIANS

EGYPT'S CURRENT STATE resembles a surrealist painting. It is difficult to decipher its components, challenging to comprehend its meaning. At the centre of the painting there are dark, abrasive lines; most onlookers would see them depicting anger, frustration and occasionally menace.

The painting's most conspicuous ominous line is the country's 45 million young Egyptians who are under thirty-five years of age (including the largest group of adolescents in the country's history). The conditions in which many of these millions live may be somewhat caricatured in much of the foreign media: neighbourhoods with absolute poverty, unreliable services and shabby buildings with peeling facades; millions of veiled young women, some as young as eight or nine years old, with long sleeves and skirts; narrow alleys with uncollected garbage and open cesspools; amplifiers and radio systems blaring out Koran recitations on every corner; disagreeable-looking crowds in vastly compacted streets; and, most strikingly, millions of young men, with wild eyes and dusty faces, usually captured on cameras shouting, screaming, burning flags and described as 'forces of menace', 'angry storms' and 'frustrated potential energy'. This caricaturing often depicts Egyptian society in lurid colours that miss its many shades and variations.

But even a more straightforward description is sobering enough.[1] More thorough observers highlight the institutionalization of corruption, the frightening increase in the rate and change in type of crime; a rooted disregard for human dignity; the descent of society's values and behaviours; and shifts in society's value system, particularly reflected in violent crimes perpetrated by teachers, students, businessmen and other members of the middle class. In 2008, a nine-year-old boy was abducted from Cairo to Tanta, where his body was found dismembered and mutilated. In the same year, a teacher was arrested for fatally injuring an eleven-year-old student for failing to do his homework. There is also a growing incidence of sexual harassment; the most notorious case was during celebrations in Cairo at the end of the holy month of Ramadan in 2007, which turned into a crazed series of sexual assaults by dozens of young men on female passers-by. 'People were just watching,' one eyewitness said. In addition, several shocking cases of sexual assault have drawn attention to a complex of social problems in Egypt, the most notable of which are street children: thousands of boys and girls, some arriving as young as five and six years old, living in dirty alleys and gritty corners under bridges, sleeping on pavements and in public gardens, begging or selling used and repackaged products at traffic lights and junctions, all fleeing poverty, abuse and exploitation.

Hardship is not only breeding crime and neglect, but also crudeness and coarseness. Cutting up and zigzag driving have become common features of Cairene and Alexandrian traffic. The sound of horns is the hysterical background music of the Egyptian street at any hour of the day and night. Drivers and passers-by typically shout at and curse each other. Standing in lines is now a rare phenomenon at any Egyptian retail or service outlet. Using profanities is very common on the Egyptian street, and increasingly among children. The street is also tense and agitated. Voices are loud. Fights begin for frivolous reasons. 'People seem ready to leap at each others' throats over seemingly trivial matters. The culture of tolerance that long existed among Egyptians is on the decline,' noted sociologist Samir Hanna.[2] And the classic Egyptian tradition of gentlemanliness (*shahama*), as featured in Egyptian black-and-white films, has died out. 'How do you expect a man who's been working sixteen hours, to leave his seat on the bus for a woman or an elderly man? Or if he stops after that long day to buy bread, why should he let a woman ahead? When you're being enslaved by the system, you don't really care about manners,' said a young man in a survey by *Al-Ahram Weekly*.[3]

'Egypt is becoming a very harsh place' is a common sentiment. Many are desperately trying to flee. In 2006, around 8 million Egyptians (more than 10 per cent of the population, the vast majority of whom were under forty years of age) applied for the American green-card lottery; Egyptians are among the top five nationalities applying to Canada's points-based immigration-approval scheme. From the mid-2000s, thousands of young Egyptians risked their lives attempting to reach the southern shores of Greece and Italy in search of work there or in countries to the north. According to a January 2008 report by the Egyptian Organization for Human Rights, 'around half a million Egyptians have successfully entered Europe illegally in the 2000s'. Increasingly, hundreds of young, poor Egyptians are picked up from tiny boats in the Mediterranean by Libyan coast guards and incarcerated in Libyan prisons (hardly an escape from their lives in Egypt).

The tough economic circumstances (official unemployment in the under-30 age group is around 21 per cent, almost double the overall total[4]) help explain this desperate response. Unemployment is partly the result of the major economic changes of the 1990s and 2000s and poor education – for example, most state universities' business graduates do not come into contact with a computer, and accordingly fail to secure jobs in the private sector. But part of the problem stems from antiquated attitudes; many university graduates prefer to remain unemployed than work in blue-collar or labouring jobs.

But such 'opting out' is not the preserve of the poor. More than a million Egyptian postgraduates now live in Europe and the United States; the vast majority will most likely never go back to live in Egypt[5] – and increasingly have very tenuous links to their original country. The range of problems inside Egypt (increasing sectarianism, the prevalence of corruption, the lack of the rule of law and the deterioration in values) compels fresh generations to emulate them. Mayar, a thirty-something economist who graduated in the top 5 per cent of her class, underwent the long administrative process to gain Canadian citizenship because she 'does not want her daughter brought up in Egypt'.

But there is another form of 'opting out', a sort of internal migration by those who stay in the country but seek to insulate themselves from its difficulties – and are prosperous enough to make the effort. Egypt's macro-economic progress has seen consumer expenditure per capita (at purchasing power parity) grow between 2000 and 2008 from $2,647 to $3,672; for the richest 20 per cent of the population, the figures were $5,770 and $8,000. Those who benefited from that wave have increasingly retreated from the hustle and bustle of society to lead secluded, isolated lives. The well-paid telecoms engineer in his mid-thirties (and his friends, the IT consultant, the accountant at a leading local company, the sales executive in a multinational, the banker, the doctor) are increasingly drawn to the Internet, to satellite dishes and even the express-delivery service of Amazon UK. If his financial situation improves significantly, his immediate objective becomes a home in one of the new, rich and isolated suburbs of Cairo, from where he and his wife will send their children to a new private school and attend a secluded, members-only sports and social club. The psychological isolation and the emotional detachment slowly, gradually and subtly instil a feeling among such people that there is a major civilization gap between them (and their neat world) and the rest of their society.

The retreat from city centres to peripheral areas is also part of a wider change in Egyptians' relationship with their land. Egypt's urban constellations (mainly Cairo and Alexandria, but also Al-Mahala, Tanta, Al-Zakazeek and Asyut) and their surrounding areas are in constant flux with both population growth and internal migration (mainly from Al-Saeed and the remote parts of the Delta – now around 800,000 annually). Egyptians were increasingly condensed in the centres as well as fragmented at the peripheries. Between the 1960s and the 2000s, Cairo grew from 6 million inhabitants to more than 15 million. The city's density, at more than 1,000 individuals per square kilometre, is among the highest in the world, and Alexandria is not far behind. The exuberance, energy and waves of creativity that characterized Cairo and Alexandria throughout the twentieth century were giving way to suffocating crowdedness, domineering compactness and stifling closeness. At the same time, the rich and the upper middle class were deserting the city centres and the old neighbourhoods for new suburbs, opting for gated communities on the outskirts, detached not only from the over-crowding and the increasingly ailing infrastructure, but also from the historic neighbourhoods and quarters that have witnessed and shaped

Egyptians' interaction with their physical space throughout decades (and at times centuries).

Cairo's centre, Zamalek, Garden City and Maadi were increasingly shadows of their former selves. New boutiques, restaurants and shopping centres continue to open up, but the city's centre of gravity has moved to the Sixth of October, Palm Hills, City Views, Allegria, the Fifth Settlement, Al-Obour and Al-Shorouk – new rich, immaculate and spacious communities, but lacking Cairo's and Alexandria's long and rich touches (and scars) of history.[6]

As a result, for the first time in Egypt's history many people live, work and socialize far from the city centre, leaving its landmarks – the centuries-old mosques and churches, the baroque buildings and palaces of Ismael Pasha, the Corniche's boulevards, the busy streets of Adly, Embaba and Shoubra – neglected. Egyptians' attachment to their physical heritage is diminishing; the burning of Al-Musafir Khana (an eighteenth-century Mameluke guest house) in 2007 and of Majlis Al-Shoura (a modern Islamic architectural gem) in 2008 went almost unnoticed (Gamal Al-Ghitanni's *Regaining Al-Musafir Khana*[7] transcends its purpose of describing the lost house, and emerges as a tribute to Egypt's 'old devotion to its emotional heritage').

In a lecture in Paris in the mid-1990s, Mohamed Hassanein Heikal offered a revealing analogy. He noted that the French urban engineer Haussmann, the designer of the Rue de Rivoli and the Boulevard de Sebastopol, was the same man who designed the Mohamed Ali Street in Cairo. But while the Rue de Rivoli and Boulevard de Sebastopol remain 'a front of civilization in the city of Light', 'lights have gone off on central Cairo's civilization fronts'; Cairo's old Opera House has been replaced by a multi-storey parking block.

It was not only the rich and the upper middle class who deserted the city centres; the newcomers (the millions who left the rural areas for Cairo and Alexandria) and the newly poor (the other millions who had crumbled under the crippling socio-economic conditions in the 1980s, 1990s and 2000s) were compelled to live in detached spaces on the peripheries of the Egyptian metropolises. Cairo's City of the Dead is the most conspicuous: an area of more than 8 square kilometres where (at least) 4 million poor Cairenes live and work in a crowded grid of tombs and mausoleums, forming a quasi-independent community. Many aspects of it are distressing, from the hundreds of thousands of children deprived of basic education to the lack of sanitation, but the city is also a beacon of creativity and make-do. Electricity is typically brought in by wires over roofs from nearby mosques or public spaces; rooms are modelled to suit living requirements;[8] and cooperative income sources are constantly invented. Similar circumstances, though on a smaller scale, exist in Garbage Village, home to more than 50,000 garbage workers (and their families), whose lives, like those of the millions living in the City of the Dead, are disconnected from proper Cairo (Mai Iskander's *Garbage Dreams*, a film independently produced in 2009, is a poignant, emotive and intriguing portrayal of life in Garbage Village).

A change in the relationship with Egyptians' physical space has also occurred in the Egyptian Delta and Al-Saeed. The fragmentation in ownership of cultivated land, the encroachment of construction on the Nile's soil and waves of internal immigration are some components of the change. Land is no longer the sole (or even the main) source of income for most Delta or Saeedi families, the quasi-sacred asset that housed the entire family to be passed from one generation to another. Yousef Chahine's 1969 film *The Land (Al-Ard)*, adapted from a novel by Abdelrahman Al-Sharkawi, brought the daily life of poor Egyptian farmers to the screen: their voices and clothes, their grinding work through sweltering days and tranquil nights, the smell of cows and chicken in their homes, their faint smiles, their dignity and poverty, their superstitiousness, and – above all – their almost-sacred attachment to their land. In the film's last scene, the ageing villager who had stood up against overlordship (played by the actor Mahmoud Al-Meligui) is brutally punished: his feet bound, his body tied to the legs of a horse ridden by the village sheriff, so that his clothes are torn and his body bleeds. Yet as he is dragged along, his hand clutches at the mud, the soil. He refuses to let go, to abandon his land, his home, his life. The audience – millions of whom wept while watching this scene – almost questioned whether Al-Meligui's hands were clutching the earth, or the earth was clutching him.[9] That deep attachment to and recognition of the sanctity of the land is vanishing.

Egypt's demographic changes have exacerbated this process. The near-doubling of the Egyptian population since the 1970s has turned the Egyptian demographic structure into a pyramid – extremely narrow at the top and enormously wide at the bottom, with very limited conduits between the few millions in their fifties, sixties and seventies and the 45 million-plus under thirty-five years of age.[10] The fading generation is carrying off with it the classic compositions of the Egyptian character and the reservoir of the Egyptian personality, while the incoming, increasingly dominant generation is hardly receiving any cultural heritage. The new generation never fought (or witnessed) a war; never lived with a national project; grew up at a time in which the country was undergoing a surgical transformation (the move from Nasserite secular, socialist Arab nationalism to Islamism, and later capitalism, through Sadat's *al-infitah*). It was a tense period. The new generation lived through an almost open war between the state and groups bent not only on overthrowing the regime, but on transforming the entire society. Sectarianism and the conspicuous withdrawal of Egyptian Christians that intensified in the same period (from the 1970s to the 2000s) deprived society of diversity and vital breathing space, previously achieved through traditional interactions with Europe and Western culture in general. Even the relationship between the regime (and especially the president) and the people during those decades was stressful: the regime asserted its authority, at times with severe coercion and utter disregard for human rights, without forging the classic emotional links between the pharaoh (or the figurehead of the Egyptian family, as President Sadat preferred to say) and his subjects. All of these factors contributed to a tense and agitated society. The millions of young Egyptians were stepping into a stressed (and stressing) social milieu.

Egyptians are keenly aware of their regression and relapse over the past four decades. And the more the regime, via its sponsored media, has stuck to notions of 'Egyptian leadership and headship', the more the realities of daily life confirmed the deterioration. Saudi's political prominence (as compared to the retreat of Egyptian foreign policy in the past three decades, discussed in Chapter 6), the Gulf's wealth, Lebanon's creativity and *joie de vivre*, Jordan's rejuvenation (under a young, energetic royal couple) and Dubai's glamour reminded Egyptians of their ailing conditions and unfortunate situation. Blame flew everywhere, from the mismanagement and corruption of successive governments to the dysfunctional system, to the regime's shady governance, to the decline in society's values. Within the many morbid symptoms of the fracturing of the social order and national regression, a shared feeling has emerged: that 'something has gone wrong' (*'fee haga ghalat'*) in society and values, and in the heritage available to the young, rising generation.

Indeed, the classic channels of cultural transmission have become seriously frayed. The 1970s and 1980s was a low period in

Egyptian culture. Many newspapers, magazines, theatres, cinemas and cultural avenues were closed down; thousands of writers, journalists, professors and artists were obliged to leave the country. Wahhabism and Salafism gained ground in social attitudes and norms as well as politics. The regime, during Sadat's last years and throughout Mubarak's containment, confrontation and coercion years, had low tolerance of dissidents and dissenters. And with the retreat in the role of Egyptian Christians and society's change of orientation from progressive liberalism and a fascination with Europe towards conservatism and religiosity, classic Egyptian culture has been hollowed out and homogenized.

The deterioration of Egypt's educational system is a further negative factor. Though elementary education (from ages six to fourteen) is compulsory in Egypt, and though more than 19 million Egyptians between the ages of six and eighteen, representing around 90 per cent of all school-age children, were enrolled in 2008 in the country's pre-university education system (taking Egypt's overall literacy rate to circa 71 per cent after decades of hovering at 50 per cent), the system as a whole is in trouble, with falling enrolments, poor teacher–student ratios and persistent gender inequality. Actual school enrolments in rural areas often fall below 50 per cent of all school-age children. School drop-outs, especially in Egypt's poorest regions (mainly Al-Saeed) or the rougher neighbourhoods of Cairo and Alexandria, reach 20–25 per cent of all enrolment figures. Gender inequality continues to persist. Girls' enrolment ratios are typically around 20 per cent lower than those of boys, and drop-out ratios are higher.

The infrastructure of schools is a chronic problem. Classes in public schools often include more than sixty or seventy students. Teacher–student ratios in most schools are around one to fifty. Playgrounds, let alone music, art rooms or laboratories, are a rarity. English is a part of the curriculum in the preparatory and secondary stages, but the quality of teaching and students' command of the language leave much to be desired. And private tutoring continues to be a major challenge: highly expensive and therefore the exclusive domain of affluent families, it disrupts the supposed equality of the educational process. In the mid-2000s, around 60 per cent of families in the major cities stated that their children had private tutoring. According to Egypt's Central Statistics and Mobilisation Agency (CAPMAS), more than 60 per cent of all investments in education are spent on private tutoring. At university level, the links to international centres of excellence and innovation are paltry; there is a major retreat in research and development, a thriving clandestine trade in class notes and examination essays and little emphasis on independent knowledge and learning as opposed to passing exams and receiving a degree.[11]

These processes – a change in the country's value system, detachment from society, the gap between generations, the weakening of Egyptian culture, the deterioration in the educational system and the damage to the most sacred of the tenets of Egyptianism, the land – have altered Egyptians' link to each other and their country. The millions of young Egyptians entering the country's public life need to re-establish these links, in order to make sense of their lives and their society. It would seem natural to look to politics as the avenue of change here; but the young generation's contribution is not welcomed in public policy or decision-making circles. Within the ruling National Democratic Party, Gamal Mubarak's wing, especially in its years of ascension (from the late 1990s to the mid-2000s) was keen on positioning itself as a wave of well-educated, young Egyptians with a strong interest in the country's public life. But with the maturing of that wing, and its establishment at the pinnacle of the party and the regime, the young faces and the youth organizations that Gamal Mubarak had championed (for example, The Future Foundation) have been relegated to the background. What remains around the regime's strong man are scions of ultra-rich families and symbols of liberal capitalism.

The same dynamics have been at work in the Muslim Brotherhood. The vigour and drive that had characterized the Brotherhood in the early 2000s (and which led to its 2005 manifesto, parliamentary election success and strong presence across a number of prominent societal circles) waned. The many young Brotherhood members, who had surrounded Mahdi Akef (the general guide) in that period, were gradually dispersed; the Brotherhood's decision-making channels, power circles and public faces remained old and tired. Even the Kefaya movement, the country's most prominent civic opposition group in the 2000s, did not manage to extend its appeal (or membership) to significant numbers of young Egyptians. Its rhetoric (highbrow and concerned with political failures rather than the ragged realities of ordinary people's daily lives) resonated with the intelligentsia much more than with the millions of university students. A partial exception has been the liberal opposition represented by Aziz Siddqui's platform of the mid-2000s and, later, Ayman Noor's *Al-Ghad* party; but they are too weak and marginalized to be a viable forum. Not surprisingly, the political participation rate of young Egyptians is dismal, even by the standards of the Arab world (according to the 2009 Arab Human Development Report, only 28 per cent participated in the 2005 parliamentary election and 23 per cent in the 2005 presidential election).

But their dynamism and activism has found other outlets – mainly cultural. The vacuum that needed to be filled stirred the creativity of thousands of young (twenty- and thirty-something) writers, film-makers, singers and musicians. Egyptian cinema in the 2000s, with new twists, stories, scripts, innovations in visual effects, shooting styles and higher production values, more than tripled its revenues from the levels of early or mid-1990s. Production budgets are now routinely US$3–5 million, if not more.[12] Distribution has expanded from the classic markets of the Gulf and Levant to North Africa, and increasingly to the world cinema circles in Europe. From 2004 onwards, at least one Egyptian film was presented every year at Cannes Film Festival. And there were serious attempts at participating in innovative gatherings such as Tribeca in New York and Sundance in Utah. The same development took place in Egyptian music: innovations (and in many cases refreshing unorthodoxy) in tones, mixes, melodies and visuals drew more listeners, opened new markets and generated more revenues. Egyptian music and artists won the prestigious World Music Award three times between 1998 and 2007.

Even reading, a long-lost cause in Egypt, has witnessed a revival. The Arabic (and in many cases illegal) translations of the Harry Potter books and *The Lord of the Rings*, the rising penetration of the Internet in cafés and public spaces, in addition to the popularity of blogs and chatrooms, triggered an enthusiasm for reading, writing and critiquing. So far another Naguib Mahfouz, Yousef Idris[13] or even Alaa Al-Aswany[14] has not emerged, but thousands of young writers are experimenting with new themes, structures and language (an evolution of Egyptian slang).[15] One refreshing example is 'El Koshary Today',[16] an English-language 'fake news website', modelled on the highly successful satirical 'The Onion' in the United States, and launched by three twenty-something Egyptians. With its tongue-in-cheek hilarity and uproarious directness, El Koshary Today has managed to attract a dedicated and increasing fan base.

Young Egyptians' dynamism has also set off a wave of innovation in Egypt's business and finance scene. The Egyptian computing and information-technology industry, though tiny in size and highly concentrated in terms of professionals and entities, boasts excellent education centres (especially at The American University in Cairo), a number of highly successful companies with international clientele and sales distribution, and an increasingly high reputation. Young Egyptians also created and led the Middle East's, the Arab world's and Africa's most successful investment bank, private equity firm, telecoms operator and construction conglomerate – all with spectacular successes throughout the 2000s. And, more interestingly, even at the core of the society's socio-economic life, away from the industries and sectors that require sophistication, exposure to the West and access to mega-funding, thousands of young Egyptians have created tens of thousands of small businesses and enterprises in numerous sectors, from small textile workshops to fast food restaurants, to taxi fleets, to diving centres. By the end of 2008, Egypt's Ministry of Trade was processing more than 2,000 new company registrations every week. Adam Smith's invisible hand was very much in action throughout the 2000s, promoting creativity, ingenuity and resourcefulness. There is a dominant view that Egyptians, as a result of their centuries-old agricultural culture, are lacking in terms of entrepreneurialism. In fact, the production of – and trading in – raw cotton, textiles, dyeing, silk, sugar and wheat gained immense economic importance through Egyptians' long experience with agriculture and farming. The concentration of funding in a few centres and circles, however, has restricted the emergence of an agribusiness culture in the country.[17]

In philanthropy and social investment, too, the new generation of Egyptians have established a large number of NGOs working with Egypt's poor and needy, including the provision of educational and vocational assistance. Among them are independent groups such as Al-Mahrousa and The American University in Cairo's Philanthropy Centre. Social work and enterprise extended to general social and environmental problems, such as efforts of independent activists to raise awareness of climate change, solve old Cairo's severe rubbish problem and confront the problem of female genital mutilation in poor rural districts.

But young Egyptians' most important contribution today is not in cinema, literature, business, philanthropy or social work; it is in formulating their own definition of Egyptianism, their own definition of a twenty-first-century Egyptian project. The fragile channel of communication between the fading generation of the 1950s and 1960s and young Egyptians, and the overall weakening of 'brand Egypt' has encouraged some of the generations taking the stage to develop their own understanding of their society and heritage. Some talented young people, depressed by the devastating decline of Egyptian culture, values, attitudes and behaviour, leapt over the past fifty years (seeing only troubles and failures), and embraced Egypt's liberal experiment of the 1920s, 1930s and 1940s. The tolerance that had characterized that experiment; the refinement, the beauty, the sophistication and the civility of the Egyptian society at the time; the cosmopolitanism of Cairo and Alexandria; and the overall *joie de vivre* of the period, intoxicated those searchers for a new identity, a new understanding of their cultural inheritance.

These young talents sought a confluence between the appeal of the liberal experiment and the energy that their coming onto the stage of Egyptian society has unleashed. The 2000s saw a plethora of films, TV series and novels glorifying and extolling the liberal experiment, especially its tolerant values, and its relaxed modus vivendi. One of the most successful TV programmes on a youth-oriented satellite channel in Egypt in Ramadan 2010 (Egyptian television's annual high season) was *Kan Yama Kan* (roughly 'was in the past') – a nostalgic show about Egyptian life and society in the 1930s and 1940s. The infatuation with the 1920s, 1930s and 1940s extended to a large number of new and exclusive restaurants in Cairo and Alexandria where the decor is 'chic 30s', the waiters wear the old fez (*tarbouche*) and the menus offer 'classic Egyptian cuisine'. Those young Egyptians, almost all hailing from Egypt's liberal capitalist camp, have been trying to summon a charming bygone past and superimpose it over the present they resent.

Some young Islamists, too, have responded to the failure of their movement by seeking inspiration (or evasion) in history: the early Islamic society of Medina, the Abbasid era in Baghdad, the Ummayad era in Andalucia, Saladin's victories or the great Mamelukes. A multitude of 'Islamic preachers' burst out on Islamist screens, programmes and chatrooms promoting 'our glorious history', 'noble values', 'the mercy and compassion of Islam' and 'the purity of earlier Islamic societies'. The return to past glories complemented the Islamic movement's missionary zeal in the present and provided it with an emotional counterpart to liberal nostalgia.

The jump to the past also stemmed from the historical and contextual vacuum from which Egyptian society suffers. The country witnessed a continuous process of repudiating the past and discrediting its leaders. Al-Wafd sidelined all of Saad Zaghloul's (and later Mustafa Al-Nahas's) challengers inside (and outside) the party – from Adly Yakan Pasha in the 1920s to Makram Ebeid Pasha in the 1940s. Nasser tarnished the 'bygone era' and silenced all of its men. Sadat sullied the entire Nasserite project and Nasser himself, throughout the second half of the 1970s, became an open target for state media. The Islamic movement shunned all of Egypt's leaders, and its militant side portrayed many of them as infidels. And recently the liberal capitalist elite disassociated itself from all of what has come before it. Even in culture, the same trend took place: Taha Hussein, Al-Akkad, Tawfik Al-Hakeem, Naguib Mahfouz, Yousef Idris, Mohamed Hassanein Heikal and others all were on the receiving end of serious smearing campaigns.

That discrediting of the past, the rapid transformations of the society over the past six decades and the major differences between the various ideologies and *projects* of the successive eras has left the people, especially the young, without national givens. Modern Egypt lacks consensus on any notion, project or person in its recent history. Its longest conflict in the past seventy years (the four wars against Israel) today seems meaningless in the context of an Egypt that is a pillar of the Pax Americana in the Middle East. The foundations of its revolution (social equality and the Arab nationalist identity) are remnants of the past, divorced from today's realities. Its hero (Nasser) is either adored or vilified without an objective assessment of his role in the country's history. Even its two traditional religions today seem entangled in a tense relationship. The young lack not only a role model or a continuous national project to which they belong, but also a nationally accepted narrative of their past.

Many observers have seen these appeals to the past in the context of the overarching political struggle in Egypt between the regime's liberal capitalists and the Islamic movement: the creative figures of cinema, music and literature were extolling liberalism's values, imposing the remnants of Egypt's liberal experiment on the country; the philanthropists were acting out of religious consciousness; the private-equity professionals, the investment bankers and the myriad businessmen (and women) were associates and junior partners of the regime, while thousands of small and medium-sized businesses were part of the economic infrastructure of the Islamic movement in the country.

But that view failed to recognise that the young's endeavours were truly independent from the liberal capitalists and the Islamists; they represented the need of millions of young Egyptians to rise above their unfortunate situation (including the struggle between the regime and the Islamic movement) and to cling to something they could be proud of, some frame of reference, a skeleton of an identity.

The more compelling criticism of today's efforts and contributions, then, is that most of them are indeed mere skeletons. The young liberals took from Egypt's liberal experiment its charming and polished facade; but they lacked the depth (or the interest) to delve into the period's realities. They ignored the plight of foreign occupation, the central political reality of Egypt's 1920s, 1930s and 1940s. They overlooked the liberal experiment's pivotal intellectual struggle between the Mediterranean-ists who wanted to place Egypt in Europe and the eastern-ists. They discounted the dramatic socio-economic gap that marked Egyptian society then (despite the similarities with today's situation). And though their packaging was attractive (such as the high production values of the TV series and films that espoused the liberal experiment), they lacked determination and intellectual courage. They invoked the facades of liberalism; but they did not go further and push for a confrontation with Salafism and its clinging to the past (as outstanding liberal intellects such as Taha Hussein had done at the height of the liberal experiment).

The young Islamists did not fare better. Their selection of the images of the purity of Prophet Mohamed's early Islamic society and the glorious victories of the Abbasids, Saladin and the Mamelukes was an example of excessive historical subjectivity that censored history and consciously (or ignorantly) overlooked the almost continuous embarrassing episodes of blood-letting and internal struggles. And as was the case with the liberals, the young Islamists excelled in packaging: young, soft-spoken, well-dressed, articulate preachers. But they lacked the solidity, audacity and scholarly vigour of Islamic thinkers such as Mohamed Abdou, Al-Akkad or even recently Seleem Al-Awaa or Gamal Al-Banna, who, courageously, delved into the realities of Islamic history and experimented with new interpretations.

There were also initiatives by young Nasserites and Arab nationalists (especially in journalism and literature) advocating a revival of Egypt's traditional role in the region. They campaigned for 'saving Gaza', made films honouring the 'martyrs of the Arab nation' and even advocated minor programmes of 'pan-Arab unity'; but there wasn't the depth and sturdiness of Nasser or the brilliance and composure of Heikal. Their message demonstrated more noise and passion than a profound understanding of the Egyptian project.

The youths' efforts were also internally focused. Their 'appeals to the past' were divorced from any creativity in terms of looking at the country's national security or strategic positioning. Neither the liberals nor the Islamists who sought solace in earlier glamour and glory put forward serious views regarding Egypt's approach to international relations. That was partly the result of the young people's exclusion from politics and the tenuous link between their creativity and enterprise and the experience of the older generation now leaving the scene. But it was also the result of languor and indolence. The loudest voices in the young liberals camp repeatedly idolized 'liberal, Mediterranean Egypt' but failed to define what kind of relationship Mediterranean Egypt should have with the United States in light of the occupation of Iraq and Afghanistan, how Egypt should position itself in (or with regard to) the Arab world and what should be the dynamics governing the relationship with Israel, given the deteriorating situation in the Palestinian territories. The young

Islamists gracefully avoided any discussion of how 'a return to our glorious Islamic past' would affect the country's foreign policy, the peace treaty with Israel or, indeed, the implications of their Islamic calling on Egypt's Arab or Mediterranean heritage.

Young Egyptians' different enterprises are only a few years old, and have a long way to go. Most of today's efforts actually reflect the consequences of the weak links between the generations, the extremely poor educational system, the denying of political participation for decades, the oppressing conservatism, the retreat of liberalism and exposure to the West and the deteriorating Egyptian culture of the past few decades. And in their attempts to make sense of their heritage, they have faced a far harder task than many of their predecessors, so consuming of the past have Egypt's recent decades been. It would be unfair to compare young Egyptians' endeavours with Egypt's liberal experiment and/or with Nasserite Arab nationalism – as some observers have done. The first, as discussed in Chapter 1, was the outcome of more than half a century of a comprehensive cultural renaissance, determined efforts at development and progress and a political and social movement inspired by 'catching up with Europe'. Arab nationalism, despite the strong momentum that Nasser personally represented, followed more than thirty years of toying with Arabism and easternism.

This generation is animated by a passion to escape the failure it feels it has inherited. Swaths of young Egyptians, across many sectors (in business, academia, entertainment, social development and the arts), dismiss their recent past and present as utter failures. The economic malfunctioning that has kept more than 40 per cent of the population under the international line of poverty; the disappointments in foreign policy and the country's international standing; the breakdown in the social contract in the country; and the feeling of an overarching defeat and almost total collapse, has driven the young (many of whom have had far better education and exposure to the wider world than their parents) to deem the previous generations' experience bankrupt, with nothing to offer or learn from.

There is a glaring disconnection between the generations, and a rejection of the old by the young. This rejection is even noticeable in fiction for adolescents. Whereas in the 1980s, the most successful series of this genre was *Ragol Al-Mustaheel* (an Egyptianized James Bond, who is part of the state's General Intelligence Agency), the 2000s witnessed the emergence of the rebel hero who snubs the state's system and society's norms. To a large extent, the rise of the new stars of business, finance, academia, entertainment and journalism has been a displacement of old norms, leaders and modus operandi, rather than a continuation and building upon of existing structures. In the public sector, entire management teams (some of them with decent track records) have been forced into retirement and replaced by young managers drawn from the private sector. State-owned banks witnessed a complete makeover with MBA graduates with stints in investment banks in London and New York replacing a generation of older bureaucrats. In government, the new 2004 administration was a breakaway from previous ways of working and thinking. Even in culture (especially in literature and cinema, two of the very few areas in which recent Egyptian heritage is commendable), Egypt's bestselling books and films in the last few years have been vastly different in terms of style, themes and even language from traditional Egyptian novels and films.

Turning to history to borrow from earlier experiences and the dismissal of the recent past as utter failure reflects a presumption that the dynamism of young Egyptians is inherently superior to that of their predecessors (by virtue of better education and exposure, and because of the widespread disregard for recent history and heritage). A prevailing line of thinking is that these new efforts could pull this 'failing society' out of its current situation and usher in a new promising future; that the new momentum in business, academia, entertainment, social development and the arts will create economic, financial and cultural centres of excellence in Egypt (in the midst of the poor masses) which will trigger positive ripple effects throughout the economy and society, and which in time will lead the country towards development and progress.

It will be a long and tough path. Almost all the contributions and initiatives mentioned above – in business, philanthropy and culture – are top-down, remain divorced from major public influence and together lack the ability to coalesce into a national project. They do not touch the vast majority of young Egyptians, whose main concerns are surviving in daily life, finding work and social opportunities and acquiring skills. Even geographically, most of those initiatives are concentrated in Cairo and Alexandria and some areas in the Delta, detached from the majority of the country's youths – for example, far away from Al-Saeed or Al-Nuba.[18] The successful business groups have become the country's main employers. The new cultural and artistic wave has found in Egyptian youths its largest market and fan base. And even the many philanthropic groups have worked with thousands of deprived young Egyptians in poor neighbourhoods. Yet the real involvement of the millions of young Egyptians remains miniscule. The vast majority of the 45 million Egyptians under thirty-five years of age are concerned with survival, trapped in circles of economic suppression and political repression; new business or work opportunities are beyond not only their capacities and acquired skills, but also their understanding; social work, activism and concern for overall social challenges are luxuries to be dismissed with smiles of scorn and bitterness; and entertainment and culture are taken in small doses when the grind of daily life permits.[19]

This severance between society's most important dynamics (which are, invariably, driven by bright young Egyptians) and the majority of the population is society's greatest loss. Millions are prevented by their crippling circumstances from participating in the most important (and promising) changes their society is undergoing. Society is thus denied their contribution. The Arab Human Development Report of 2009 concluded that the young are insecure in 'almost all living aspects'; their lives render them 'hardly free' to make their own decisions; their socio-political environments disfavour any meaningful social participation, whether political or economic; and the abuse of their rights drives them to reject not only the governing regime, but the entire society in which they feel imprisoned and humiliated.[20]

There are nonetheless some positive trends. For the first time since the 1950s, the private sector in Egypt now employs more Egyptians than the public sector. This significant shift coincides with the regime's subtle but consistent lifting of the social safety net that Egyptians have enjoyed since the 1960s. This means that the prices of staple foodstuffs are increasing (which provoked serious demonstrations and riots in early 2008); healthcare is effectively becoming privatized; the government's guarantee to create job opportunities for new graduates is all but null and void; and the dominant operating mode of the entire economy is unmistakably capitalist. Many observers highlight the corruption and vast income differentials that are among the by-products of these changes. As important, however, is the emergence of a new and broad-based class of engaged economic agents who participate in and have stakes in the country's economic system. These businesspeople (owners and shareholders, as well as managers and employees) are economically independent of the government's and the public sector's schemes, and this encourages a much more assertive and outspoken attitude towards the elements holding the country back. It is notable, for example, that new and relatively insignificant associations of small- and medium-sized business entities are actively involved in drafting laws, in the tradition of white papers pursued by Western governments. Also of significance is that the government's new universal tax system is based on participatory contribution, whereby industry and special-interest groups have a say in various details and schemes.

The effects of that stakeholder mentality are mounting. It is common for observers to hail new media and the Internet, satellite TV channels and greater openness to the outside world as central to the wave of political activism that Egypt has witnessed since 2003–4 (involving active professional syndicates, flourishing universities and a multitude of bloggers). All true, but arguably more fundamental is the factor of self-assurance that comes from being economically independent. The spreading realization among many young Egyptians (in the higher as well as lower socio-economic segments) that they will never work for the government or the public sector – because these are no longer the main providers in Egyptian society – has been the trigger of the new activism. That trend is now irreversible – and is gaining momentum. One of the most important dynamics in Egypt today is how (no longer if) the private sector and its agents will transform their economic power into political power.

Another major trend among young Egyptians concerns the areas where the new Egyptian capitalism meets young people's creativity and thirst for change. For example, three investment funds were launched in 2009 that focus solely on the most deprived areas in Al-Saeed; all are managed by thirty-something young Egyptians who have returned to the country from New York and London. The information-technology sector in Egypt is also witnessing a wave of entrepreneurialism, capital investment and exposure to advanced technologies. The same trend is taking place in the tourism, food and beverage, transportation, real-estate and consumables sectors. There is a fusion here of personal incentive and social improvement that is a potential source of development and progress.

The country is also experiencing a revival in the role of (and respect for) civil society. Long ignored and demonized during the decades of the rise of Islamism, civil society is regaining some of its lost ground. While the Islamic movement's (and the Church's) social infrastructures continue to be the country's most widespread and effective social networks, private groups are active today in trying to supplement the government's ailing public social services. The rise of private universities, businessmen associations, chambers of commerce, consumer protection groups and the multitude of independent press and TV channels that Egypt has seen in the 2000s are part of the trend. All are assertive of Egyptianism (as opposed to Islamism or Christianism) in various social aspects and endeavours. For example, the country's most generous and sought-after scholarships today are offered by three private, independent trusts, rather than the government or a religious body; the professional syndicates and the Judges' Club front today's wave of political activism; the four independent Egyptian newspapers with the highest circulation (especially among young Egyptians) are determinedly secular. For example, *Al-Dostour, Al-Masry Al-Youm, Sout Al-Ummah* and *Al-Shorouk* are able to combine a firmly secular line with intelligent and invigorating coverage of Islamic (and Christian) topics of interest.

Even Islamism is changing. There is a recurring tendency among analysts to simplify political Islamism by reducing it to the Muslim Brotherhood; but this is not (as is often stated) the most important or pervasive Islamic force in the country. This description more accurately defines the Salafist movements (discussed in Chapters 1 and 3). Salafists, who regard early pious Muslims and their communities as exemplary models, command major followings among young Egyptians. They are not politically active and have a relatively blank record: no history of violence, no organizational structure, no manifestos and no obvious political ambitions, and that is why they are tolerated (and sometimes encouraged) by the regime; that is also why they do not feature in news bulletins or reports on the country. Their influence, however, is many times more than that of organized political Islam. Their presence has traditionally been much more diverse than political or militant groups.

Political and militant Islam, as a result of its organizational structures, has grown through geographic expansion. In the case of militant Islamism, for example, the growth was from Al-Saeed (where the police's presence in the mid- and late 1970s was relatively light) to Cairo and Alexandria. Salafist groups, however, because they mostly lack organizational structures, expand haphazardly and rapidly. Salafist thinking, which has been proliferating in Egypt for more than three decades, is based on a religious view of life and a strict and highly conservative social code, and inherently advances an Islamist foreign policy. Unlike political Islamism, which has clear objectives, Salafism is an abstract current that is flexible enough to accommodate and absorb different ambitions and orientations. The accumulating influence of this significant Salafist sway on Egyptian society is making many young Egyptians more anti-secular, anti-liberal and anti-Western.

Yet, at the other end of the social spectrum, millions of young Egyptians, Egypt's first digital generation, are highly westernized; there are very liberal sparks in music, films and literature, and in attitudes, styles of living and tastes. But the most interesting changes are taking place in some of Cairo's and Alexandria's poorest neighbourhoods and deep in Saeedi villages. Millions of youths from disadvantaged backgrounds are, for the first time, exposed to the world in ways that expand aspirations and ambitions. Though more than 50 per cent of them are still without access to modern schools and hospitals, let alone a personal computer, the openness to the world makes them realize that there is much more to life than the immediate circumstances they have been born into. One result is that demand for English-language, personal-computing, secretarial and business-basics courses is mushrooming in the unlikeliest of places in Egypt. For example, the British Council in Egypt is the largest of its operations worldwide. Professional apprenticeships are also growing. Behind the wild eyes, dusty faces and crowds that many in the West associate with conservatism, anger and potential menace, there are millions, in the midst of devastating conditions, who are admirably striving for better futures.

These more positive trends in today's Egypt interact with the contributions in business, finance, culture, social investment and philanthropy. The results remain unclear. There is a chance that the new dynamism that Egyptian society is currently experiencing, after the turbulent times of the past sixty years, will bring about development and progress phases that Egyptian society has not yet undergone. In the same way that the Great Depression, the two world wars and a period of dynamism and youth rebellion (in the late 1960s) steered Western societies towards social maturity, the dominance of a solid and colossal middle class, a national focus on quality of living, a respect for individualism and the enshrining of democracy, the current interactions in Egypt could be that last developmental phase – after the Nasserite expansion, *al-infitah*'s shockwaves, militant Islamism and sectarianism and religious conservatism – enabling Egyptian society to reach the same final destinations. The new developments could evolve to become the next phase of progress that Egypt was denied by the liberal experiment's abrupt end sixty years ago. The wager would be on the expansion and growth of an increasingly secure and economically independent (from the state) middle class that would recognize its rights and have the sophistication and means to demand them, and the maturity (and stake in the country) to achieve these rights through peaceful changes.

But the same interactions and dynamics could prove to be false promises. They might remain sparks and green shoots in the midst of a dismal present. The independent and increasingly assertive private sector could recoil from enhancing its role and confronting Egypt's various socio-economic problems; fortify itself in free zones, export-driven industries and sectors; and link its revenues and cash flows to international, mobile circles, rather than commit them to its home market. The daring young creative types could fail to grow into a serious social force able to effect change in their society, and remain confined to entertainment, content with ballooning box offices. Social workers, philanthropists and the hundreds of engaged activist groups could also remain marginal to society's gruelling realities, satisfied with disparate projects with limited, localized results. Adam Smith's invisible hand could stop working, and society could plunge further into despair. The detachment of the majority of young Egyptians, amid crushing living conditions and the absence of a national project to ignite energy and momentum, could instead – at a moment at which the regime fails to grab hold of the country – rouse a tornado of turmoil in which anger and despair trump hope.

Today, Egypt resembles the agonized Egyptian at the beginning of Naguib Mahfouz's novel *Autumn Quail*, seemingly 'standing in the middle of nowhere and everywhere'.[21] The direction in which young Egyptians will drive their society is yet to emerge.

CONCLUSION

Egypt's Different Worlds

KING AHMOSE, EFFECTIVELY the founder of Ancient Egypt's New Kingdom,[1] described his pharaonic mandate as 'maintaining order (*maat*) and averting chaos (*isfet*)'. Today, at the beginning of the second decade of the twenty-first century, three dynamics determine whether or not the country will fall into *isfet* or grab hold of its future and establish *maat*.

At the moment, any planning at the top of the Egyptian hierarchy for the period post-President Mubarak is shrouded in mystery. Since the 1952 coup that established Egyptian republicanism, the military establishment (the armed forces and the intelligence services) has provided the framework within which Egyptian presidents rule. Despite Nasser's popularity and appeal, Sadat's transformative changes and Mubarak's long reign, all three have relied on their military credentials, war-experience gravitas and the unquestioned support of the military establishment – the only institution in the country that is able to effect change by force – to buttress their rule. And in return, the three presidents have presented themselves (genuinely) as the 'sons' of the military establishment and, to a large extent, its representatives in leading the country. That positioning, though flexible (Nasser graduated from being a coup leader to the country's hero; Sadat changed his image from the victorious leader of the 1973 (Yom Kippur) war[2] to that of the president bringing peace and prosperity), underscored the power dynamics in the country. Egypt was arguably never a military dictatorship in the way a number of Latin American countries were from the 1960s to the 1980s; the military establishment never assumed the role of 'the guardian of the state', as was the case in Turkey. But though it never ruled per se (the presidents have always retained all power levers), the military establishment enjoyed a detached, exceptional status – ahead of and superior to any other organization in the country.[3]

That power dynamic has been shaken (though far from broken) over the past decade. The liberal capitalist elite, led by the president's son Gamal Mubarak, has emerged as a conspicuous power group working within the state, very rapidly rising within the regime's ranks and increasingly taking hold of entire power domains: economics (from the country's key resources – most notably the public sector – to strategic economic planning), finance (from internal and external trade to budgeting and fixed and monetary policies) and services (from education to health care, to transportation, to telecommunications). These sectors, though never (at least since the introduction of *al-infitah*) under the direct control of the military establishment, were, because of their importance, subject to its overarching sponsorship and supervision.

Throughout the 1960s, 1970s, 1980s and well into the 1990s, Egypt's National Security Council, which consists almost entirely of military and intelligence professionals, had expansive powers over vast areas of the country's public life. Throughout the 2000s, however, the liberal capitalist elite asserted not only its influence, but complete control over these areas. The change that the Egyptian economy and society witnessed in that decade (the economy's integration into global markets, the rise of financial services and capital markets, the real-estate boom and the increasing links to highly capitalist centres such as Dubai) widened the dimensions and reach of the liberal capitalists' power; they seemed to be at the forefront of the sectors shaping society's future. Increasingly, the capitalists appeared to have graduated into ruling partners, carving out for themselves specific power domains (in the areas directly affecting Egyptians' daily lives) and leaving to the military establishment only the areas of state sovereignty (defence, national security and foreign policy).

The balance of power between the military establishment and the liberal capitalist elite has only been achieved through the presence of President Mubarak. With his unrivalled influence and ability to pull any string, President Mubarak has ruled supreme; his presence and unsurpassed authority has indicated clearly (to the liberal capitalists) who is boss, which in turn has lessened any apprehension felt by the military establishment; he has maintained an exclusive veto on any potentially destabilizing economic policy; and frequently intervened (sometimes subtly, sometimes less so) to rein in some of the excesses of the liberal capitalists. But that balance is not sustainable, especially when President Mubarak leaves the scene.

Many observers in and outside of Egypt engage in creative scenario planning regarding power dynamics in Egypt post-Mubarak. But at the heart of most scenarios, one variable predominates: would the military establishment accept Gamal Mubarak as Egypt's next president? Is the military establishment willing to hand over the grasp on authority it has enjoyed for the past six decades to the liberal capitalist elite?

A number of factors could lead to that potential willingness. The military establishment, though the cornerstone of the Egyptian regime since 1952, has effectively been confined to barracks since the mid-1970s (with the end of the Yom Kippur War) and its influence restricted to issues of national security (and not much else) for more than a decade. There has also been a deliberate effort to ensure that the establishment is not breeding potential challengers, and so unlike the situation in the 1960s, for example (when Field Marshal Abdelhakim Amer, with far-reaching influence and popularity over the whole military establishment at the time, was the de facto supreme commander of the army), the Egyptian army is not now coalesced around a single strong man (or a small group of leaders) who can effect change. The military establishment has also enjoyed a rapid and rejuvenating flow of cadres which has resulted in relatively young leaders, with specialized mandates and limited areas of control and command, which have precluded the emergence of entrenched influences and power centres. And, most importantly, the establishment at its core (at the individual's level), and despite the benefits allocated to officers and army professionals which shelter them from the economic difficulties that most Egyptians confront, is a representative of the society's middle class, which is increasingly seeking change from the modus operandi that has governed the country for decades. These factors might lead the establishment to decide to refrain from imposing itself on the country's future, leaving the stage open for the group closest to the upper echelons of power: Gamal Mubarak and the liberal capitalist elite.

Regional changes could also encourage that outcome. Almost all military establishments in the region are opening up to civilian rule. In Turkey, the military establishment's most influential figures seem to be giving in to publicly elected politicians, even if they are of unmistakable Islamic orientation, such as the AK Party. In Israel, quasi-civilians such as Benjamin Netanyahu and Tzipi Livni seem to be assuming the leadership mantle from the military establishment's trusted sons, the generation of Shimon Peres and Ariel Sharon.

Yet other factors could lead to a different conclusion. Seeing the meteoric rise of the liberal capitalists over the past decade and sensing the middle class's resentment of the prevailing corruption and excesses that are linked to the liberal capitalists (and especially to leading members of the ruling National Democratic Party's elite), the military establishment might decide to refrain from imposing itself, yet lend its support – albeit subtly – to other contenders for the top job. Increasingly, there are established Egyptians with credible experience, gained and developed outside the country's framework, and therefore untainted by any real or perceived corruption, who are at considerable distance from the liberal capitalist elite in Egypt and who are putting themselves forward as potential presidential candidates – for example, Amr Mousa, the secretary general of the Arab League, and Mohamed Al-Baradei, the ex-director general of the International Atomic Energy Agency, in addition to a number of prominent figures in the country's civic arena. The genuine, almost intuitive, and substantial welcome that Al-Baradei received upon returning to Egypt in February 2010 might confirm to observers within the military establishment that vast sectors of Egyptian society (especially the young) yearn for new faces and a complete change. By subtly accepting either of these contenders (or another proven figure from outside the liberal capitalist camp), the military establishment would effectively be relinquishing its grasp on power and satisfying the middle class's desire to see real change, while, at the same time, vetoing the liberal capitalists' rise to power.

There are also a number of observers who argue that the country still has not developed its institutional base or educational and social infrastructure, and that it is therefore unable to handle genuine democracy or purely civilian rule. That view goes on to argue that the liberal capitalists, despite their apparent influence and far reach across the economy, draw all of their power from President Mubarak's support. And were that support to be lifted or withdrawn, the only way to avert the establishment of the Islamic Republic of Egypt (the Islamists winning in any free election held after President Mubarak leaves the scene) would be for the military to intervene, uphold the secular nature of the state and install its candidate as the country's new president – whether the ultra-influential General Omar Suleiman, the head of the General Intelligence Agency, or another respected and experienced general.

The military could also decide on a compromise: gracefully veto Gamal Mubarak's ascent to the presidency, install a temporary government of bureaucrats (or support the existing one led by the information-technology professional Dr Ahmed Nazif) and lead the way toward genuinely free elections. This scenario resembles the situation that developed in a similar country, Morocco, at a similar moment in history, a period of delicate political crossing from one era to another. In the last few months before his death in 1999 (and after his cancer was diagnosed as terminal), King Hassan II entrusted his government's premiership to Abdelrahman Al-Yousufi, a respected politician from outside the establishment that had ruled Morocco for decades and from outside the country's military and security forces. Choosing Al-Yousufi was seen as an attempt at placating the masses, sidelining very unpopular forces and sanctioning a new beginning in an effort to smooth the way for the transfer of power to the next King, Mohamed VI. The Egyptian military, acting as the warden of stability in the country, could decide to adopt a similar role.

These debates are twenty years late. As discussed in Chapter 6, President Mubarak came to the presidency to calm and soothe the nation after Nasser's and Sadat's tumultuous and radical changes. The end of President Mubarak's first term (at the end of the 1980s) or even the end of his second term (in the early 1990s) would have been ideal times for the country to engage in such debates on its future. President Mubarak could have established himself as the country's safe conduit from quasi-pharaonic times (Nasser's and Sadat's absolutism) towards a new era of civic institutionalization, detached from the reliance on the military establishment. But he did not. Now, the country must confront these issues and changes without his support. The delay, however, has had two benefits. After the long (and tough) fight with militant Islamism and the changes that the political Islamic movement has undergone, society is wiser than it was at the end of the 1980s or the early 1990s. The exacting price of the confrontation between the regime and militant Islamism has convinced most Egyptians of the need for smooth, peaceful change.

The society is also freer. Globalization, free media, satellite channels and the Internet have opened up the political debate; the fact that these debates and interactions will take place after President Mubarak (with his authority and power) leaves the scene means that refreshing views can be debated, free from the influence of a super powerful president; the rise of the private sector and the waves of creativity and civic activism that Egypt is currently experiencing will promote innovation and novelty in a political process that has been stagnant for decades. If the military establishment decides not to suppress this potential process for change, the society's dominant force (young Egyptians) will almost certainly shape its future; real political representation, the beginning of serious democracy, *could* commence.

There is much in Egyptian history and traditions that predisposes Egyptians to expect and accept authoritarian rule. The country has no experience of orderly transfer of power governed by an institutional system of checks and balances. Egyptian history teaches its readers that political stability in the country is best assured by a powerful, benign dictator. But the vigour of today's young Egyptians and their disillusionment with authority and recent history could mark a departure from that long-standing tradition and see the introduction of a people-led transformation.

The fact remains, however, that the dynamics at the top of Egypt's political hierarchy will be determined by the military establishment's course of action. After almost sixty years since the 1952 revolution against the country's 'corrupt political system' (the liberal experiment of monarchical Egypt), the country's institutional infrastructure is still unable to develop, let alone guarantee, a smooth and clear transfer of authority.

A number of observers believe that Egypt has completed 'a full circle': it has returned, after sixty years of failed experimentation, to staggering inequality, political paralysis, a potentially hereditary regime and an unstable situation in which the army holds the key levers of power. This view argues that this full circle, combined with the rising anger on the Egyptian street, could herald an era of chaos.

Potentially there are real triggers for chaos in Egyptian society today, as I have demonstrated throughout this book. Yet political disorder and the fall of the state remain very unlikely scenarios. The Egyptian regime, with its (so far) effective containment and confrontation modus operandi (and highly efficient security apparatuses), is controlling the street and the various manifestations of popular anger.

The real victim of the full circle, however, is the accumulated experience of society over the past six decades. The sense of rejection, especially among young Egyptians, of all of that has taken place from the 1950s to the 2000s could potentially leave society devoid of accrued wisdom – a monumental loss given society's very rich experience over the past 150 years. And, as discussed in Chapter 7, young Egyptians with different allegiances and worldviews are leaping over the past six decades and returning to earlier times (the days of nascent Egyptianism in the early years of the twentieth century) when society was trying to figure out its identity, frame of reference and direction. The journey over the past half century seems to have offered many lessons and created many scars, but has left the passengers today (especially young people) stranded at a junction, a fork in the road, pondering where to go from here. Egyptians are asking – themselves more than any specific political party – quo vadis?

The Islamists and the liberal capitalists, after their respective turns over the past decades, dominate the struggle for the hearts and minds of young Egyptians, and have ventured, through their different programmes, to answer society's question. Leading wings within the Islamic movement believe that the Islamists, plagued by the experience of militant Islamism from the 1970s to the 1990s and increasingly unable to mount an existentialist threat to the regime, should move towards a more liberal framework. Influenced by the seemingly successful Turkish experience under the AK Party in the 2000s, these wings advocate a return to the thinking of the liberal Islamists of the early decades of the twentieth century (most notably Sheikh Mohamed Abdou); they try to put together and advocate an overarching Islamic social umbrella, hoping that their new modus operandi and positioning will be perceived as a marriage between political Islam and the waves of creativity shaping tomorrow's society. The liberal capitalist elite, on the other side, in their continuous betting on an economic solution to society's problems, are championing as their own many of the younger Egyptians' initiatives (especially the remarkable waves of entrepreneurialism) and so in their own way also offer a framework for young Egyptians' inventiveness and enterprise.

But the Islamists' and the liberal capitalists' claim on young Egyptians' efforts is but political expediency, ignoring fundamental internal weaknesses on both sides. The liberal Islamists, at the time that their message is increasingly gaining resonance among the upper (and rich) segments of the youth sector and the middle class, are facing internal resistance (and at times outright hostility) from the more conservative wings in the Salafist movement (and especially within the Muslim Brotherhood). The enforced change in October 2009 at the Office of the Brotherhood's general guide as a result of the promotion of a number of liberal members to the supreme council is but the clearest example of the intellectual (and political) struggle within the Brotherhood. Those conservative wings cling to jihadist, confrontational and backward-looking views that are at odds with the demands and aspirations of a growing middle class and a forward-looking youth sector. To a large extent, today's Salafists seem to be making the exact same mistake that their predecessors in the 1920s and 1930s made: championing a move to the past at a time when the active forces in the society are eagerly looking to the future. The Brotherhood, in the words of the prominent Egyptian journalist Ibrahim Eissa, 'looks as if it has the body of a dinosaur and the brain of a bird'. That internal struggle consumes the energy of the liberal Islamists; they appear exhausted and cornered, unable to assume the mantle of leadership in a pulsating, young society.

On the liberal capitalists' side, there is growing concern and worry over the regime's ability to stand up to the mounting anger and frustration of the country's poor and middle class. And with colossal economic empires shooting up in different corners of the economy, increasing numbers of liberal capitalists are graduating from being beneficiaries of the regime's largesse into established powers with entrenched interests. Increasingly, some are repositioning themselves for a potentially different future – a potential weakening of the ruling elite of the NDP and lower chances of Gamal Mubarak securing the presidency. Over the past twelve months, a number of leading capitalist forces have diluted their links to the NDP; and some are considering running in national or municipal elections as independents as opposed to NDP candidates. Many established capitalist centres 'do not want to find [themselves] betting on yesterday's force or, worse, be considered guilty by association'.

The liberal capitalist elite also have a difficult positioning problem: their remaining at the top of the Egyptian scene entails an antiquated, almost tribal, hereditary transfer of power which flies in the face of the spirit of change and modernity that young Egyptians' endeavours represent. Some strategists within the NDP have proposed a new 'post-President Mubarak structure' where executive power is to be transferred from the presidency to the prime-ministerial office. In that structure, Gamal Mubarak would become Egypt's prime minister, leaving the then ceremonial presidency to a less-contentious figure. But that structure, as a number of NDP loyalists have rightly commented, is cosmetic. It does not solve the positioning dilemma of a hereditary transfer of power in a sixty-year-old republic, driven by young people with aspirations for genuine change.

And despite the 1990s economic reform programme and the 2000s' 'new thinking', the liberal capitalist elite's economic strategy remains without tangible effects on ordinary Egyptians' daily lives. Indeed, the conditions of the country's poor are excruciating, while the suffering of the middle class intensifies. It is difficult to envisage new programmes or thinking with any ground-breaking results in the short or medium terms. It seems that after more than thirty years since the introduction of *al-infitah* and the confluence of power and wealth, the law of diminishing returns has begun to bite.

And now that the challenges of the post-Mubarak period are increasingly difficult to ignore, the legitimacy problem discussed in Chapters 4 and 6 is pressing. A number of judges and movements within the country's judicial community have attacked the various constitutional changes that they believe were introduced to support the liberal capitalist movement.[4] Prominent members of the Judges' Club and leading constitutional experts have severely criticized the alteration of clauses 76 and 77 (which stipulate that presidential candidates should either be leaders of a party represented in the parliament or receive the endorsement of a significant quota of parliamentary legislators and members of municipal councils), which they believe were introduced to smooth Gamal Mubarak's route to the presidency.[5]

These internal pressures and challenges are very difficult to diffuse; and their dynamics are too complex to predict. They would be compounded, however, by external pressures brought upon by the departure of President Mubarak. As discussed in Chapter 6, Egypt's foreign policy over the past thirty years has been based on the decision to become a pillar of the Pax Americana in the Middle East. Mubarak's foreign policy never followed a populist course that focused on playing an (as it were) 'heroic' role. Rather, it has sought to become the Arab world's ultimate pragmatist, irrespective of the views of its citizens. This doctrine has been workable, despite immense popular rejection, because of President Mubarak's authority and control. The post-Mubarak administration – especially if it turns out to be a dynasty, headed by Gamal Mubarak – will be politically much more lightweight and have very limited military capital (even if the military establishment does not veto its installation) to adopt a similar strategy. The administration would also have no illusions about the real dynamics of power – military, economic, political – in the Middle East.

The situation in Israel will compound the problem, for the character of decision-making there is changing. The founding generation that witnessed the creation of Israel as a tiny, vulnerable state has left or is leaving the scene – the eighty-five-year-old Shimon Peres (who won election to the ceremonial presidency in mid-2007) is its last prominent figure. That Israeli generation, which lived through the wars of the 1940s to the 1970s – when Egypt was Israel's greatest threat – recognized the invaluable strategic gain to be made in sidelining its giant neighbour. Israel's more recent ruling generation has not experienced the difficult years of 1948–73; has not fought a real war against a serious, sizable enemy; has never seen Israel in serious danger; does not share the wisdom of its predecessor; and is haughtily aware of Israel's unrivalled power (economic, scientific and, of course, military) in the region. It is more than capable of using every opportunity to exercise this power, especially at a time when the Arab world seems exposed and helpless. That was as evident in the Gaza War as it was in the war in Lebanon in the summer of 2006. In both cases, the unapologetic use of extreme violence reflected Israel's awareness of its own power and its opponent's feebleness. How would Gamal Mubarak's untested administration – with a very tenuous legitimacy – respond if and when Israel acts in similar fashion against the Palestinians (again) or Lebanese or Syrians – or indeed Iranians?

Maintaining the regime's traditionally pragmatic course will be far from easy. The new administration might find itself compelled to respond to pressure applied by the masses (and by its internal opponents, mainly the Islamists). The administration might increasingly detach itself from the highly pragmatic foreign-policy doctrine, and adopt a gradually confrontational approach. That is already happening. In the midst of the Iranian nuclear dilemma, Gamal Mubarak sponsored an initiative to build 'Egypt's own nuclear capability'; and even in the wake of the silly confrontations in November 2009 between Egyptians and Algerians after their World Cup qualifying football match, Gamal Mubarak took a noticeably hawkish stand, aligning himself with sentiments on the street.

This hawkishness has a precedent in Egyptian foreign policy. In the early 1950s, in the midst of its internal meltdown and evaporating popularity, Al-Wafd (and more specifically a wing very close to Mustafa Al-Nahas) sought a diversion in a forceful (some would argue aggressive) foreign policy. Al-Nahas' foreign minister, Mohamed Salah-El-Din, brought the negotiations with the British to an end a number of times. Al-Wafd almost sanctioned the military insurgency against the British in the Suez Canal region. And for the first time, Al-Wafd seemed open to Egypt's involvement with the 'problem in Palestine'.[6]

Opportunity could also bring about a change in Egyptian foreign policy. Today the Middle East's geostrategic scene is empty. Saudi Islamism has long retreated; the Israeli Middle Eastern project fell because of the realities of the Israeli–Palestinian conflict. With the disappearance of King Hussein, Hafez Al-Assad and Yasser Arafat, and the internal political civil war between Palestinian leaders, the Levant lacks any unifying figure or political force. Iraq is effectively divided into three political entities and its fraught situation will keep it consumed with its internal problems for many years to come. Iran is embroiled in its confrontation with the West over its nuclear programme as well as its internal tensions, and, because of its Shi'ite identity and the wounds of its war against Iraq, its reach in the heart of the

Arab world remains (and will continue to be) very limited. Turkey is arguably the one rising player in the Middle East. But modern Turkey is not the Ottoman Empire; Turkey's aspiration to join the European Union, the internal social strains between the secularists and the Islamists, and the fact that Turkey is a staunch ally of the United States and the second largest professional army in NATO, would limit its involvement in the Middle East. This emptiness could seduce the new Egyptian administration to seek diversions and breathing spaces in an energetic, different foreign policy that would mobilize the people, coalescing them behind rousing stances, and confer legitimacy.

It is very unlikely that Egypt's new administration, especially if it was led by Gamal Mubarak, would adopt a foreign policy that would antagonize the United States, let alone jeopardize the Egyptian–Israeli peace treaty. And it is almost inconceivable that such an administration would undertake hard-line positions especially in the context of the Arab-Israeli conflict – not only because it would be a stark move away from the country's modus operandi over the past thirty-five years, but also because the tenuous legitimacy of the administration (and its increasing confrontation with various forces inside the country) would necessarily deepen the dependence on the United States' approval and tacit support. Also the tenets of liberal capitalism in Egypt (open markets, free trade and of course intricate – and, in many cases, personal – economic interests) necessitate stability and integration in the world economy, rather than confrontation and antagonism.

And as such, the regime's political schemes continue to espouse its pragmatist doctrine. Some political observers close to the NDP repeatedly cast the regime's siding with the United States against Iran as protecting Arabism and Egypt's 'strategic role in the Arab world' against 'Persian intrusion' and Iran's 'exporting of the revolution'. Also Egypt's passive role in the Gaza War in December 2008/January 2009 and the continuous closure of the Rafah border crossing is presented as 'secular Egypt' – the pillar of the Arabic (as opposed to Islamic) project – 'controlling' the activities of 'loose jihadist agents' (Hamas) working for 'countries with expansive agendas' (Iran).

But the regime's foreign-policy rhetoric (and calculations) aside, the current emptiness in the Middle East's geostrategic scene does indeed present Egypt with a historic opportunity to resuscitate its 'project in the Arab world', the defining feature of its foreign policy and regional role. Despite Egypt's closeness to Israel over the past few years, almost all serious Palestinian leaders look to Egypt to direct an acceptable reconciliation between the fractious factions. The weighty voices inside the Palestinian Liberation Organization, after two decades of fruitless negotiations with Israel, are revisiting 'the Palestinian Option' (defining their conflict as a Palestinian, as opposed to Arab, problem); increasingly they are returning to the notion that their predicament is, indeed, the Arab central struggle, that their limited resources fail to confront Israel and that Egypt, with its demographic size and intrinsic leadership role, should be at the centre of managing the conflict. In Syria, Bashar Al-Assad, still a long way from his late father's power and influence and crammed in between a perilous inherited alliance with Iran and a dangerous vulnerability to Israel, is subtly trying to mend his regime's relationship with Egypt. A working relationship with Egypt (with its strategic weight and – relatively – better reach in Washington and a number of European capitals) could improve Syria's positioning and hedge against the exposure to Israel. Also in the Levant, a number of key Lebanese players (from Walid Jumblatt, the Druze's leader, to Saad Al-Hariri, the Sunni prime minister), after experimenting with an American–Saudi alliance that promised them revenge for the murder of prime minister

Rafik Al-Hariri in 2005 and a power base to confront Hezbollah, have realized that their gamble has not paid off. An engaged, but not intrusive, Egyptian role seems to them (and to many of their advisors who reminisce about 'Nasser's golden days') the 'perfect equalizer' between America's incentivizations and Iran's intimidations. In the Arab Maghreb, the renewed tensions in Algeria (especially given the uncertainty over the period post the ailing President Boutaflika), a similar situation in Tunisia and Gaddafi's continuously purposeless forays in international relations all call upon Egypt's guiding role in the region and summon its presence. Interestingly, Gaddafi keeps reminding his listeners of Egypt's galvanising sway.

Egypt's foreign policy also faces threats that could incentivize the country's next administration to look for a new direction. Egypt's over-zealousness in becoming a pillar of the Pax Americana has alienated the Arab streets. In 2009, Egypt's embassies in Yemen and Jordan were attacked by protestors. In Lebanon, a number of the country's leading politicians publicly blamed Egypt for the suffering of Gazans. Al-Jazeera, the highly influential pan-Arab TV station, broadcast a number of programmes on 'the absence of Egyptian role'.[7] The threats extend beyond 'brand Egypt' to some of the country's most vital interests. In April 2010, six of the River Nile source countries signed an agreement that effectively challenges Egypt's 'historical rights' to more than 50 per cent of the Nile's water and its veto over any upstream project. Egypt refused to sign or even acknowledge the agreement. Now, the country faces a major challenge of immense strategic importance: how to confront the signatories to that agreement and what to do about it – a challenge that the country's diplomacy and decision makers have ignored for decades. Egyptian foreign policy faces embarrassing situations as well. In the mid-2000s, Egypt's regime repeatedly stated that the country is a claimant to a permanent

Security Council seat. Now it appears that were Africa to get a permanent seat, it would most likely be South Africa's. And whereas Brazil, South Africa, Turkey, and Saudi Arabia are regular attendees at the G20 conferences, Egypt is hardly ever invited.

Changes in the regional landscape also augment the prospects of a new foreign policy. China is increasingly a major importer from and investor in Egypt. Its expanding companies are among the largest employers in the country. In telecommunications and information technology, for example, two Chinese companies are the employer of choice of some of the best Egyptian engineers. Chinese development banks are actively seeking financing opportunities in the country's flourishing and growing infrastructure sectors; China Africa Development Fund is increasingly a leading investor in the country. China is building Egypt's largest industrial park. Russia is also charting its re-entry into the Middle East. Russians are among the largest real-estate investors in the Gulf and increasingly in Egypt's Red Sea region. The country is now Egypt's number-one tourism market. A number of Russian investment banks featured regularly in mega Egyptian deals in the mid- and late 2000s, especially in the energy sector. China's and Russia's increasing presence in Egypt (and other parts of the Middle East and Africa) will gradually alter the country's geostrategic outlook. The next Egyptian administration could conceive a new course in a regional scene that will be less dominated by the United States, and therefore more accommodating of the classic Egyptian project.

The next administration's foreign policy (especially if it was headed by Gamal Mubarak) would be a highly difficult balancing act between, on one side, the need to placate the 'street' and avoiding, as much as possible, an embarrassing exposition of the regime's dependence on the United States or (from the street's standpoint) lack of resolve, and on the other side, maintaining the liberal capitalist doctrine with its needs for stability, away from any assertive regional role, geostrategic opportunities or historical echoes. Foreign policy might become just another major challenge for the liberal capitalist elite – exacerbating their legitimacy dilemma and aggravating the predicament of how to secure their ascent to power (and maintaining it) without relying entirely on coercion, confrontation and containment.

On almost every front, the liberal capitalist elite seem to be pushing the boundaries of normalcy: a hereditary power transfer in a republic; an extension of an almost thirty-year-old reign notwithstanding deafening calls for change; an alliance of money and power in the face of pervasive poverty and a distressed middle class; an unpopular foreign-policy doctrine without the foundations for endorsing (or even selling) it; and a self-proclaimed mandate amid a sea of rejection and an evaporating legitimacy. The ruling elite are not even trying to ingratiate themselves with the enraged masses. As Robert Fisk, the most renowned of Middle East correspondents, once put it: 'can a regime survive without some form of acknowledgement of sins past?'

This approach strains society at a time when its dominant force (young Egyptians) is striving to transcend the difficulties of the present and build better lives and futures. The ruling elite, with their quest for power, are effectively hindering society from progressing, positioning themselves against its interests, further attenuating their legitimacy and placing themselves (and society) in a vicious circle.

It is regrettable that, after the various experiments of the past hundred years, Egyptian society finds itself in this position. The vicious circle could continue; the society's winds of change could lose their force; and, as was the case with the liberal experiment in the early twentieth century, young Egyptians' enterprise and creativity could disintegrate into disparate endeavours unable to coalesce into the foundations of a sizable and engaged middle class; and once again society would miss a historic opportunity for fundamental change.

But that need not happen. Whether as a result of free elections, the internal confrontations between the different political movements, the military establishment's decision to step back or the attractions and calls of a historic opportunity to resuscitate Egypt's strategic role in the Middle East, society could potentially manage to solve the dilemma that the ruling elite have created for the country (and for themselves). As discussed at the end of Chapter 7, the increased role of the private sector and thereby economic independence from the state, the rise of the civic society, new exposure and development within traditionally deprived classes, the different innovations in business, culture and the arts and the creative initiatives in social work and philanthropy could (with time) bring about an expansion in society's middle class, enable it to build real stakes in its society and as such be incentivized to effect change in a smooth and peaceful way. Young Egyptians, in their efforts to make sense of the unfortunate present they have inherited and build a promising future of their own, could conceive a new Egyptian project.

Egypt is in dire need of that new project. Mohamed Ali's ambition to build a state for his family ushered in modern Egypt but ended when the Pasha's descendants' dreams went beyond their state's resources and capacities. The early twentieth-century liberal experiment took the state from Mohamed Ali's family and (at least in theory) gave it to the people, and the country enjoyed the beginnings of democracy, true representation, constitutionalism and crucially the notion of equal rights and obligations in contemporary citizenship. But the experiment crumbled when its leaders detached themselves from the realities of their constituency and nurtured the illusion of a 'Paris on the Nile'.

Nasser, unlike his predecessors, built a project 'by, for and of the people', the first truly Egyptian developmental enterprise since the fall of the pharaonic state. But by centring his efforts on his 'heroic role', Nasser failed his people. Lacking an institutional support base, the project disintegrated when the hero fell.

In the last thirty years, the Egyptian regime has aimed to transform the country by embracing a distorted form of liberal capitalism and a relentlessly realist world outlook. The former is on the verge of blowing up from the internal pressures of poverty and anger and the latter seems lost in an avalanche of rejection and resentment, the tail end of which Egypt is still experiencing. Now, after more than three decades without a direction, a consensus or even a dream, the country needs a new project. The waters of the Nile that slink between muddy banks and twirl through creamy sand have been stagnant for a long time; the 'eternal brown land' needs a deluge of energy. Young Egyptians need to chart their route to the future.

In her novel *The Cairo House*,[8] Samia Serageldin reflects that 'for those whose past and present belong to different worlds, there are places and times that mark their passage from one to the other, a transitional limbo'. Egypt today is in such a transitional limbo. The hope is that its future will be a different world from its recent past and present.

NOTES

Introduction

1. Artemis Cooper, *Cairo in the War: 1939–1945* (Penguin Books, 1998).
2. *The Economist*, 'A Special Report on the New Middle Classes in Emerging Markets', 12 February 2009, which drew on Carol Graham's 'Patterns of Middle Class Consumption in India and China', World Economics, July–September 2005.
3. Paul Amar and Diane Singerman (eds), *Cairo Cosmopolitan: Politics, Culture, and Urban Space in the New Globalised Middle East* (The American University in Cairo Press, 2006).
4. This is not based on an official statistic, but on the observation of a medical professional with a long history at the Mayo Clinic.
5. *Sunday Times*, 19 October 2008.
6. Mohammed El-Erian, Co-Chief Executive Officer and Chief Investment Officer of PIMCO, the world's largest manager of fixed-income funds. El-Erian's book *When Markets Clash* won the Financial Times/Goldman Sachs Best Business Book Award in 2008.

Chapter 1: Egypt's World

1. The Mamelukes ('*owned*' in classical Arabic) were slave soldiers brought to Egypt by the Ayyubids. They were raised, educated and trained as professional soldiers whose loyalty was exclusive to the Sultan. Over time, and especially towards the end of the Ayyubid Empire, the Mamelukes became Egypt's most powerful military caste. Always consumed with internal fighting, the Mamelukes never established a state or a dynastic empire. They ruled Egypt, however, from 1250 to 1517 (when the Ottoman Sultan Selim I conquered

Egypt and the Levant after his victory over Sultan Al-Ghouri in Marg-dabek). To a large extent, the story of the Makelukes in Egypt resembles that of the Janissaries within the Ottoman Empire. Thomas Philipp (ed.), *The Mamlukes in Egyptian History and Politics*, published in 1998 as part of the Cambridge Studies in Islamic Civilisation, provides a concise yet comprehensive account of their era. Old Cairo, and especially Al-Moaz Street, features a large number of monuments erected by Mameluke sultans.

2. See G. Baer's *A History of Landownership in Modern Egypt: 1800–1950* (Oxford University Press, 1962), and Assem Desouki's "Large Landowners in Egypt", Dar Al-Shorouk, Cairo, 2006.

3. Caroline Fenkel, *Osman's Dream: The Story of the Ottoman Empire* (John Murray, 2005) and M.W. Daly (ed.), *The Cambridge History of Egypt*, Volume 2: *Modern Egypt from 1517 to the End of the Twentieth Century* (Cambridge University Press, 1998) offer two different views of that period's dynamics – the first focuses on how the Ottomans viewed Egypt at the time; the second on the details of the situation in Egypt.

4. In Arabic, Dar Al-Maaref, Cairo, 1984.

5. The various writings of Khaled Fahmy (at the history department of New York University) are a detailed source on Mohamed Ali's reign. See *All the Pasha's Men: Mohamed Ali and the Making of Modern Egypt* (The American University in Cairo Press, 2002).

6. Egyptians are ambivalent towards the French expedition. On the one hand, it is indisputable that the campaign, and especially the scores of scientists and administrators that Napoleon had brought with him from France, triggered the waves of modernity that Egypt witnessed throughout the nineteenth century. On the other hand, there is a strong hostility to it as a violent occupation. Invariably, Egyptian history books, especially in educational syllabi, emphasize the French 'insensitivity to Egyptian sensibilities', and stress the people's defiance and 'the flame of resistance that flared up in Cairo against the occupiers'. State history books also point out that though the French 'opened the door to modernity', it was the Egyptians' self-reliance and ingenuity that launched the country on the development trajectory.

7. Khedive Abbas and Khedive Said ruled in the fifteen years between Mohamed Ali's death and Ismael's accession to the throne. Zein-Al-Abdedeen Nigm's *Egypt During Abbas's and Said's Reigns* (in Arabic, Dar Al-Shorouk, 2007) recounts those fifteen years.

8. Samir Raafat's *Cairo: The Glory Days* (Harpocrates, Alexandria, 2003) discusses the architectural jewels of the era. Galila El-Kadi and Dalila El-Kerdany's 'The Politics of Refurbishing the Downtown Business District', in Paul Amar and Diane Singerman (eds), *Cairo Cosmopolitan*, discusses the different Egyptian and international attempts at preserving those jewels.

9. Dr Younan Rizk's several studies on monarchical Egypt and the writings of Dr Mursi Saad El-Deen in *Al-Ahram* are expansive sources on the period of Ismael's reign.

10. Based on Ilias Ayoubi's *Egypt during the Reign of Khedive Ismael* (in Arabic, Cairo, 1923).

11. Based on 'Social Change in the Nineteenth Century', in Helen Metz's *Egypt: A Country Study*, a report commissioned by the Library of Congress in 1990.

12. See Robert Hunter's 'Egypt Under the Successors of Mohamed Ali', in M.W. Daly (ed.), *The Cambridge History of Egypt*, Volume 2.

13. For more information, see Hassan Ibrahim's 'The Egyptian Empire: 1805–1885', in Daly (ed.), *The Cambridge History of Egypt*, Volume 2 and Caroline Fenkel's *Osman's Dream*.

14. Abdullah Al-Nadeem was Egypt's most prominent orator in the 1880s. See Radwan Al-Kashef's *Freedom and Justice in the Thought of Abdallah Al-Nadeem*, General Egyptian Book Organisation, Cairo, 2005.

15. The 1923 constitution remains a highly debatable topic in Egypt. For some, it represents the epitome of Egypt's liberal democratic experiment. To others, especially the Nasserite camp, it was a facade for the control of Egypt's monarchy and major landowners.

16. Any serious study of Egypt's liberal experiment or of the Arabs' early encounter with Europe would study the thinking and role of Sheikh Al-Tahtawi. Ira Lapidus's *A History of Islamic Societies* (Cambridge University Press, 1988) and M. Moaddel's *Islamic Modernism, Nationalism, and Fundamentalism: Episode and Discourse* (Chicago University Press, 2005) tackle the impact of the Sheikh's thinking in different contexts and compare him to other modernists. The writings of Gamal Al-Banna (an Islamist writer in Egypt) are an example of a modern liberal Islamist's view of Sheikh Al-Tahtawi's ideas. Mohamed Emara's *Sheikh Refae Al-Tahtawi* (in Arabic, Dar Al-Shorouk, 2007) is a journey into Al-Tahtawi's role in modernizing Islamic thinking and guiding it in its early encounters with Europe.

17. See Caroline Fenkel's *Osman's Dream*.

18. Though there is a wealth of Arabic sources on Mohamed Abdou's thinking (for example, the work of Dr Mohamed Emara on Islamic rationality), there appears to be a dearth of English-language sources on Abdou and his work. In the series *Making of Sociology*, published by Routledge in 2000, Volume 6, Bryan Turner presents a detailed view of how the Western world viewed Mohamed Abdou's thinking. Also the writings of Rachid Al-Ghanouchi, a Tunisian Islamic scholar, present an expansive and insightful assessment of Sheikh Mohamed Abdou's ideas. Ghanouchi's writings are especially interesting because he represents a very progressive, yet highly politicized, school of thought within the Islamic movement in the Arab world. Al-Ghanouchi was a political exile in London for many years.

19. In his *The End of a Regime* (in Arabic, Dar Al-Shorouk, 2002), Mohamed Hassanein Heikal elaborates on the foundations and manifestations of Egypt's seductive soft power. Artemis Cooper's *Cairo in the War* provides an interesting portrait of the cosmopolitanism of the Cairene social scene at the height of Egypt's liberal experiment.

20. The marriage of King Farouk's sister, Princess Fawzia, to Iran's then Crown Prince Mohamed Reza Pahlavi. Rawia Rashed's *Nazi, a Queen in Exile* (in Arabic, Nara Publishing, Cairo, 2008) recounts the story of the royal marriage in detail.

21. Ali Maher Pasha was the most notable of those. See Mohamed Al-Gawadi's *Ali Maher Pasha and the End of Egyptian Liberalism* (in Arabic, Dar Al-Shorouk, Cairo, 2009).

22. Malak Badrawi's 'The Egyptian Parliament: 1924–1952', in Arthur Goldschmidt, Amy Johnson and Barak Salmoni (eds), *Re-Envisioning Egypt: 1919–1952* (The American University in Cairo Press, 2005) presents a number of those parliamentary rows with a focus on the state's finances.

23. Afaf Lutfi Al-Sayyad-Marsot's *Egypt's Liberal Experiment* (University of California Press, 1977) remains the quintessential source on the period's

politics. Abdesalam Al-Maghraoui's *Liberalism without Democracy: Nationhood and Citizenship in Egypt, 1922–1936* (Duke University Press, 2006) provides an analytical view of how the period's political system established liberalism but failed to achieve real democracy and representation in society. Anshuman Mondal's *Nationalism and Post-Colonial Identity* (Routledge, 2003) is an interesting study (on Egypt and India), but it focuses on only two aspects of that experiment: how Egyptian liberalism was detached from Islam and how that detachment resulted in a 'crisis in Egyptian secular liberal nationalism'; and how liberalism influenced Egyptian literature in the 1920s, 1930s, and 1940s, especially the works of Tawfik Al-Hakeem and Naguib Mahfouz. Israel Gershoni's and James Jankowski's *Egypt, Islam, and the Arabs: The Search for Egyptian Nationhood 1900–1930* (Oxford University Press, 1986) focuses on Egyptian liberalism from a political angle and how the dynamics of that rich period were pulling the Egyptian identity in different directions. It is interesting, however, that the international library still lacks a serious book on the story of Al-Wafd and how it embodied the political facet of the period's liberal experiment – and how and why that venerable political party failed to keep the momentum of its founding fathers and descended into just another political party controlled by large landowners.

24. See 'Social Change in the Nineteenth Century', in Helen Metz, *Egypt: A Country Study*; Joel Beinin's *The Dispersion of Egyptian Jewry* (The American University in Cairo Press, 2005); and Ayman Zohry's *Armenians in Egypt*, a study presented at the 2005 International Union for the Scientific Study of Population.

25. Abdel Wahab (1907–91) is considered by many to be Egypt's greatest musician.

26. A Syrian–Lebanese singer, composer and virtuoso oud player, Al-Attrash (1915–74) is considered one of the greatest Arab musicians; his career boasted a large number of highly successful movies.

27. Umm Kulthoum (who was dubbed 'the planet of the Orient') is Egypt's and the Arab world's most famous and distinguished singer.

28. Esmat Dawestashi's *Mahmoud Saeed* (in Arabic, Cairo, 1999) is a comprehensive source on Saeed and how his work managed to capture the 'layering' of Egyptian society at the time.

29. In Arabic, Dar Al-Maaref, Cairo, 1938.

30. Many books have studied Hussein's role in the Egyptian liberal experiment, but few have ventured to study Hussein's intellectual journey and his invaluable contributions to 'the search for Egypt's identity' and Islamic thinking. Megahed Megahed's *A Journey in the Thinking of Taha Hussein* (in Arabic, Dar Al-Thaqafi Lel-Nashr wal-Tarzee, 2001) is a rigorous study of his work. Albert Hourani's *Arabic Thought in the Liberal Age: 1798–1939* (Cambridge University Press, 1983) puts Hussein's thinking in the context of the era's cultural and intellectual flow, and links his thinking to that of other icons of the liberal movement.

31. Mustafa Al-Nahas Pasha, leader of Al-Wafd Party from the 1930s to the 1950s, had a number of debates with leading Salafists, including Sheikh Hassan Al-Banna, the founder of the Muslim Brotherhood, in which Al-Nahas emphasized that liberal, constitutional democracy is the embodiment of Islam's 'good governance'.

32. Judge Tariq Al-Bishri studied that period and Al-Wafd's assertion of nationalism (uniting Muslims and Christians together) in *Democracy in the Framework*

of the Nationalist Movement and *The Muslims and the Copts* (in Arabic, Kitab
Al-Hilal, Cairo, 2005).

33. Mohamed Hassanein Heikal's *The End of a Regime* presents a concise yet
insightful view of the transformations that Al-Wafd and the Palace underwent
at the time.

34. We discuss the social inequality that Egypt suffered in the 1930s and 1940s of
the twentieth century in Chapter 2: Nasser and Arab Nationalism. For a detailed
view of the Egyptian economy in that period and its development under Nasser,
see Khalid Imran's *The Egyptian Economy: 1952–2000* (Routledge, 2006).

35. See Magda Baraka's *The Egyptian Upper Class between Revolution 1919–1952*
(Ithaca Press, Reading, 1998).

36. The story of King Farouk, and how he fell from grace as a symbol of hope and
nationalism when he ascended to the throne in 1936 to being seen as a corrupt
monarch, is a moving drama. Dr Latifa Salem's *Farouk from the beginning to the
end* (in Arabic, Dar Al-Shorouk, Cairo, 2005) recounts the political background of his reign. Karim Thabet's *Memoirs: Farouk as I Knew Him* (in Arabic,
Dar Al-Shorouk, Cairo, 2000) provides an account of Farouk's character, from
one of the late King's closest advisors (though the account is hardly flattering).
Mohamed Heikal's *The End of a Regime* covers the personal as well as political
reasons behind the King's descent.

37. For a detailed review of that sad incident, see Anne-Claire Kerbouef's 'The
Cairo Fire of 26 January 1952', in Arthur Goldschmidt, Amy Johnson and
Barak Salmoni (eds), *Re-envisioning Egypt: 1919–1952*. On the fiftieth anniver-
sary of the Cairo Fire, 30 January 2002, *Al-Ahram Weekly* published an expan-
sive report on it with Maurice Guindi giving a personal witness account and
Fayza Hassan investigating who was behind it.

Chapter 2: Nasser and Arab Nationalism

1. The numbers in this paragraph are mostly drawn from Dr Assem Al-Desoky's
Major Landowners in Egypt: 1914–1952 (in Arabic, Dar Al-Shorouk, Cairo,
2007). Part of Al-Desoky's work has been conducted alongside Dr Roger
Owen at St Antony's College, Oxford University.

2. Salah Jahin (1930–86) is generally known for the nationalistic (mainly
Nasserite) songs that he wrote throughout the 1950s and 1960s, to the extent
that many dubbed him 'the revolution's poet'. But Jahin, alongside a number
of other poets (most prominently Abdelrahman Al-Abnudi and Sayyid Higab),
pioneered colloquial Arabic poetry. Jahin's most famous work is 'Al-Rubayiat'
in which he expressed his views on a vast number of topics.

3. The High Dam, which was built between 1955 and 1970, is Egypt's key
modern engineering accomplishment. Before it was built, the Nile flooded the
valley each year; following its building, Egypt began to manage the flow and
reservation of the Nile water. The Dam is roughly 4km long, 1km wide at the
base and 40m wide at the crest, and stands 111m tall. It comprises more than
40 million cubic metres of material. It manages around 10,000 cubic metres of
water per second (in high season), in addition to having three main reservoirs,
of which Lake Nasser is the largest.

4. See D. Turnham's *The Employment Problem in Less Developed Countries: A
Review of Evidence*, published in the OECD's 1971 Economic Development

Papers. Between 1960 and 1970, employment across 'all manufacturing sectors' grew faster than during any period from 1947 to 1985 (Norman Gemmell, 'The Growth in Employment in Services in Egypt', *Developing Economies*, vol. 23, issue 1, 1985). The percentage of general employment in agriculture went down by around 12 per cent in roughly the same period.

5. Khalid Imran's *The Egyptian Economy* is an extensive source on the different cycles through which the Egyptian economy has passed in the past five decades. Interestingly, one of the very insightful studies on the Egyptian economy during Nasser's era was conducted at Ben-Gurion University in the Negev in Israel, by Suleiman Abu Bader and Aamer Abu Qarn at the University's Department of Economics. Another (more comprehensive) Israeli-linked study on Nasser is Shimon Shamir's *Egypt from Monarchy to Republic* (Westview Press, 1995).

6. There are many studies on the Suez Crisis. From a Western standpoint, the memories of Sir Anthony Eden, *Full Circle* (Cassell, London, 1960) and Sir Anthony Nutting's *Nasser* (E.P. Dutton, London, 1972) provide an inside record of how the key participants viewed not only the war, but Nasser's entire project. From an Egyptian standpoint, Mohamed Hassanein Heikal's *Cutting the Lion's Tail* (Andre Deutsch, London, 1986) is a comprehensive account from Nasser's closest advisor.

7. Said Aburish's *Nasser: The Last Arab* (Thomas Dunne Books, 2004) traces the development of Nasser's appeal within and without the Arab World, throughout the 1950s and 1960s.

8. Education at Al-Azhar was governed by Al-Azhar Law of 1910 that organized its curricula, examinations and the state's recognition of its certificates.

9. Abdallah Imam's *Nasser and the Muslim Brotherhood* (in Arabic, Dar Al-Mawqif Al-Arabi, 1986) is a detailed account of Nasser's struggle with the Brotherhood.

10. Mohamed Heikal's *Nasser: The Cairo Documents* (New English Library, 1972), though not necessarily an analysis of Nasser's relationship with the United States, provides a comprehensive view of how the entire Nasserite project was destined to clash with US interests in the Middle East. Charles Glass's *The Tribes Triumphant* (Harper Press, 2006) and Lawrence Freedman's *A Choice of Enemies: America Confronts the Middle East* (Weidenfeld & Nicolson, 2008) offer relatively updated views of US interests in the Middle East. Freedman's book touches, in more detail, on how the United States has traditionally viewed the threat of a united Arab world.

11. Yevgeny Primakov's *The Middle East: The Known and the Unknown* (in Arabic, Dar Iskandaroun, 2006).

12. Said Aburish details the story in *Nasser*.

13. Avi Shlaim's *The Iron Wall: Israel and the Arab World* (W.W. Norton & Co., 1999) is a comprehensive view of the development of Israeli foreign policy (and strategic thinking) throughout the last century (going back to the period before Israel's creation, when the International Jewish Agency was spear-heading the 'Zionist Project').

14. For a detailed review of the story of the Six-Day War, see Michael Oren's *Six Days of War: June 1967 and the Making of the Modern Middle East* (Oxford University Press, 2002).

15. From Kabbani, 'Marginal Notes in the Book of Defeat', first published in *Al-Adab* magazine, Beirut, August 1967. Translation from fen.wordpress.com, adapted by author.

16. Michael Oren's *Six Days of War* delves into the differences in the 'strategic relationships' between Israel and the United States on one side and Egypt and

the USSR on the other. Heikal's *The Sphinx and the Commissar* (HarperCollins, 1978) tells the story of the Soviet's engagement with the Arabs in general and the Arab nationalist project in particular.

17. A Nasserite doctrine stipulating that at least 50 per cent of all parliamentary seats are reserved for candidates running as either 'peasants' or 'labourers'. Not surprisingly, the system was repeatedly abused in the following decades. For example, a business millionaire would run as 'a labourer' on the premise of 'owning a factory in which he works'. The validity of the doctrine in today's capitalist times has been one of the major debatable and contentious issues in parliamentary discussions.

Chapter 3: The Islamists

1. This paragraph draws on information and descriptions in the *New York Times'* and *Ahram Weekly*'s coverage of Sheikh Sharaawi's funeral.

2. Most notably those of Al-Imam Al-Hussein, the Prophet's grandson and Al-Shia's most venerated Imam, in Fatimid Cairo; Al-Sayyda Zainab, Al-Hussein's sister in Cairo as well; Al-Sayyed Al-Badawi in Tanta in the heart of the Nile Delta; Al-Morsi Abu-Al-Abbas in Alexandria; and Ibrahim Al-Desouki in Desouk. See Anna Madoeuf's 'Mulids of Cairo', in Paul Amar and Diane Singerman (eds), *Cairo Cosmopolitan*. Salah Jaheen's and Sayed Mikawi's operetta *Al-Leila Al-Kabeera* is the most popular artistic expression of the Egyptian Mwaled. For a view on the origins (and accuracy) of the accounts behind Ahl-Al-Bayt's mosques in Cairo, see John Renard's *Friends of God: Islamic Images of Piety, Commitment, and Servanthood* (University of California Press, 2008).

3. Valerie Hoffman's *Sufism, Mystics, and Saints in Egypt* (University of South Carolina Press, 1995) studies Egypt's Shi'ite heritage.

4. Mohammed Ayoub and Hasan Kosebalaban (eds), *Religion and Politics in Saudi Arabia* (Lynne Rienner Publishers, 2008) and Madawi Al-Rasheed (ed.), *Kingdom without Borders* (Hurst, 2008) recount the story of Wahhabism's religious expansionism.

5. Nashwa Al-Hoofi, an Egyptian journalist, conducted a study on the subject, which was published in *Al-Sharq Al-Awsat* newspaper in November 2006. The study highlights the fact that most Egyptian women, due to their economic conditions, cannot keep pace with fashion or afford regular visits to hairdressers, and as such the veil becomes an economically attractive option. Also, the highly condensed neighbourhoods with very limited, if any, private space necessitate more modesty. *A Veiled Revolution*, a film made by Elizabeth Fernea in 1982 as part of a study titled 'Reformers and Revolutionaries: Middle Eastern Women' (funded by the UK's National Endowment for the Humanities and Channel 4), features interviews with women from different walks of life and their personal feelings about 'the meaning of the veil'. Shereen Abu-Al-Naga's *Al-Hijab between the Local and the Global* (in Arabic, Arab Cultural Centre, 2008) is an expansive study on the subject.

6. The late 1970s and 1980s witnessed the emergence of a large number of influential writers and commentators advocating 'women's return to their rightful kingdom: the home'. Sheikh Al-Sharaawi blessed the trend. The Islamic female scholar Zaynab Al-Ghazali asserted the different roles of the two

genders in society and offered examples from the Koran to emphasize gender equality, yet also the natural different social preoccupations of the two sexes. Yvonne Haddad and John Esposito's *Islam, Gender, and Social Change* (Oxford University Press, 1998) discusses the topic in detail.

7. Based on the *New York Times'* series of articles 'Stalled Lives', serialized in the first half of 2008.

8. Gilles Kepel's *The Prophet and the Pharaoh* (University of California Press, 1984) is a classic source on the origins and development of the Muslim Brotherhood. Saad El-Din Ibrahim's *Egypt, Islam, and Democracy* (The American University in Cairo Press, 2002) traces the development of the Brotherhood's thinking.

9. Hisham Al-Awadi discusses this point in depth in *A Struggle over Al-Shariaa* (in Arabic, The Centre for Arab Unity Studies, 2009).

10. Those Brotherhood-controlled student unions proved to be highly effective in tackling students' problems. But, increasingly, some of them were more assertive than many observers (or electors) expected. In 1980–1, several unions demanded the deletion of Darwin's evolution theory from the educational curricula in some colleges. In other colleges, some groups implemented a policy of gender segregation in lecture halls.

11. In *The New Renaissance*, Sheikh Hassan Al-Banna wrote that there is a 'necessity for a return to the principles, teachings, and ways of Islam, as a prelude to the final Islamisation of the society'.

12. In *Whatever Happened to the Egyptians* (The American University in Cairo Press, 2002), Galal Amin elaborates on how the Egyptian psyche was increasingly looking to the wealthy centres of the Gulf, and not the cultural capitals of Europe, for social trends and orientations.

13. Not necessarily a reflection of improved living conditions. Most of that new consumerism was in non-durable goods: food and beverages, cosmetics and low-end entertainment (for example the exponential penetration of VCRs).

14. In his panoramic book *The Great War for Civilisation: The Conquest of the Middle East* (Harper Perennial, 2006), Robert Fisk recounts how in 1991, in the midst of America's war to liberate Kuwait, a group of Saudi officials had mistaken him for an American official and presented him with a document entitled 'The Sword of Islam' that claimed that 'the mere shine of the sword eliminates falsehood just like light wipes away darkness'; the document was intended to convince Americans to convert to Islam. The irony was that the Saudis were riding an American truck, carrying American helmets and were operating under American command.

15. From the writings of Al-Sanhouri Pasha, the main drafter of the Egyptian Civil Law, and an authority on Islamic Sharia. Al-Sanhouri Pasha's work was an admirable attempt at mixing the foundations of Islamic law with the necessities of modernity, and the new ideas gained from Egypt's modernization and exposure to the West in the last few decades of the nineteenth and the first half of the twentieth century.

16. The Syrian Reda is one of Sheikh Mohamed Abdou's leading disciples. Though a reformist, he is a darling of some of the most conservative forces in the Islamic movement because, in his later years, he changed his position and sang the praises of Wahhabist thinking. In October 2007, Mashari Al-Zaydi published a refreshing essay ('In Search of the Early Rachid Reda') on the evolution of Reda's thinking in *Al-Sharq Al-Awsat* newspaper (English edition).

17. Mohamed Saeed Al-Ashmawi was a leading Egyptian judge and a scholar of Islamic jurisprudence. His book *The Essence of Islam* (in Arabic, Madbouli,

Cairo 1996) triggered a stimulating discussion in Egyptian newspapers. Unfortunately, some of his ideas turned him into a target for militant Islamic groups. He was also a key advisor to the prosecution team at the trial of the assassins of President Sadat in 1982.

18. Shahrour is a Syrian mathematician with creative and revolutionary new interpretations of the Koran, especially with regard to women's roles in Islamic society. His book *The Jurisprudence of Women* (in Arabic, Al-Ahali Printing, Damascus, 2000) is his most popular book. His views put him at odds with the Islamic establishment in most Arab countries.

19. Al-Awaa was the General Secretary of the International Union for Muslim Scholars. He has emerged as one of the most poised Islamic scholars in Egypt in the last two decades. His book *On the Political System of the Islamic State* (American Trust Publications, 1980) studies Islam as a political framework in today's world. In his book *Egypt after Mubarak: Liberalism, Islamism and Democracy in the Arab World* (Princeton University Press, 2009), Bruce Rutherford studies Al-Awaa's thinking in detail.

20. Al-Ghazali was one of the most popular and prominent Azhar scholars in Egypt in the second half of the twentieth century. However, he was vilified, especially in the Western media, for testifying on behalf of the assassins of the secularist writer Farag Fouda.

21. Most of Howeidy's work appeared as articles in *Al-Ahram*. For example, see 'Liberating the Question of Secularism' (in Arabic, *Al-Ahram*, 1 September 1992) and 'Reviewing Secularism' (in Arabic, Al-Ahram, 21 June 1994). He currently writes for the Cairene *Al-Shorouk* newspaper.

22. Al-Banna is the younger brother of Hassan Al-Banna, the founder of the Muslim Brotherhood. He is a rare example of a Salafist scholar with highly liberal views on political and societal frameworks. His latest book *Islam, Faith and Nation, Not Faith and State* (in Arabic) was published by Dar El-Shorouk in 2008.

23. Naguib Mahfouz, the winner of the Nobel Prize in Literature in 1988, was throughout the 1950 and 1960s one of Egypt's most productive novelists and writers.

24. For example, Ahmed Bahaa El-Din, a highly respected editor-in-chief of *Al-Ahram*, found intellectual refuge in Kuwait. Most of Mohamed Hassanein Heikal's articles at the time were published in Beirut and London. Alaa Al-Deeb's *A Pause before the Plunge* (in Arabic, Dar El Shorouk) is a moving exposition of the alienation of Egyptian intellectuals at that time.

25. Viola Shafik's writings, for example *Popular Egyptian Cinema* (The American University in Cairo Press, 2007), are expansive sources on the main trends in Egyptian cinema's over 100-year-old history.

26. Dr Soheir Lotfy, a sociologist at the Egyptian Centre for Criminal and Social Research, has made a number of studies on the rise of violence in Egyptian society.

27. The Brotherhood's initial response to the negotiations with Israel was subdued and cautious. But in March 1979, the group called for a holy war against the Jews. John Esposito elaborates on the Brotherhood's gradual (and changing) response to the negotiations and the peace process in *Unholy War: Terror in the Name of Islam* (Oxford University Press, 2003).

28. That logic of claiming the mantle of Jihad from the ruling regime, and fighting the authority for its lack of jihadist mettle became a recurring argument for many of the militant groups that emerged in Egypt and other parts of the Arab

and Muslim worlds. Gilles Kepel elaborates on that point in *Jihad: In the Trail of Political Islam* (Harvard University Press, 2002).

29. The Egyptian regime's decision to support the US–Saudi effort in Afghanistan and facilitate the move of thousands of Egyptians to Peshawar (the heart of the struggle against the USSR) was fundamentally a strategic decision. However, there was also a strong economic incentive. Egypt's large reserve of old Soviet weaponry (guns, rifles, ammunitions, artillery, mortars and anti-aircraft missiles) was no longer in line with the new militarization programme based on American weaponry. The Afghanistan War was an opportunity to dispose of those old weapons in profitable transactions.

30. James Bruce's 'Arab Veterans of the Afghan War', *Jane's Intelligence Review*, April 1997, is a long study of the thinking and the modus operandi of the tens of thousands of 'Arab Afghans', as they came to be known.

31. Ahmed Rashid's *Taliban: Militant Islam, Oil, and Fundamentalism in Central Asia* (Yale University Press, 2001) is a detailed and thought-provoking exposition of how Islam is interpreted, practised and expressed in that part of the world. The book also provides a detailed account of the cultural interaction between the Arab Afghans and the indigenous warriors of the region. John Esposito's *Unholy War* gives a historical account of the genealogy of Islamic jihad, drawing on the concept's evolution in the context of cultural circumstances.

32. Taha Hussein's *The Great Sedition* (in Arabic, Dar Al-Maaref, Cairo, 1938) explores the theological and intellectual foundations and circumstances from which the Assassins sprang up. In a departure from historical consensus, Hussein argues that Hassan Al-Sabbah's Assassins, as well as other rejectionist and violent groups of the time, were in fact political players impassioned by nationalist, rather than religious, causes. In the case of the Assassins, Hussein argued that the Arabs' dominance over the Persians in the Abbasid Empire, and even within the Shii Fatimid Caliphate, fuelled resentment that manifested itself in aggression. Bernard Lewis's *The Assassins: A Radical Sect in Islam* (Phoenix, 2003) is a study on the Assassins and their leader, Hassan Al-Sabbah, 'the Old Man of the Mountain'.

33. Most of the Brotherhood's members continue to refer to Qutb as 'the martyr'. It is not clear how the Brotherhood currently views Qutb's thinking. The group has never disowned his ideas or books, yet Maamum Al-Hodeiby, the second general guide of the Brotherhood after Hassan Al-Banna, indirectly attacked Qutb's ideas in his book *Preachers, not Judges* (without once mentioning his name). Emmanuel Silvan's classic *Radical Islam: Medieval Theology and Modern Politics* (Yale University Press, 1985) remains a leading source on Qutb's views. Gilles Kepel's *Jihad* is another expansive source. Rudolph Peters' *Jihad in Classic and Modern Islam* (Princeton University Press, 1996) presents modern militant Islamism drawing on its theological origins towards the end of the Abbasid period. Adnan Musallam's *From Secularism to Jihad: Sayyid Qutb and the Foundation of Radical Islamism* (Greenwood Press, 2005) is a detailed study of his life and work. Albert Bergesen's *The Sayyid Qutb Reader* (Routledge, 2007) analyses Qutb's writings.

34. There are many sources on militant Islamism in Egypt and elsewhere. Oliver Roy's *Globalized Islam: The Search for a New Ummah* (Columbia University Press, 2004) addresses the topic from multiple angles and offers insightful analyses on the thinking of many of the leading figures of militant Islamism with a special focus on the historical context of many of those violent ideologies.

35. The group played a significant role in the assassination of President Sadat, and led a number of attacks on Egyptian assets abroad (for example attacks on the Egyptian embassies in Pakistan and Albania). The group was also behind the attacks on the US's embassies in Kenya and Tanzania. In 1998, Al-Jihad merged with Al-Qaeda, and the group's leader Dr Ayman Al-Zawahiri became the deputy leader of the combined group.

36. In *Autumn of Fury* (Random House, 1983) Mohamed Hassanein Heikal recounts the shocking ease with which the assassination of President Sadat took place. Also review the memories of General Al-Nabawi Ismael, Egypt's minister of the interior at the time.

37. See Saad El-Din Ibrahim's *Egypt, Islam, and Democracy*.

38. The book was serialized in the London-based *Al-Sharq Al-Awsat*. Though his influence on the Egyptian scene has diminished significantly in the last decade, Ayman Al-Zawahiri remains a key figure in 'international' militant Islamism. Montasser Al-Zayat, the Islamic movement's most prominent lawyer in Egypt, published *Al-Zawahiri as I Knew Him* (in Arabic, Dar Misr Al-Mahrousa, 2002), a book about Dr Al-Zawahiri's background and thinking.

39. The most notable of them was Major General Raouf Khayrat. The story of his assassination was considered for a film; the project was later aborted as 'too sensitive'. That was not a new development in Egypt. The Muslim Brotherhood, during Egypt's monarchical era, assassinated a number of prominent judges and policemen such as Seleem Zaki and Ahmed Al-Khazindar.

40. Shaymaa fell in a crossfire during an attempt on the life of Dr Atef Siddqui, Egypt's prime minister at the time. Her death triggered exchanges between Egyptian intellectuals and some of militant Islamism's leading theorists. A number of observers believe her death was among the factors that drove some of those theorists into the self-critique that eventually resulting in them discarding violence at the end of the 1990s.

41. Egypt witnessed few and sporadic terrorist attacks in the mid- and late 2000s, and not comparable with the 1990s' wave in terms of frequency, intensity or organization. For example, in October 2004, a bomb exploded near Taba Hilton (which is a regular destination for Israeli tourists in Egypt); in 2005, a suicide bombing in Khan Al-Khalili in Fatimid Cairo killed three tourists; and in 2006, three bombs were set up in southern Sinai killing two tourists.

42. That specific point was the centre of a heated debate between Dr Essam El-Erian, a leading member of the Brotherhood, and Dr Abdel-Moneim Saeed, the director of Al-Ahram Centre for Political and Strategic Studies.

43. Between January and May 2009, *Egypt Today* ran a number of stories on developments within the Brotherhood, including some interviews with second- and third-tier leaders. The interviews reveal the change in the Brotherhood's tone as well as their rising confidence.

44. Raymond William Baker's *Islam without Fear: Egypt and the New Islamists* (Harvard University Press, 2003) is an expansive study of the underlying changes in ideology.

45. Timothy Garton Ash at the London *Guardian* wrote a number of articles on that 'engaged' variant of political Islam.

46. See the writings of Mohamed Seleem Al-Awaa and Tariq Al-Bishri on the history and legal framework of the relationship between Egyptian Muslims and Christians.

47. Bernard Lewis elaborated on that feeling across the Islamic world in *What Went Wrong?: The Clash Between Islam and Modernity in the Middle East*

(Weidenfeld & Nicolson, London, 2002) and *The Crisis of Islam: Holy War and Unholy Terror* (Modern Library, 2003). The Tunisian scholar Abdelwahab Meddeb discussed a similar theme: the difference between the 'powerful positivist Muslim giver' at the height of the Islamic civilization and the 'weak negativist Muslim receiver' today in a number of essays, lectures and in his book *Islam and Its Discontents* (William Heinemann, 2003).

48. Gilles Kepel used that term in describing swaths of young Muslims in countries such as Algeria, Pakistan and Egypt in his discussion of the reasons behind the radicalization of many middle-class members in *Jihad*.
49. Abdelwahab Meddeb elaborates on the analogy of terror as a nihilistic force in *Islam and Its Discontents*. Here he compares some of the terrorist groups working under Islamic banners to the nihilists of Dostoyevsky's *The Possessed*.
50. Yasser El-Sheshtawy and Mona Abaza studied that development in detail in Paul Amar and Diane Singerman (eds), *Cairo Cosmopolitan*.
51. Abdelkadir Shoheib's *The Breakthrough* (in Arabic, Sinaa Publishing, 1989) is a detailed account of the story of Islamic money management companies in Egypt.
52. Joel Beinin, the professor who specializes in the study of Egypt at Stanford University's history department, has written extensively on the topic – for example, 'The Islamists' Economy', in *Al-kotob Weghat Nathar*, December 2008 issue, and 'Political Islam and the New Global Economy', in the Spring 2005 issue of the *New Centennial Review* (vol. 5). Samia Imam's *Who Owns Egypt* (in Arabic, Dar Al-Mostaqbal Al-Arabi, 1987) discusses the situation in the late 1970s (especially during the *al-infitah* years) and well into the 1980s.
53. Rupe Simms' 'Islam is Our Politics', (*Social Compass*, vol. 49) analyses the Brotherhood's ideas in the period from 1928 to 1953. Hassan Al-Banna's *The New Renaissance* is the original source.
54. The latest development was the decision of the Shuraa Council (the upper house of the parliament), in May 2009, to forward the 'party's folder' to an independent judge to assess its merit.

Chapter 4: The Rise of Liberal Capitalism

1. In Egypt, where venture capital and private equity investments are still nascent and where the capital markets are relatively shallow and suffer occasional liquidity crunches, bank credit is the key factor that enables medium-sized companies to grow. In the 2000s, the Egyptian credit market went through two stages. In the period from late 2001 and up to late 2004, the market tightened due to the severe impacts of the world contraction followed by the flotation of the Egyptian pound. The international economic boom that followed from 2004 and up to mid-2008 (which resulted in exponential growth in Egyptian remittances to the economy and the receipts from tourism, oil exports and capital gains in industry and capital markets) led to a significant credit expansion in the country's monetary system. The Egyptian Centre for Economic Studies published two white papers on the country's credit market (in July 2006 and June 2008).
2. Reuven Brenner's *The Force of Finance* (Texere Publishing, 2002) is a theoretical framework for Sadat's vision for *al-infitah*. In the book, Reuven argues that proper implementation of capitalism and genuinely open and free markets are the route to building democracy and developing a society.

3. Dr Gawdat Al-Malt, ex-head of the Central Auditing Agency, has made inform-ative, and at many times harsh, assessments of how the government approached the allocation of economic rents in Egypt over the past few decades.

4. By the late 2000s, the region was contributing around 50 per cent of all of the country's tourism revenues. Egypt's total receipts from southern Sinai grew from virtually zero in the mid-1970s to around US$4 billion in 2007. More than US$3.8 billion has been invested in tourism in Egypt in 2008 – a signifi-cant percentage of which was invested in southern Sinai. Around 1.5 million Egyptians were employed in the sector in the same year, of whom around 35 per cent were working in southern Sinai.

5. Eric Denis has written a number of papers on the topic, for example 'Cairo Reversed: Values and Spaces' (Symposium for Urban Trajectories in Cairo, Princeton University, January 2009). He has also written expansively on the same topic in Paul Amar and Diane Singerman (eds), *Cairo Cosmopolitan*. See also Mona Abaza's 'Consumer, Culture and the Reshaping of Public Space in Egypt', *Theory, Culture and Society*, August 2001, vol. 18, Sage, UK).

6. See Charles Issawi's *Egypt in Revolution* (Oxford University Press, 1963).

7. See Heba Handousa, Maryse Louis and Alia Al-Mahdy's 'Foreign Direct Investment in Egypt', in Saul Estrin and Klaus Meyer's *Investment Strategies In Emerging Markets* (Edward Elgar Publishing, 2004).

8. Abdel-Khalek Farouk's *The Roots of Administrative Corruption in Egypt* (in Arabic, Dar Al-Shorouk, 2008) tackles the incentivization angle but does not link it to the overall deterioration of the management of the sector and the entire government.

9. Farha Ghannam's 'Keeping Him Connected: Globalization and the Production of Locality in Urban Egypt', in Paul Amar and Diane Singerman (eds), *Cairo Cosmopolitan*, presents, through a detailed case study, how the absentee fathers and brothers in the Gulf remained connected to their envi-rons back at home. Through 'letters, phone calls, photos, and tapes' the fami-lies managed to overcome the physical distance that separated them; 'besides the flow of money and goods, there was also a continuous flow of ideas, news and information' that enabled the absentee family members to 'participate effectively in making decisions related to daily lives'.

10. There do not appear to have been any serious studies on the diaspora of Egyptian capital during Nasser's years. However, various artistic works (for example, a number of films by Atef Al-Tayeb and Radwan Al-Kashef) have tackled the theme of Egyptian capital fleeing to Europe during Nasser's rule in the 1950s and 1960s, only to return to Egypt at the beginning of *al-infitah*.

11. Amira Al-Azhari's *The New Mamlukes: Egyptian Society and Modern Feudalism* (Syracuse University Press, 2000) is an elaborate study of political and economic corruption in Egypt. She compares the capitalist elite that sprang up during and after *al-infitah* to the sixteenth-century Mamelukes. See also Abdel Khaled Farouk's *The Roots of Administrative Corruption in Egypt*. Also the intro-duction of Joel Beinin and Joe Stork (eds), *Political Islam – Essays from Middle East Report* provides a succinct view of corruption at the Egyptian public sector at the time.

12. See *Al-Ahram Weekly*, 28 September 1995.

13. In *My Conversations with Sadat* (Dar Al-Hilal, Cairo, 1987), Ahmed Bahaa Al-Din explains how the events of those two days shocked President Sadat who repeatedly tried to describe the incident as 'a thieves' intifada'. Bahaa Al-Din

and many other observers believe the incident had a lasting impact on Sadat, and was a catalyst to his rapid moves in the negotiations with Israel and later his surprising trip to Jerusalem in the same year.

14. Mohamed Hassanein Heikal put a scathing argument against *al-infitah* in *Autumn of Fury*.

15. Ibrahim Aoude's 'From National Bourgeois Development to Al-infitah: Egypt 1952–1992', *Arab Studies Quarterly*, January 1994, is a detailed source on the issue.

16. The Suez region oil fields resumed production after almost a complete stop in the 1960s and early 1970s. In 1972, the receipts of Egyptian oil were circa US$40 million, in 1980, they were circa US$3 billion. Remittances surged from US$189 million in 1974 to US$2.85 billion in 1981. See Khalid Imran's *The Egyptian Economy*.

17. For example, US$2 billion in 1976 from the Gulf Organization for the Development of Egypt.

18. In his article 'What Have We Done with US Aid', in *Al-Ahram Weekly* (issue 539, June 2001), Mustafa Kamal presented a detailed and historical view of the size and deployments of US aid to Egypt from the late 1970s to 2000.

19. For a rigorous study of the dynamics and consequences of the economic policies of *al-infitah*, see Khalid Imran's *The Egyptian Economy* and Riad Ghonemy's *Egypt in the Twenty First Century: Challenges for Development* (Routledge Curzon, 2003).

20. President Sadat used to refer to army officers as 'my boys'.

21. In a long article in the June 2000 issue of *Weghat Nathar* (in Arabic), Mohamed Hassanein Heikal argued that prioritizing economic over political reform raises questions of legitimacy. The severe social consequences entailed in any serious economic reform programme (at least in the short and medium terms) should not be taken by government employees or economic experts, but by elected politicians with a legitimate mandate from the people to make strategic decisions.

22. Mainly utilities (expanding the electricity grid and the water distribution system), health care (especially in the areas of infant mortality and family planning), transportation (the rail and road networks connecting Cairo with the Delta), telecommunications (predominantly the public switched telephone network) and education (the number of schools in the Delta and Al-Saeed). The results were indeed very encouraging: a dramatic improvement in the provisioning of utilities throughout the country, a major reduction in infant mortality, a noticeable decrease in the pace of population growth, a rise in life expectancy at birth and a major upgrading of the transportation and telecoms networks.

23. By the early 1990s, the economic pressures on the Egyptian budget were intolerable. The budget deficit had reached more than 15 per cent of GDP; inflation was running at circa 14 per cent for a few years in a row; foreign exchange reserves were dwindling to around US$4 billion; and crucially the debt service ratio had climbed to roughly 55 per cent of the GDP.

24. Subsidies are one of the major burdens on the Egyptian government's budget. The Atef Siddqui measures were successful in reducing total subsidies from 5.2 per cent of GDP in 1991 to roughly 1.5 per cent by 1996. They, however, remain a major problem. The World Bank estimates that only 17 per cent of subsidies benefit the poorest 20 per cent of the population, while 25 per cent of subsidies go to the richest 20 per cent of the population.

25. In her book *IMF-Egyptian Negotiations* (The American University in Cairo Press, 2005), Basma Momani studies the protracted negotiations between the

IMF and the Egyptian government: the 1983 and 1987 Structural Studies, the 1991 Restructuring Assessment and the 1993 and 1996 Protocols.

26. Khalid Imran's book *The Egyptian Economy* is an expansive source on the details of that programme.

27. The term was coined by Khalil Al-Anani, a writer at *Al-Ahram*.

28. Based on a study conducted by Sara Bjerg Moller, a research associate at the Council on Foreign Relations, for *World Politics Review*, Spring 2008.

29. Some of those papers, most of which were published by the Egyptian Centre for Economic Studies, were insightful expositions on the country's socio-economic conditions at the time. For example, see Moheideen's paper with Mohamed El-Erian (at the time at the International Centre for Economic Growth) *Financial Development in Emerging Markets: The Egyptian Experience* (International Centre for Economic Growth, 1998).

30. One of the most interesting political stories in Egypt in the early and mid-2000s was the subtle struggle between the old guard of the NDP (the old stalwarts of President Mubarak's regime) and Gamal Mubarak. The story is full of court intrigue and plots, but, fascinating as it is, it is not directly related to the flow of narrative here. As far as it is known, no serious investigative journalistic work has covered that story yet.

31. Gamal Mubarak's main initiatives within the NDP were summarized in the party's booklet *New Thinking* (*Fikr Gadeed*), which was published in 2005.

32. The writings of Judge Tariq Al-Bishri (the leading writer of the manifesto, which was later published in a number of opposition newspapers in Egypt) throughout the 2000s show the dynamics within the judicial community.

33. The most notable change was President Mubarak's decision, in February 2005, to amend Article 76 of the constitution allowing for directly contested presidential elections.

34. Peter Gran's *Islamic Roots of Capitalism* (Syracuse University Press, 1998) studies the role of capitalism within Islam and provides a thorough analysis of the economic underpinnings of different Islamic societies across the ages.

35. See Noami Saqr's *Arab Television Today* (I.B. Tauris, 2007).

36. The privatization of the Bank of Alexandria in an international bidding process was an interesting case in point.

37. The Egyptian Central Bank continues to face significant challenges and restraining legacies. However, the development of the Bank since the early 2000s is a successful case study. The OECD's Development Cooperation Report commented positively on three cases of admirable change in the management of monetary policy in emerging economies: the work of the finance department of South Africa under Manuel Trevor, the replenishment of the Lebanese Central Bank under its impressive governor Reyad Salama and the Egyptian Central Bank's management of the country's monetary policies, especially after the floatation of the Egyptian pound.

38. 'Outrage over 2006 Egypt ferry disaster acquittals', AFP 27 July 2008.

Chapter 5: Egyptian Christians

1. *The Memoires of Nubar Pasha* (Library of Lebanon, 1983) offer an insightful view on Egyptian society in the second half of the nineteenth century, and of the struggle between foreign interests in the country and the rising Egyptianism.

2. Birger Pearson and James Geohring (eds), *The Roots of Egyptian Christianity* (Fortress Press, 1986) is a comprehensive source on that period.
3. Following the Council of Nicaea in 325, and the inter-church conflicts that accompanied and followed it, two new patriarchates were established at the expense of Antioch: Constantinople and Jerusalem.
4. Mainly as a result of the division of the Roman Empire by Diocletian (284–305) into two great halves: the Eastern one centred in Constantinople and the Western around Rome.
5. The Second Council of Lyons in 1274 and the Council of Florence in 1439 tried to effect some form of reunion between the churches.
6. See Euan Cameron's *Interpreting Christian History: The Challenge of the Churches' Past* (Wiley-Blackwell, Massachusetts, 2005).
7. Arabizing state and administrative matters started in 697 CE when the Ummayad Caliph Abdel-Malek Ibn-Marwan Arabized the administrative structure of the Islamic Empire (*diwan*). The process continued and was later intensified during the early years of the Abbasid Empire. Gershoni and Jankowski's *Egypt, Islam, and the Arabs* tells the story of Egypt's slow move from Christianity to Islam.
8. Patrick Manning's *Migration in World History* (Routledge, 2005) discusses migration to (and from) Egypt – mainly from the Arabian peninsula to Egypt and, later, the Beni Hilal migration from Egypt to North Africa. Less scholarly but highly engaging is *Siret Al-Hilali*, Abdel-Rahman Al-Abnoudi's long poem-play on the Hilali's migration to and from Egypt.
9. In her major study *Osman's Dream*, Caroline Fenkel elaborates on the efforts of the Ottomans, especially during the reign of Sultan Mohamed the Fourth, to convert Christians throughout the empire to Islam.
10. Fenkel, *Osman's Dream*.
11. Mohamed Hassanein Heikal discussed that relationship at length in *End of a Regime*.
12. Mervat Hatem discussed that trend in her study of secularist and religious trends and discourses in post-colonial Egypt. See 'Secularist and Islamic Discourse on Modernity in Egypt', in Haideh Moghissi (ed.), *Women and Islam: Images and Realities* (Routledge, New York, 2005). See also Fadwa Numeirat's *Arab Christians and the Idea of Arab Nationalism in the Levant and Egypt* (in Arabic, Centre for Arab Unity Studies, 2009). For a wider picture of the social change of that era (including the impact of Arab nationalism on Egyptian society and on Egyptian Christians), see Yvonne Haddad and John Esposito's *Islam, Gender, and Social Change*.
13. Following the inauguration of the new Orthodox Cathedral in 1969, the Patriarch's official title was changed to Pope.
14. Building churches in Egypt remains a contentious issue. It is still governed by the Hamayouni Law and its 1934 corollary, the Al-Ezabi Decree, which legislates the existence of non-Muslim places of worship. The legislation stipulates that 'concerned authorities' need to be consulted before any governorate issues an approval for a new church. But the legislation fails to identify those 'concerned authorities'. That vague wording, let alone the existence of the legislation itself, has frustrated Christians for decades. Youssef Sidhom, the editor of the Christian daily *Watani*, has written a number of articles on the issue.
15. Sana Hasan's *Christian versus Muslims in Modern Egypt* (Oxford University Press, 2004) is an expansive study on the causes and development of that positioning.

16. Originally built in 684, and then rebuilt in 1857, this church is the most famous Christian archaeological monument in 'Misr Al-Qadima' (Old Egypt), Cairo's oldest part.

17. This paragraph is based on reporting by Gawdat Gabra of the Centre for Coptic Studies at Macquarie University in Australia, reports of the Egyptian Centre for Human Rights and Tariq Al-Bishri's The National Group: Isolation and Integration, Copts and Muslims within Civil Society (in Arabic, Kitab Al-Hilal, Cairo, 2005). The interview with Nevine was published in Dina Ezzat's 'Blessed be the People of Egypt', an article in issue 929, 8 January 2009, Al-Ahram Weekly, part of Ezzat's wide reporting on Egyptian Christians' conditions in Egypt.

18. There are few solid sources on the Mubarak regime's strategy towards Egyptian Christians. Fouad Ajami's article 'The Sorrows of Egypt', in Foreign Affairs, 1995, touches on the political background of that relationship. David Zeidan's 'The Copts: equal, protected, or prosecuted', in Islam and Christian-Muslim Relations, vol. 10, issue 1 (1999), offers a more socio-economic and historical perspective.

19. See Bahaa Tahers Khalti Safeya wa-el-Dir (Dar Al-Shorouk, Cairo, 2007), and Yousef Zidan's Arabic Booker winner Azazel (Dar Al-Shorouk, Cairo, 2008). The latter, however, caused strife. The book's focus on the theological turbulences that followed the Arian controversy in the third and fourth centuries led to theological confrontations in a number of Egyptian magazines.

20. For a long assessment of that line of thinking, see Gamal Al-Banna's Islam: Religion and Nation, not Religion and State.

21. Abu Al-Ela Madi's The Coptic Question, the Sharia, and the Islamic Renaissance (in Arabic, Dar Safeer, 2007) is a study on the topic from a leading politician within the Islamic movement.

22. There do not appear to have been any serious studies conducted on the political strategy of the Egyptian Church, and how it has changed over the last five decades of the twentieth century.

23. The numbers are derived from the International Religious Freedom Report 2007, the US Department of State Background Notes Website, Euromonitor International's The Future Demographics of Egypt, published in February 2009, and Dina Ezzat's article 'Blessed be the People of Egypt', issue 929, 8 January 2009, Al-Ahram Weekly.

24. Kamal Ghobrial skilfully presented many of those trends in his book Copts and Liberalism (in Arabic).

25. William Kelada's The Copts from Minority to Citizenry. Egypt in the Twenty First Century (in Arabic, Al-Ahram Centre for Publishing and Translation, 1996).

Chapter 6: The Mubarak Years

1. Jonathan Fenby, France on the Brink (Arcade Publishing, 2000).

2. President Mubarak was the commander of the Egyptian air force during the Yom Kippur War in 1973. Prior to that, he was the commander of the country's Air Force College. And as many of his colleagues and students emphasize, he was one of the country's most able military commanders.

3. In the May/June 1998 issue of the Washington Report on Middle East Affairs, James Napoli analysed the complicated dynamics between the Egyptian press

and the Mubarak regime, and elaborated on the Mubarak regime's mixed record on 'free' press.

4. Osman Ahmed Osman was one of Egypt's most successful entrepreneurs (the founder and chief executive officer of the mammoth Arab Contractors) and a close friend of President Sadat. His autobiography, *Pages from My Experience* (in Arabic, Al-Maktab Al-Masri, Cairo, 1981), sheds light on various dynamics in the 1960s and 1970s. Despite his role in designing (and executing) *al-infitah*, he remains a highly respected figure among large groups of Egyptians.

5. Gregory Aftanadilian's weighty report *Egypt's Bid for Arab Leadership: Implications for US Policy* (Council on Foreign Affairs Press, 1993) provides a detailed assessment of the Egyptian role in the Iraq–Kuwait crisis of 1990. Majid Khadduri and Edmund Ghareeb's *War in the Gulf* (Oxford University Press, 2001) tackles the same crisis (and Egypt's role in it), though with much more emphasis on the inter-dynamics within the Arab world. Gil Feiler's *Economic Relations between Egypt and the Gulf Oil States, 1967–2000* (Sussex Academic Press, 2003) is an expansive source on the economic consequences of the war and especially the cancelation of debt.

6. Heikal's most important books – specifically *The 30 Years War* series – emphasize 'Egypt's historical role' through its involvement in the various wars in the Middle East in the last fifty years. Itamar Rabinovich's *Waging Peace: Israel and the Arabs, 1948–2003* (Princeton University Press, 2004) offers the exact opposite view of the Egyptian project, Israel's view of the future of the Middle East and how that view has shaped the negotiations between the two parties over the past six decades. Kenneth Stein's *Heroic Diplomacy* (Routledge, 1999), though, focuses on the Egyptian–Israeli peace process and later the peace accord and provides an interesting assessment of American and Israeli views of the Egyptian project.

7. There are a number of publications on the US–Egyptian strategic relationship. For example, see the study *Strengthening US–Egyptian Relationship*, published by the Council on Foreign Affairs in 2002. From an Egyptian standpoint, the writings of Dr Abdel-Monem Saiid, the director of Al-Ahram Centre for Political and Strategic Studies in Cairo, offer insightful assessments, especially given his closeness to the Mubarak regime.

8. George Fawaz discusses the immediate impacts of that Casablanca conference and the Egyptian–Israeli tension at the time in 'Egyptian Israeli Relations Turn Sour' in the May/June 1995 issue of *Foreign Affairs*. For a detailed exposition on the Israeli project, see Shimon Peres's book *The New Middle East* (Henry Holt & Co., 1993).

9. The different Israeli projects can be discerned from two books: Shimon Peres's *The New Middle East* and Netanyahu's *A Durable Peace, Israel and its Place Among the Nations* (Grand Central Publishing, 2000).

10. The dilution of Egypt's strategic importance, mainly in the United States's list of priorities, can be discerned from Zbigniew Brzezinski's *The Grand Chessboard: American Primacy and its Geostrategic Imperatives* (Basic Books, 1997) and Brzezinski's and Brent Scowcroft's *America and the World*, edited by David Ignatius (Basic Books, 2008).

11. There appears to be a dearth of sources on Egypt's new foreign-policy doctrine. Perhaps the most weighty source on the development of the thinking that has led to the new approach is Boutros Boutros Ghali's *Egypt's Road to Jerusalem* (Random House, 1997). Ghali was, throughout the second half of the 1970s, a very close foreign-policy advisor to President Sadat and one of the

architects of Egypt's strategy in the negotiations that led to the Camp David peace accord. The writings of Dr Mustafa El Fiqui, an ex-senior assistant to President Mubarak and a member of parliament, shed light on the regime's more recent modus operandi. Also, the more than ten hours of TV interview that Egyptian journalist Emad El-Din Adeeb conducted with Dr Mustafa Khalil, one of the closest advisors to Presidents Sadat and Mubarak and a key designer of Egyptian–Israeli relationships, is a valuable source.

12. In *A Choice of Enemies*, Lawrence Freedman studies the strategic scene in the Middle East, including the changing mood in key Arab countries, including Egypt.

13. Curtis Ryan, in his 'Political Strategies and Regime Survival in Egypt', *Journal of Third World Studies* (Zeidan, Fall 2001), argues that that weakening of state institutions was intentional and carried out throughout the reigns of Nasser, Sadat and Mubarak. There are difficulties with this assessment, given that the three presidents' approaches to governance were vastly different. As explained in different chapters, each of the three presidents tried to assert his control through different modus operandi. Arthur Goldschmidt's *Modern Egypt: The Formation of a Nation State* (Westview Press, 1988) is a comprehensive source on how Nasser's and Sadat's efforts had sometimes helped and sometimes hindered the formation of viable institutions in the country.

14. Based on the Egyptian Organisation for Human Rights' report on 8 August 2007.

15. The International Crisis Group reported on Kefaya's different initiatives and some of the regime's responses in *Reforming Egypt: In Search of a Strategy*, report no. 46 (October 2005). Mohamed Al-Sayyed, at *Al-Ahram Weekly*, reported on the same topic in December 2006.

Chapter 7: Young Egyptians

1. For example, see Michelle Dunne's study, 'A Post-Pharaonic Egypt', *American Interest*, September–October 2008, Aladdin Elaasar's 'Is Egypt Stable?', *Middle East Quarterly*, Summer 2009, in addition to various reports by the International Crisis Group, the *Economist* newspaper, Care International, the UN Development Programme and others.

2. Sociologist Samir Hanna quoted in *Al-Ahram Weekly*, 3 December 2008.

3. A respondent in a survey by the same publication.

4. See the Egyptian Information and Decision Support Centre's June 2009 report on unemployment in Egypt.

5. According to a study by the Arab Labour Organization, at least 50 per cent of students who take up postgraduate studies in Europe or the US do not return to live in Egypt.

6. Max Rodenbeck's *Cairo: The City Victorious* (Picador, 1998) is a tour de force of old Cairo's history and geography, the attitudes and behaviours of its people and the 'feel' and character of the city.

7. Gamal Al-Ghitanni, *Regaining Al-Musafir Khana* (in Arabic, Dar Al-Shorouk, Cairo, 2007).

8. Most Egyptian cemeteries are different in design and construction from Western ones. Since ancient Egyptians believed that the deceased's family would 'accompany' him in the first forty days after his soul's death (or the first

forty days of his voyage into the other world), Egyptians built their burial sites in multiple rooms that could sustain living and even social interaction. John Foster's *Ancient Egyptian Literature: An Anthology* (Texas University Press, 2001) shows how Egyptians, even in their poems, commemorated death and dealt with it as a phase within a long journey.

9. The work of the Swiss painter and photographer Margo Veillon, who spent years travelling around the Egyptian countryside, is a detailed and visual reflection of the Egyptian peasants' relationship with their land.

10. Business Monitor's Q2 2009 Report on the Egyptian economy has a detailed analysis of the Egyptian demographic pyramid.

11. See the US State University Directory on the Egyptian Education System, Business Monitor International's 2009 report on Egypt's infrastructure, Karima Korayem's *The Research Environment in Egypt* (Research for Development in the Middle East and North Africa at the International Development Research Centre, 2000), the UN Arab Human Development Report 2005, and a number of lectures by Dr Ahmed Zewail, the winner of the 1999 Nobel Prize in Chemistry.

12. *Leilat Al-Baby Doll*, a 2007 movie produced by GoodNews4U, cost more than US$8 million, a staggering budget by Egyptian cinema standards.

13. Idris (1927–91) is Egypt's most prominent short-story writer (his most famous collections include *The Cheapest Nights, A House of Flesh* and *I am the Sultan of the Law of Existence*). He is also an innovative playwright and satirist with experimentations such as *Al-Farafeer* (a sensational theatrical success in the 1960s). According to the Cultural Bulletin of Egypt's State Information Service, his work has been the subject of about ninety-five PhD theses in and outside Egypt.

14. Al-Aswany came to prominence through his highly successful novel *The Yacoubian Building* (published in Cairo by Merit Publishing in 2002; the English-language translation, by Humphrey Davies, was published by The American University in Cairo Press in 2004). *The Yacoubian Building* has been translated into twenty-three languages.

15. For example, Khaled Al-Khamissi's *Taxi* (translated into English as *Taxi: Cabbie Talk*, Aflame Books, 2008) and Osama Ghareeb's *Egypt is not My Mother, but My Stepmom* (Dar Al-Shorouk, 2008).

16. Al-Koshary is the quintessential Cairene dish (a mixture of pasta, rice and lentil in a hot tomato and garlic sauce).

17. Dr Raouf Abbas Hamed, ex-chair of the History Department at Cairo University, wrote extensively on the socio-economic implications of the country's agricultural heritage.

18. The detachment of Al-Saeed was also the result of rising tribal solidarity during the 1980s and 1990s. Diane Singerman and Paul Amar state that rising Saeedi solidarity was also influenced by their experience of migration to the Gulf, where tribal values shape society. See the introduction of *Cairo Cosmopolitan*.

19. The difficulty of life in Egypt for ordinary individuals sometimes touches on the bizarre and depressing. In its September 2009 issue, *Egypt Today* ran a reportage on Al-Barada, a village in Al-Qalyoubia (one of the nearest gover-norates to Cairo). The sole source of drinkable water for the village's 30,000 inhabitants has, for ten years, been neighbouring villages or a water tanker that comes once a day to the village. After the government inaugurated a new project to supply the village with drinkable water, 'we found the water yellow

as mango juice, and it smelled awful', one villager said. Soon the 'drinkable' tap water spread typhoid across the village's families. It later transpired that the predicament in Al-Barada was a common problem across other villages and towns. Typhoid rates, which are universally estimated to be a total of around 21 million cases, spread in a number of Egyptian governorates at the rate of 59 cases for every 100,000 people, a frightening ratio.

20. The report offers a lengthy and comprehensive review of how Arab regimes in general, not only in Egypt, have developed into threats to the ordinary Arab, rather than the guardians of his/her rights, independence and dignity. The discussion on the impacts of the obsession with security among Arab regimes is particularly illuminating, albeit chilling.

21. Mary Anne Weaver used a similar analogy in *A Portrait of Egypt: A Journey through the World of Militant Islam* (Farrar, Straus, and Giroux, 2000).

Conclusion

1. The New Kingdom was Ancient Egypt's golden age. The traditionally isolated country grew into an empire stretching from Sudan to Syria. That was the age of Egypt's most famous pharaohs – Tuthmosis the Third (the great warrior and empire builder), the female king Hatshepsut, Akhenaten (the so-called Egyptian prophet) and his wife Nefertiti, the boy-king Tutankhamen, the 'guardian' Hur-Muheb and Ramses the Second (the great).

2. Every year Egypt celebrates 6 October, the day the hostilities began; the war is considered the country's greatest modern military success. Henry Kissinger's *Crisis: The Anatomy of Two Major Foreign Policy Crises* (Simon & Schuster, 2004) is a detailed account of the development of the war.

3. The defence minister, though officially a member of the cabinet, is appointed by and reports mainly to the president. The military budget is a state secret. There are clear limitations to the powers of the police over military officers. Robert Satloff's study 'The Army and Politics in Mubarak's Egypt' (Washington Institute of Near East Policy, 1988) is one of the very few sources on the topic.

4. For example, a number of judges attacked 'law 203' governing privatization as well as the whole legal framework for the country's capital markets.

5. Mohamed Seleem Al-Awwa's *The Judge and the Sultan* (in Arabic, Dar Al-Shorouk, 2006) exposes the legal interactions between the regime and the judicial community. The Egyptian journalist Sahar Al-Gaara has also written extensively on those two articles. Also see Gamal Essam El-Din's 'Opposition Vs El-Baradei', an article in *Al-Ahram Weekly*, issue 4 March 2010.

6. Tariq Al-Bishri's *The Political Movement in Egypt between 1945 and 1953* (in Arabic, Dar Al-Shorouk, 2002) is a rigorous study of the changes in Al-Wafd's (and other parties') stance on foreign policy.

7. For example, a number of episodes of *Fi-Al-Omoq* or the *Daily News Analysis*, e.g. that of 26 June 2010.

8. Samia Serageldin, *The Cairo House* (Fourth Estate, 2004).

BIBLIOGRAPHY

Abaza, Mona, *Consumer, Culture and the Reshaping of Public Space in Egypt*, Theory, Culture and Society, Sage, vol. 18, London, 2001

Abdelraziq, Ali, *Islam wa Usul Al-Hokm: Bahith fi Al-Khilafa wa Al-Hukuma fi Al-Islam*, Matbaat Misr, Cairo, 1925

Abu-Al-Naga, Shereen, *Al-Hijab between the Local and the Global*, Arab Cultural Centre, Morocco, 2008

Abu-Lughod, Lila, ed, *Remaking Women: Feminism and Modernity in the Middle East*, Princeton University Press, New Jersey, 1998

Aburish, Said, *Nasser: The Last Arab*, Thomas Dunne Books, London, 2004

Aftanadilian, Gregory, *Egypt's Bid for Arab Leadership: Implications for US Policy*, Council on Foreign Affairs Press, New York, 1993

Ahmed, Leila, *A Border Passage: From Cairo to America, A Women's Journey*, Penguin Books, New York, 2000

Ajami, Fouad, 'The Sorrows of Egypt: A Tale of Two Men', *Foreign Affairs*, September/October 1995

——, *The Arab Predicament*, Cambridge University Press, Cambridge, 1985

Al-Ashmawi, Mohamed Saeed, *Gawhar Al-Islam*, Madbouli, Cairo, 1996

Al-Awaa, Mohamed Seleem, *Al-Qadi wa Al-Sultan*, Dar Al-Shorouk, Cairo, 2006

——, *On the Political System of the Islamic State*, American Trust Publications, Illinois. 1980

Al-Awadi, Hisham, *Siraa ala Al-Shariaa*, Centre for Arab Unity Studies, Beirut, 2009

Al-Azhari, Amira, *The New Mamlukes: Egyptian Society and Modern Feudalism*, Syracuse University Press, New York, 2000

Al-Azm, Sadiq, *Al-Naqd Al-Dhatti Bad Al-Hazima*, Dar Al-Taleeia, Beirut, 1969

Ali, Arafa, *Rehla fi Zaman Al-Qahira*, Madbouli, Cairo, 1990

Amar, Paul & Diane Singerman, *Cairo Cosmopolitan: Politics, Culture, and Urban Space in the New Globalised Middle East*, The American University in Cairo Press, Cairo, 2006

Amin, Galal, *Whatever Happened to the Egyptians*, The American University in Cairo Press, Cairo, 2002

——, *Been Holm Abdel Nasser wa Holm Al-Sadat: Thulatheyat al-Sulta wa al-Mal wa al-Nagah fi Tagrobat Osman*, Al-Kotob Weghat Nazar, vol. 1, issue 5, Cairo, June 1999

Aoude, Ibrahim, 'From National Bourgeois Development to Al-Infitah, Egypt 1952–1992', *Arab Studies Quarterly*, Illinois, January 1994

Ayoub, Mohammed & Hasan Kosebalaban (eds), *Religion and Politics in Saudi Arabia*, Lynne Rienner Publishers, Boulder, Colorado, 2008

Ayoubi, Illias, 'Misr fi Ahd Al-Khediwei Ismael (1923)', in Iman Farag, *Les Manuels D'Histoire Egyptiens: Genese et Imposition d'une Norme*, Geneses, issue 44, Paris, March 2001

Badrawi, Malak, 'Financial Cerberus: The Egyptian Parliament 1924–1952', in Arthur Goldschmidt, Amy Johnson & Barak Salmoni (eds), *Re-Envisioning Egypt: 1919–1952*, The American University in Cairo Press, Cairo, 2005

Baer, Gabriel, *A History of Landownership in Modern Egypt 1800–1950*, Oxford University Press, New York, 1962

——, *Studies in the Social History of Modern Egypt*, University of Chicago Press, Chicago, 1969

Bahaa-El-Din, Ahmed, *My Conversations with Sadat*, Dar Al-Hilal, Cairo, 1987

Baker, Raymond William, *Islam without Fear: Egypt and the New Islamists*, Harvard University Press, Massachusetts, 2003

Bakhtiar, Laleh, *Sufi: Expressions of the Mystic Quest*, Thames & Hudson, London, 1976

Al-Banna, Gamal, *Al-Islam Din wa Ummah, lais Din wa Dawlah*, Dar Al-Shorouk, Cairo, 2008

Baraka, Magda, *The Egyptian Upper Class between Revolutions 1919–1952*, Ithaca Press, Reading, 1998

Beinin, Joel, *The Dispersion of Egyptian Jewry*, The American University in Cairo Press, Cairo, 2005

——, 'Political Islam and the New Global Economy', *New Centennial Review*, vol. 5, Missouri, 2005

Beinin, Joel & Jackary Lockman, *Workers on the Nile: Nationalism, Communism, and Islam on the Egyptian Working Class, 1882–1954*, Princeton University Press, New Jersey, 1987

Beinin, Joel & Joe Stark (eds), *Political Islam: Essays from the Middle East Report*, University of California Press, California, 1996

Bent, Hansen, 'Capital and Lopsided Development in Egypt Under British Occupation', in Georges Sabagh (ed.), The *Modern Economic and Social History of the Middle East in Its World Context*, Cambridge University Press, Cambridge, 1989

Bergesen, Albert, *The Sayyid Qutb Reader*, Routledge, New York, 2007

Al-Bishri, Tariq, *Al-Jamaa Al-Wataniyya: Al-Uzla wa Al-Indimaj*, Kitab Al-Hilal, Cairo, 2005

——, *The Political Movement in Egypt between 1945-1953*, Dar Al-Shorouk, Cairo, 2002

Bonney, Richard, *Jihad from Qu'ran to Bin Laden*, Palgrave Macmillan, New York, 2004

Boutros-Ghali, Boutros, *Egypt's Road to Jerusalem*, Random House, London, 1997

Brandsma, Judith & Laurence Hart, *Making Microfinance Work Better in the Middle East and North Africa*, World Bank Institute, Washington, 2002

BIBLIOGRAPHY

Brenner, Reuven, *The Force of Finance*, Texere Publishing, New York, 2002

Bruce, James, 'Arab Veterans of the Afghan War', *Jane's Intelligence Review*, Bracknell, April 1997

Cameron, Euan, *Interpreting Christian History: The Challenge of the Churches' Past*, Wiley-Blackwell, Massachusetts, 2005

Cooper, Artemis, *Cairo in the War: 1939–1945*, Penguin, London, 1995

Cotran, Eugene & Mai Yamani (eds), *The Rule of Law in the Middle East and the Islamic World*, I.B. Tauris, New York, 2000

Daly, M.W., *The Cambridge History of Egypt, Volume 2: Modern Egypt from 1517 to the end of the twentieth century*, Cambridge University Press, Cambridge, 1998

Davison, Roderic, *Reform in the Ottoman Empire, 1856–1876*, Princeton University Press, New Jersey, 1963

Dawestashi, Esmat, *Mahmoud Saeed*, Cairo Cultural Development Fund, Cairo, 1999

——, The Political Movement in Egypt between 1945–1953, Dar Al-Shorouk, Cairo, 2002

Al-Deeb, Alaa, *Waqfa Qabl Al-Munhadar*, Dar Al-Shorouk, Cairo, 2004

Denis, Eric, *Cairo Reversed: Values and Spaces: Symposium for Urban Trajectories in Cairo*, Princeton University Press, New Jersey, 2009

Al-Desouky, Assem, *Kibar Mulak Al-Aradi Fi Misr*, Dar Al-Shorouk. Cairo, 2007

Diamond, Larry, Marc Plattner & Daniel Brumberg (eds), *Islam and Democracy in the Middle East*, Johns Hopkins University Press, Maryland, 2003

Dunne, Michelle, 'A Post-Pharaonic Egypt', *The American Interest*, Washington, September–October 2008

Eban, Abba, *Personal Witness: Israel Through My Eyes*, Putnam, New York, 1992

Eden, Anthony, *Full Circle*, Cassell, London, 1960

El-Shazly, Saad, *The Crossing of Suez*, American Mideast Research, San Francisco, 1980

Elaasar, Aladdin, 'Is Egypt Stable?', *Middle East Quarterly*, Summer 2009

Emara, Mohamed, *Sheikh Refaa Al-Tahtawy*, Dar Al-Shorouk, Cairo, 2007

Empereur, Jean-Yves, *Alexandria: Past, Present and Future*, Thames & Hudson, London, 2002

Esposito, John, *Unholy War: Terror in the Name of Islam*, Oxford University Press, New York, 2003

Ezzat, Dina, 'Blessed Be the People of Egypt', *Al-Ahram Weekly*, Cairo issue 929, 8 January 2009

Fahmy, Khaled, *All the Pasha's Men: Mohamed Ali and the Making of Modern Egypt*, The American University in Cairo Press, New York, 2002

Farghali, Mohamed, *Eshto Hayati Bayna Haoulaa*, Cairo, 1984

Farouk, Abdel-Khalek, *Gozour Al-Fasad Al-Idari Fi Misr*, Dar Al-Shorouk, Cairo, 2008

Farrell, Diana, Jaana Remes & Heiner Schulz, 'The Truth about Foreign Direct Investment in Emerging Markets', *McKinsey Quarterly*, 2004

Fawaz, George, 'Egyptian–Israeli Relations Turn Sour', *Foreign Affairs*, May/June 1995

Feiler, Gil, *Economic Relations between Egypt and the Gulf Oil States, 1967–2000*, Sussex Academic Press, Sussex, 2003

Fenkel, Caroline, *Osman's Dream: The Story of the Ottoman Empire*, John Murray, London, 2005

Field, Michael, *Inside the Arab World*, Harvard University Press, Massachusetts, 1994

Fisk, Robert, *The Great War for Civilisation: The Conquest of the Middle East*, Harper Perennial, London, 2006

Foster, John, *Ancient Egyptian Literature: An Anthology*, Texas University Press, Texas, 2001

Freedman, Lawrence, *A Choice of Enemies: America Confronts the Middle East*, Weidenfeld & Nicolson, London, 2008

Gardezi, Hassan, *The Political Economy of International Labour Migration*, Black Rose Books, Montreal, 1995

Gemmell, Norman, 'The Growth in Employment in Services in Egypt', *Developing Economies*, vol. 23, issue 1, Chiba, Japan, 1985

Ghonemy, Riad, *Egypt in the Twenty First Century: Challenges for Development*, Routledge Curzon, London, 2003

Glass, Charles, *The Tribes Triumphant*, Harper Press, London, 2006

Goldschmidt, Arthur, *Modern Egypt: The Formation of a Nation State*, Boulder, Colorado, Westview Press, 1988

Gershoni, Israel & James Jankowski, *Egypt, Islam, and the Arabs: The Search for Egyptian Nationhood 1900–1930*, Oxford University Press, New York, 1986

Gran, Peter, *Islamic Roots of Capitalism*, Syracuse University Press, New York, 1998

Haag, Michael, *Alexandria: City of Memory*, Yale University Press, New Haven, 2005

Haddad, Yvonne & John Esposito, *Islam, Gender, and Social Change*, Oxford University Press, New York, 1998

Halliday, Fred, *Nation and Religion in the Middle East*, Saqi Books, London, 2000

Hamouda, Adel, *Hariboun Bemiliarat Misr*, Dar Al-Foursan, Cairo, 2000

Hamouda, Sahar & Colin Clement (eds), *Victoria College: A History Revealed*, The American University in Cairo, Cairo, 2004

Hasan, Sana, *Christian versus Muslims in Modern Egypt*, Oxford University Press, New York, 2004

Heikal, Mohamed Hassanein, *Nehayat Nizam*, Dar Al-Shorouk, Cairo, 2002

——, *Cutting the Lion's Tail*, Andre Deutsch, London, 1986

——, *The Road to Ramadan*, Quadrangle, New York, 1975

——, *Nasser: The Cairo Documents*, New English Library, London, 1972

——, *The Sphinx and the Commissar*, HarperCollins, London, 1978

——, *Autumn of Fury*, Random House, London, 1983

Hoffman, Valerie, *Sufism, Mystics, and Saints in Egypt*, University of South Carolina Press, South California, 1995

Hourani, Albert, *Arabic Thought in the Liberal Age, 1798–1939*, Cambridge University Press, Cambridge, 1983

——, *A History of the Arab Peoples*, Warner Books, New York, 1991

Hussein, Taha, *Mustakbal Al-Thaqafa Fi Misr*, Dar Al-Maaref, Cairo, 1938

Ibrahim, Saad El Din, *Egypt, Islam, and Democracy*, The American University in Cairo, Cairo, 2002

Imam, Abdallah, *Nasser wa Al-Ikhwan*, Dar Al-Mawqif Al-Arabi, Cairo, 1986

Imam, Samia, *M'an Yamlok Misr*, Dar Al-Mostaqbal Al-Arabi, Cairo, 1987

Imran, Khalid, *The Egyptian Economy: 1952–2000*, Routledge, London, 2006

International Crisis Group, *Reforming Egypt: In Search of a Strategy*, report no. 46, New York, October 2005

Irwin, Robert, 'Burying the Past: The Decline of Arab History and the Perils of Occidentosis', *Times Literary Supplement*, 3 February 1995

Ismail, Mohamed Hussam Al-Din, *Madinat Al-Qahira min Welayat Mohamed Ali ila Ismael*, Dar Al-Afaq Al-Arabeya, Cairo, 1997

BIBLIOGRAPHY

Issawi, Charles, *Egypt in Revolution*, Oxford University Press, New York, 1963

Kamal, Mustafa, *What Have We Done with US Aid?*, *Al-Ahram Weekly*, issue 539, June 2001

Kelada, William, *The Copts from Minority to Citizenry. Egypt in the Twenty-First Century*, Al-Ahram Centre for Publishing and Translation, Cairo, 1996

Kepel, Gilles, *The Prophet and the Pharaoh*, University of California Press, Berkeley, 1984

——, *Jihad: In the Trail of Political Islam*, Harvard University Press, Massachusetts, 2002

Khadduri, Majid & Edmund Ghareeb, *War in the Gulf*, Oxford University Press, New York, 2001

Kissinger, Henry, *Crisis: The Anatomy of Two Major Foreign Policy Crises*, Simon & Schuster, New York, 2004

——, *Years of Upheaval*, Little, Brown, Boston, 1982

Korayem, Karima, *The Research Environment in Egypt*, Research for Development in the Middle East and North Africa, International Development Research Centre, Ottawa, 2000

Landes, David, *Bankers and Pashas: International Finance and Economic Imperialism in Egypt*, Heinemann, London, 1958

Lane, Edward William, *Manners and Customs of the Modern Egyptians*, Cossimo Classics, New York, 2005

Lapidus, Ira, *A History of Islamic Societies*, Cambridge University Press, Cambridge, 1988

Lewis, Bernard, *The Crisis of Islam: Holy War and Unholy Terror*, Modern Library, New York, 2003

——, *The Assassins: A Radical Sect in Islam*, Phoenix, London, 2003

——, *What Went Wrong?: The Clash Between Islam and Modernity in the Middle East*, Weidenfeld & Nicolson, London, 2002

Madi, Abu Al-Ela, *Al-Masala Al-Qibteya*, Dar Safeer, Cairo, 2007

Al-Maghraoui, Abdesalam, *Liberalism without Democracy: Nationhood and Citizenship in Egypt, 1922–1936*, Duke University Press, North Carolina, 2006

Manning, Patrick, *Migration in World History*, Routledge, London, 2005

Meddeb, Abdelwahab, *Islam and Its Discontents*, William Heinemann, London, 2003

Megahed, Megahed, *Rihla Fi Fikr Taha Hussein*, Dar Al-Thaqafi Lel-Nashr wal-Tawzee. Cairo, 2001

Mernissi, Fatima, *Islam and Democracy: Fear of the Modern World*, Virago, London, 1993

Metz, Helen, *Egypt: A Country Study*, US Congress, Washington, 1990

Mitchell, Timothy, *Colonising Egypt*, University of California Press, California, 1991

Moaddel, M., *Islamic Modernism, Nationalism, and Fundamentalism: Episode and Discourse*, Chicago University Press, Chicago, 2005

Moghissi, Heidi, *Women and Islam: Images and Realities*, Routledge, New York, 2005

Moheideen, Mahmoud & Mohamed El-Erian, *Financial Development in Emerging Markets: The Egyptian Experience*, International Centre for Economic Growth, Cairo, 1998

Momani, Basma, *IMF–Egyptian Negotiations*, The American University in Cairo Press, Cairo, 2005

Mondal, Anshuman, *Nationalism and Post-Colonial Identity: Culture and Ideology in India and Egypt*, Routledge, New York, 2003

Mortimer, Edward, *Faith and Power: The Politics of Islam*, Vintage Books, New York, 1982

Musallam, Adnan, *From Secularism to Jihad: Sayyid Qutb and the Foundation of Radical Islamism*, Greenwood Press, Westport, 2005

Myntti, Cynthia, *Paris Along the Nile: Architecture in Cairo from the Belle Epoque*, The American University in Cairo Press, Cairo, 1999

Netanyahu, Benjamin, *A Durable Peace: Israel and Its Place Among the Nations*, Grand Central Publishing, New York, 2000

Nigm, Zein-Al-Abdedeen, *Misr fi Ahd Abbas wa Saeed*, Dar Al-Shorouk, Cairo, 2007

Numeirat, Fadwa, *Arab Christians and the Idea of Arab Nationalism in the Levant and Egypt*, Centre for Arab Unity Studies, Beirut, 2009

Nutting, Anthony, *Nasser*, E.P. Dutton, London & New York, 1972

Oren, Michael, *Six Days of War: June 1967 and the Making of the Modern Middle East*, Oxford University Press, New York, 2002

Osman, Osman Ahmed, *Safahat min Tagribati*, Al-Maktab Al-Masri, Cairo, 1981

Parker, Richard, *The Politics of Miscalculation in the Middle East*, Indiana University Press, Bloomington, 1993

Pearson, Birger & James Geohring (eds), *The Roots of Egyptian Christianity*, Fortress Press, Goehring, Philadelphia, 1986

Peres, Shimon, *The New Middle East*, Henry Holt & Co, New York, 1993

Peters, Rudolph, *Jihad in Classic and Modern Islam*, Princeton University Press, New Jersey, 1996

Philipp, Thomaas (ed.), *The Mamlukes in Egyptian History and Politics*, Cambridge, University Press, Cambridge, 1998

Pipes, Daniel, *The Hidden Hand: Middle East Fears of Conspiracy*, St Martin's Press, New York, 1998

Primakov, Yevgeny, *Russia and the Arabs: Behind the Scenes in the Middle East from the Cold War to the Present*, trans. Paul Gould, Basic Books, New York, 2009

Pryce-Jones, David, *The Closed Circle: An Interpretation of the Arabs*, Phoenix Press, London, 2002

Al-Qaradawi, Yousef, *Oumatana bayna Qarnein*, Dar Al-Shorouk, Cairo, 2000

Qutb, Sayyid, *Maalim fi al-Tariq*, translated as *Milestones*, International Islamic Federation of Student Organisations, Kuwait, 1978

Raafat, Samir, *Cairo: The Glory Days*, Harpocrates, Alexandria, 2003

Rabinovich, Itamar, *Waging Peace: Israel and the Arabs, 1948–2003*, Princeton University Press, New Jersey, 2004

Rashed, Rawia, *Nazli, Malika Fi Al-Manfa*, Nara Publishing, Cairo, 2008

Rashid, Ahmed, *Taliban: Militant Islam, Oil, and Fundamentalism in Central Asia*, Yale University Press, New Haven, 2000

Renard, John, *Friends of God: Islamic Images of Piety, Commitment, and Servanthood*, University of California Press, California, 2008

Rodenbeck, Max, *Cairo: The City Victorious*, Picador, London, 1998

——, 'Islam Confronts Its Demons', *New York Review of Books*, 29 April 2004

Roudi, Farzaneh Nazy, *Population Trends and Challenges in the Middle East and North Africa*, Population Reference Bureau, Washington, 2001

Roy, Oliver, *Globalized Islam: The Search for a New Ummah*, Columbia University Press, New York, 2004

Rugh, Andrea, *Family in Contemporary Egypt*, The American University in Cairo Press, Cairo, 1985

BIBLIOGRAPHY

Russell, Thomas, *Egyptian Service, 1902–1946*, John Murray, London, 1949

Ryan, Curtis, 'Political Strategies and Regime Survival in Egypt', *Journal of Third World Studies*, Fall 2001

Sadat, Anwar, *In Search of Identity*, Harper & Row, New York, 1977

Said, Edward, *Orientalism*, Vintage, New York, 1979

——, *Reflections on Exile and Other Literary and Cultural Essays*, Granta Books, London, 2001

——, *Culture and Imperialism*, Knopf, New York, 1994

——, *Representation of the Intellectual: The 1993 Reith Lectures*, Vintage, London, 1994

Said, Rushdi, *Rushdi Said: A Life's Journey*, Dar Al-Hilal, Cairo, 2000

Salem, Latifa, *Farouk: min al-milad ila al-rahil*, Dar Al-Shorouk, Cairo, 2005

Saqr, Noami, *Arab Television Today*, I.B. Tauris, London, 2007

Satloff, Robert, *The Army and Politics in Mubarak's Egypt*, Washington Institute of Near East Policy, Washington, 1988

Al-Sayyad-Marsot, Afaf Lutfi, *Egypt's Liberal Experiment*, University of California Press, California, 1977

Al-Sebaei, Labib, *Al-Gameat Al-Mesreya Eind Mouftarak Al-Torouk*, Al-Kotob Weghat Nazar, vol. 13, issue 31, Cairo, August 2001

Serageldin, Samia, *The Cairo House*, Fourth Estate, London, 2004

Shafik, Viola, *Popular Egyptian Cinema*, The American University in Cairo Press, Cairo, 2007

Shamir, Shimon (ed.), *Egypt from Monarchy to Republic: A Reassessment of Revolution and Change*, Westview Press, Boulder, 1995

Shlaim, Avi, *The Iron Wall: Israel and the Arab World*, Allen Lane, London, 2000

Shoheib, Abdelkadir, *Al-Ikhtiraq*, Sinaa Publishing, Cairo, 1989

Shoman, Mohamed, 'The Cairene Street: Order, Chaos, and Power Struggle', *Al-Kotob Weghat Nazar*, vol. 11, issue 124, Cairo, May 2009

Siegman, Henry, 'Israel: The Threat from Within', *New York Review of Books*, 2 February 2004

Silvan, Emmanuel, *Radical Islam: Medieval Theology and Modern Politics*, Yale University Press, New Haven, 1985

Soueif, Ahdaf, *The Map of Love*, Bloomsbury, London, 2000

Starett, Gregory, *Putting Islam to Work: Education, Politics, and Religious Transformation in Egypt*, University of California Press, Berkeley, 1998

Stein, Kenneth, *Heroic Diplomacy: Sadat, Kissinger, Carter, Begin and the Quest for Arab-Israeli Peace*, Routledge, New York and London, 1999

Talani, Leila, *Out of Egypt: Globalisation, Marginalisation, and Illegal Muslim Migration to the European Union*, UCLA Center for European and Eurasian Studies, UCLA International Institute, University of California, Los Angeles, California, 2005

Thabet, Karim, *Memoirs: Farouk As I Knew Him*, Dar Al-Shorouk, Cairo, 2000

Turnham, D., *The Employment Problem in Less Developed Countries: A Review of Evidence*, OECD, Economic Development Papers, Paris, 1971

Turner, Bryan, *Making of Sociology*, Routledge, New York, 2000

Viorst, Milton, *In the Shadow of the Prophet: The Struggle for the Soul of Islam*, Westview Press, Boulder, 2001

Weaver, Mary Anne, *A Portrait of Egypt: A Journey through the World of Militant Islam*, Farrar, Straus, and Giroux, New York, 2000

Wright, Lawrence, 'The Man Behind Bin Laden', *New Yorker*, 16 September 2002

Zaghloul, Naayem Saad, *The Decision Support Centre Monthly Reports*, The Egyptian Cabinet Decision Support Centre, Cairo, 2009

Zayat, Montasser, *Ayman Al-Zawahiri As I Knew Him*, Dar Misr Al-Mahroussa, Cairo, 2002

Al-Zaydi, Mashari, 'In Search of the Early Rachid Reda', *Al-Sharq Al-Awsat*, London, October 2007

Zeidan, David, 'The Copts: Equal, Protected, or Prosecuted', *Islam and Christian–Muslim Relations*, vol. 10, issue 1, 1999

Zohry, Ayman, *Armenians in Egypt*, International Union for the Scientific Study of Population, Paris, 2005

INDEX

INDEX

INDEX

INDEX